The "Sign" of the Last Days

—When?

THE "SIGN"

OF THE LAST DAYS

—WHEN?

CARL OLOF JONSSON
WOLFGANG HERBST

COMMENTARY   PRESS ◆ ATLANTA

Unless otherwise indicated, Scripture quotations in this book are from the *American Standard Version*. Abbreviations of other Bible translations referred to are:

AT	*An American Translation*
JB	*The Jerusalem Bible*
NAB	*The New American Bible*
NASB	*The New American Standard Bible*
NEB	*The New English Bible*
NIV	*The New International Version*
NW	*The New World Translation*
RSV	*The Revised Standard Version*
TEV	*Today's English Version*

Copyright © 1987 by
Commentary Press, P.O. Box 43532, Atlanta, Georgia 30336

Manufactured in the United States of America
Typography by Graphic Composition, Inc.
Printing & binding by Arcata Graphics

ISBN: 0-914675-09-5
Library of Congress Catalog Card No.: 86-72140

Be careful that you are not deceived. . . . There will be many coming in my name, saying "I am he" and "The time is very near now." Never follow men like that.

      —Words of Jesus Christ recorded at Luke 21:8,
        The New Testament in Modern English.

CONTENTS

PREFACE

> What terrible wars, both foreign and domestic!
> what pestilences, famines . . . and quakings of
> the earth has history recorded!—Tertullian, in
> *Ad Nationes,* writing in the year 197 A.D.

THE COMING of Jesus Christ on earth and the promise of his return awakened great expectations in human hearts. In the nineteen centuries that have followed from then till now, not all of the expectations people have embraced have proved to be healthful ones, solidly based on either Scripture or fact.

A characteristic among a large segment in every generation seems to have been the belief that their day was unique. Though aware of the hardships and calamities that have been the common lot of people in all ages, they have nonetheless concluded that their times were worse—that troubles and dangers were mounting rapidly toward the extreme calamity that could, and would, end the world.

We often hear the expression, "the good old days." Nostalgia makes the past seem better and the present to be getting worse. This attitude calls to mind the Biblical admonition, "Do not say: 'How is it that former times were better than these?' for it is not in wisdom that you ask about this."—Ecclesiastes 7:10, *The New American Bible.*

Commenting on this text, one scholar says:

> The supposition is a foolish reflection upon the providence of God in this world. . . . One is so much a stranger to the times past, and such an incompetent judge even of the present times, that he cannot expect a satisfactory answer to the enquiry and therefore he 'does not enquire wisely.'[1]

---

1 *Matthew Henry's Commentary* on Ecclesiastes 7:10.

Perhaps because we are to such an extent 'strangers to the past,' we easily read into the events and circumstances of our own day a distinctiveness and uniqueness that may not actually be there.

In the minds of many religious people there is a belief that the final war of Armageddon, the coming of Christ Jesus for the final judgment, is sure to occur in their day. It is hard for a person to accept that an event of such momentous importance should not happen in his or her lifetime. One inwardly resists the thought of missing out on it, of not experiencing a personal 'rendezvous with history,' particularly divine history. Doubtless this is why books that feed and stimulate such expectations often enjoy great popularity. As just one example, the book *The Late Great Planet Earth,* by Hal Lindsey, reached a circulation of over 18 million copies in a number of languages. People obviously *want* to believe that their day is unique, singled out in Bible prophecy as special.

Yet, history shows that generation after generation has fixed high hopes on certain dates or predictions, only to suffer disappointment, many becoming seriously, even bitterly, disillusioned when their expectations failed to materialize.

Quite in contrast to such attitude, the Bible sets out the plain reality of matters as relates to human life in general, saying:

> **What has happened before will happen again. What has been done before will be done again. There is nothing new in the whole world. 'Look!' they say, 'here is something new!' But no, it has all happened before we were born. No one remembers what has happened in the past, and no one in days to come will remember what happens between now and then.**—Ecclesiastes 1:9–11, *Today's English Version.*

Whether in the Dark Ages, the Middle Ages, the Age of Discovery, the Industrial Age, the Atomic Age, the Space Age, the events of the day are essentially repetitions, variations, elaborations or extensions of the past, and life on earth, the overall course of humankind, human nature itself and mankind's relationships with one another continue very much the same as they were in the past. What appears momentous, even stupendous, to one generation is not to the next, and rarely figures in the daily thoughts or concerns of people living in such later time. Spectacular though a lunar landing may be, today how many persons remember the name of the first man to set foot on the moon? The past fades from human thoughts that are immersed in the present and grappling with the future.

Scripture, in reality, shows that the only genuinely complete change takes place at the revelation of God's Son, who can make all things truly new.

If history has any lesson for us, it makes no stronger point than the unwisdom of "date-setting" for the end. Editorial writer Noel Mason says:

> The history of Jewish and Christian 'date-setters' with all its bitter disappointment and disillusionment has not curbed the desire of many Christians to calculate the end. Some groups continue to cling to their dates in spite of the embarrassment created by the continuation of history. Rather than acknowledging their interpretations of Daniel and Revelation as wrong, many simply avoid the embarassment by reinterpreting the supposed 'fulfillment.'[2]

Such date-setting and religious alarmist writings are thus very "old news," repeatedly occurring throughout the nineteen centuries of the Christian era. Already in the first century we find the apostle Paul writing to fellow believers in Thessalonica:

> Now we implore you, brothers, by the certainty of the coming of our Lord Jesus Christ and of our meeting him together, to keep your heads and not be thrown off your balance by any prediction or message or letter purporting to come from us, and saying that the day of the Lord has already come. Don't let anyone deceive you by any means whatever.— Second Thessalonians 2:1–3, *The New Testament in Modern English* by J. B. Phillips.

Despite that plea, the conjecture and predictions did not end. In the third century, for example, we find church father Cyprian painting this ominous picture to Christians of his day:

> That wars continue frequently to prevail, that death and famine accumulate anxiety, that health is shattered by raging diseases, that the human race is wasted by the desolation of pestilence, know that this was foretold; that evils should be multiplied in the last times, and that misfortunes should be varied; and that the day of judgment is now drawing nigh.[3]

In the sixth century, in a powerful, stirring sermon, Pope Gregory the Great proclaimed:

> Of all the signs described by our Lord as presaging the end of the world some we see already accomplished. . . . For we now see that nation arises

---

2 *Good News Unlimited* magazine, September, 1984, p. 4.

3 Cyprian, Treatise 5, "An Address to Demetrianus," *The Ante-Nicene Fathers*, edited by A. Roberts and J. Donaldson, Eerdmans, 1978, Vol. V, p. 459.

against nation and that they press and weigh upon the land in our own
times as never before in the annals of the past. Earthquakes overwhelm
countless cities, as we often hear from other parts of the world. Pestilence
we endure without interruption. It is true that we do not behold signs in
the sun and moon and stars but that these are not far off we may infer
from the changes in the atmosphere.[4]

History thus records the long and dismal list of predictions and
failures of countless "prophets" of the end times. It seems hardly necessary to go into detail about all the last-days proclaimers who in our
own time have—both by printed word and radio and television ser-
mons—stirred up excited expectations with their eschatological
alarmist predictions.

Does this mean that a sense of expectancy is wrong? By no means,
for we are constantly urged in Scripture to stay "on the watch." On
the watch for *what* then? Do the failures of past predictions necessarily
mean that our generation may not be the exception, that our twentieth
century may not indeed contain events that definitely mark our time
as that in which Bible prophecy will reach final fulfillment? If the
Bible actually sets out a certain "sign" (perhaps composed of a number of individual "signs") that enables us to identify such a period and
if that "sign" is now visible, it would be disastrous for us not to acknowledge it, reprehensible not to contribute toward making it known.
On the other hand, if such claims are nothing more than the result of
manipulation of fact and, worse, manipulation of Scripture, then it
would be equally disastrous and reprehensible for us to promote trust
in such claims, to contribute toward their spread. Reprehensible, because it would mean disobeying the Word of God which warns against
practicing deception on others, deception which can not only be hurt-
ful emotionally, materially and physically, but can also cause devastating erosion of faith in the genuine message of God.

The claim is certainly made that we today are seeing such a "sign"
or "signs" identifying our generation as living in the end-time of the
world.

In his best-selling book, *Approaching Hoofbeats, The Four Horsemen of the Apocalypse,* Dr. Billy Graham states:

We have to ask ourselves: Is this the time of 'the end' that the Bible
speaks of so graphically in so many places? . . . The Bible teaches that
there will be a number of signs that are easily discernible as we approach

4 Quoted in *His Appearing and His Kingdom,* by T. Francis Glasson, M.A., D.D., The
Epworth Press, London, 1953, p. 45.

the end of the age. All of these signs seem currently to be coming into focus.—Pages 126, 127.

Under the heading "Watch for These Signs," in *The Promise*, published in 1982, Hal Lindsey refers to Jesus' words in Matthew chapter twenty-four and lists these signs as wars, famine, plagues, lawlessness and earthquakes. He likens these and other features of prophecy to pieces of a "great jigsaw puzzle" and then goes on to say that, following the establishment of the Jewish state in Israel in 1948, **"the whole prophetic scenario began to fall together with dizzying speed."**—Pages 197–199.

In *Good-bye, Planet Earth,* a book that in some respects seems to be patterned after Hal Lindsey's *The Late Great Planet Earth,* Seventh-Day Adventist author Robert H. Pierson cites the disciples' question about Jesus' coming and then says:

> **Read what Jesus answered—what He had to say about your day and mine—the latter part of the twentieth century. . . .**
> **Read these words in the light of current world events.**

Then follows the subheading:

> **The Phenomenal Increase of War, Crime, Violence and Fear Are All Signs of Jesus's Second Coming![5]**

The now-deceased Herbert W. Armstrong, founder and leader of the Worldwide Church of God, in a letter to subscribers of *Plain Truth* magazine, wrote:

> **. . . let me give you a brief preview of the world YOU live in today, and what the next very few years are going to bring into YOUR life and mine. We are living in a time of extreme DANGER! . . . All evidence seems to indicate it—pollution, unprecedented crime and violence, family life breaking down, morals in the cesspool, terrorism, local wars in Asia, the Middle East, South America. ALL signs point to the fact that we are living in the TIME OF THE END of this present civilization! . . .**
> **We are living in the most tremendous days of world history—the very END TIME, the END of this present evil, unhappy, violent world—just prior to the Second Coming of Jesus Christ.**

While numerous sources proclaim that our day is indeed different from any past time and that we do indeed see events and conditions

---

5 *Good-bye, Planet Earth,* Pacific Press Publishing Association, 1976, p. 48. As will be seen in Chapter 8, not all Seventh Day Adventist sources take the same position as author Pierson.

that positively mark our era as the foretold and final one, probably none is more vocal in this claim than the international organization known as Jehovah's Witnesses. Their leadership, through its agency the Watch Tower Society, with headquarters in Brooklyn, New York, has built up a worldwide publishing empire rarely equalled for sheer volume of output. The millions of persons among the organization's membership are continually exhorted to be conscious of the 'urgency of the time.' In response, members are to be found knocking at the doors of homes in all lands where such activity is allowed, offering literature which declares as indisputable fact that the last days began in the second decade of this century, and that some of the people living then will positively still be alive when the final end arrives.

More than this, their Governing Body makes belief in such teaching an article of faith, essential to acceptance by God and Christ and therefore necessary for anyone to gain salvation. For that reason, any member who seriously questions the soundness of such teaching—on the basis of Scripture and fact—is subject to disfellowshipment, thereafter to be considered, and totally shunned, as an "apostate" from the true faith.

Because of such factors, and particularly because their claims regarding the "uniqueness" of our times often surpass—both in boldness and extent—those of other sources, in its comparison of scriptural teachings and historical facts this book may at times focus somewhat wider consideration on the claims and predictions made by the Governing Body of Jehovah's Witnesses and their Watch Tower Society as to the times we live in.

In so doing the views of other widely publicized sources are by no means lost from sight, for the same facts here considered generally have a strong bearing on the claims and predictions made by those other sources.

Whatever the source, the essential question is: **Are such claims truly authorized by Scripture? Do the events and conditions so dramatically pointed to actually constitute a Biblical "sign"? Are they truly unique to our century and distinctive of our generation? What do the facts show?**

We believe that the material prepared by the authors of this book will bring home to the great majority of us just how much we have been 'strangers to the past,' and therefore how easily we may have shown ourselves to be 'incompetent judges of the present.' The histor-

ical evidence resulting from the authors' intensive research will doubtless be surprising for many, yet it is carefully and authentically documented. We are pleased to publish this work, trusting that it will
greatly clarify some very crucial questions.

The Editors

CHAPTER 1

Our 20th Century—Time of the End?

THE REMAINING years of the twentieth century are rushing toward their close. Our century has already been the stage for some monumental events and may see still more.

If we accept the claims made by a number of religious sources, this century is the scene of the last days. Books circulate earthwide that dramatically describe events and circumstances of our time as visible proof of the immediacy of "the end." Their claims are seriously made and often accompanied by impressive evidence as proof of their validity. Some of these religious sources even assign a specific starting point for the last days within the context of this century.

1914—The Start of the Last Days?

Doubtless the most highly visible and publicly vocal of these sources is the worldwide religious movement known as Jehovah's Witnesses. The year 1914 plays a very key role in all their public preaching. The circulation of millions of copies of books by certain end-times authors is easily eclipsed by the hundreds of millions of copies of Watch Tower publications that go out each year in scores of languages, all heralding the significance of the year 1914.

That year, it is claimed, Jesus Christ's promised return to earth took place, starting his *parousia* or "presence." In that year, we are told, the kingdom of God was established and the "last days" began. This, according to Watch Tower teaching, means that the generation that experienced 1914 will not, in fact *cannot,* pass away until the final end has come. It is a claim presented, not as a mere possibility or even a probability, but as an absolute certainty!

Yet people ask, "How can 1914 have this significance when no man has actually seen Jesus or his kingdom?"

1

Because Jesus came *invisibly* and his kingdom was set up *in God's invisible heavens,* replies the Watch Tower Society.

If true, these claims obviously have vital importance to each of us. What evidence is there to support them? On examining that claimed evidence, we will at the same time examine the views published by a number of other religious sources in our time, with their resulting excitement of expectation. For, although differing widely in many areas, the evidence they offer for the nearness of the end is often remarkably similar.

In proof of their claims, the Watch Tower Society, the publishing agency of Jehovah's Witnesses, uses two lines of argument: 1) Bible chronology, and 2) what they describe as the "signs" since 1914.

Briefly put, according to the Watch Tower Society's understanding the "times of the Gentiles," or as they prefer to translate it, "the appointed times of the nations," referred to at Luke chapter twenty-one, verse 24, is a period of 2,520 years that began in 607 B.C. and ended in 1914 A.D. During this period it is understood that the nations would be allowed to rule without interference from God.

But, again, people ask, "How could the times of the Gentile nations have ended in 1914?" After all, the nations are still ruling this planet as much as they did before that date. The *number* of nations, in fact, has nearly tripled since 1914! How, then, could their times have ended in that year? For almost two-thirds of existing nations today, their times have *begun,* not ended, since 1914.

Another problem, a major one, is that the *starting point* for this calculation—the year 607 B.C., claimed as the date for the destruction of Jerusalem—is in conflict with a long string of historical facts, as well as with a number of passages in the Bible.[1]

Rather than struggle with these chronological difficulties, the Watch Tower Society, therefore, prefers to concentrate on the "signs" since 1914. In this they are not alone, for well-known writers of a number of other religious organizations focus on the very same signs as proof of the nearness of the end. What are these "signs"?

---

1   For a full presentation of these facts, see Carl Olof Jonsson, *The Gentile Times Reconsidered*, 2nd edit., Commentary Press, Atlanta, 1986.

What sign did Jesus actually give?

A few days before his death, Jesus predicted the coming destruction of the temple of Jerusalem. (Matthew 24:1, 2) Because of this prediction some of his disciples put a couple of questions to him:

> **Tell us, when will these things be, and what will be the sign of your coming, and of the end of the age?**—Matthew 24:3, NASB.[2]

Before actually answering these questions, Jesus gave some warnings to his disciples:

> **'Be careful that no one misleads you,' returned Jesus, 'for many men will come in my name saying "I am Christ", and they will mislead many. You will certainly hear of wars and rumours of wars—but don't be alarmed. Such things must indeed happen, but that is not the end. For one nation will rise in arms against another, and one kingdom against another, and there will be famines and earthquakes in different parts of the world. But all this is only the beginning of the birth-pangs.'**—Matthew 24:4–8, *The New Testament in Modern English* by J. B. Phillips, Revised Edition.

In addition to wars, famines and earthquakes, Jesus, in the following verses, mentions persecutions, false prophets and increasing lawlessness. Were all these occurrences to be understood as the positive, identifying signs of Christ's return and the end of the age? Or, to the contrary, did Jesus in fact warn his disciples *not to let themselves be led astray* by such events?

Careful and discreet Bible commentators have often pointed out that Jesus nowhere identifies these events as the "sign" of his coming, but rather appears to warn his disciples not to draw such a conclusion when disasters or catastrophes of this kind take place. From the very start of his reply, his admonishment was: "Don't be misled. Don't be terrified. Such things must take place, but the end is not yet." They also point out that the Greek word for "sign" (*to sēmeíon*) at Matthew

---

2 In the Watch Tower Society's *New World Translation* this text has been rendered so as to support the idea of Christ's being invisibly present: "Tell us, when will these things be, and what will be the sign of your *presence* and of the conclusion of the system of things." However, although "presence" is the primary meaning of the Greek word *parousía*, it was also used in a technical sense as meaning "the visit of a ruler." Practically all NT Greek scholars today agree that the word *parousía*, when used in connection with Christ's second coming, is used in its technical rather than its primary sense. The context and manner of its usage in this connection in the Bible itself harmonizes with this view. This topic will be dealt with later in this publication. (See Appendix B.)

24, verse 3, is *in the singular* and therefore could hardly refer to *a number* of different events.

They have further observed that Jesus actually does not describe his return until his words in verses 27 to 31, following his prediction of the destruction of Jerusalem. Then, for the first time, he starts to talk about the sign of his coming, "the *sign* of the Son of man" (verse 30), here again in the *singular* precisely as in verse 3.

This "sign," according to Jesus' words, was to "appear in heaven," not on earth. The Watch Tower Society admits this. They are, therefore, forced to make a distinction between "the sign of the Son of man . . . in heaven," appearing when he comes for the final judgment, and the "sign" of his coming (*parousía*), which they say is to be found in the wars, famines, pestilences, earthquakes, and so forth, since 1914.[3] In this way they not only get *two different types of "signs"* of Christ's coming—they also have *two different comings,* one in 1914 and another at the "great tribulation."

However, Jesus' introductory words should evidently be understood as *warnings* against false conclusions—"watch out that no one deceives you . . . see to it that you are not alarmed." There would be wars, famines, pestilences, earthquakes and other troubles. His followers would also have to meet hatred and persecution, not only once but many times in the future. They would have to endure such things all the time right up to the end. Before that the gospel of the kingdom preached by Jesus and his disciples would reach all nations of earth. Not until after this would the end come. (Matthew 24:4–14) After giving this general survey of future history, Jesus then began to answer the questions of the four disciples: their question about the destruction of the temple (verses 15 to 22), and their question about his return and the end of the age (verses 27 onward).

End-times proclaimers as a rule do not accept this natural understanding of Jesus' reply. Many popular expositors of the prophecies today insist on interpreting Jesus' initial words about the coming troubles, not as a preliminary introduction, but as **the answer** to the question about the sign of his coming and the end. The Watch Tower Society, for example, explains away the *singular* form of the Greek word for "sign" by saying that the sign itself consists of *a number of different features*. They speak of the sign as "the *composite* sign." When all the events—wars, famines, pestilences, earthquakes and

---

3 *God's Kingdom of a Thousand Years Has Approached* (1973), pp. 326–328.

THE LAST DAYS AND THEIR SIGN
as depicted by one religious source

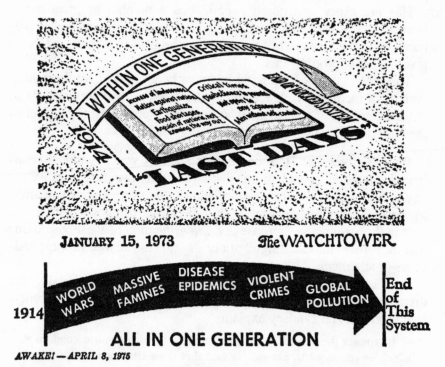

JANUARY 15, 1973   *The*WATCHTOWER

AWAKE! — APRIL 8, 1975

Jesus' words about wars, famine, pestilences, earthquakes, lawlesssness and so on, are understood by many expositors to be the "sign" of his coming. The Watch Tower society claims that we have seen this "composite sign" on an unprecedented scale since 1914. This, it is held, means that Christ's *parousía* and the last days began with that year, and that Armageddon will come within the generation of 1914.

other tribulations—appear *at the same time, during the same generation,* then we are able to discern the "sign," the sign proving that Christ has come and is invisibly present.

Against this interpretation it might be objected: Has not *every* generation seen such a "composite sign"?

Have we not always had wars? Some historians point out that in the past 5,600 years we have had only a total of 292 years *without* wars. Others feel there may not have been any such war-free years at all!

Has not every generation been afflicted by famines and pestilences? As history demonstrates, wars have characteristically had famines and pestilences in tow. The three scourges have virtually always been inseparable, and as a rule more persons have died in the famines and pestilences than were killed in the wars.

Has not every generation experienced a number of great earthquakes "in one place after another"? The catalogs of earthquakes prepared by modern experts and covering the past two thousand years give abundant proof of this.

The past history of mankind has also been marked by fluctuating periods of increased violence and lawlessness, as also persecutions of different groups of Christians who have been preaching the gospel of the Kingdom.

We therefore ask: How can events such as wars, famines, pestilences, earthquakes and so on, distinguish this twentieth century (or any period within it) when history shows that *every generation* since the time of Jesus has been hit by this so-called "composite sign"?

It is the astounding *increase* and *intensification* of these visitations that turns them into the "sign" of our days, is the answer of most end-times proclaimers.

In *The Late Great Planet Earth,* for instance, on discussing the disciples' inquiry for a sign as recorded at Matthew chapter twenty-four, verse 3, Hal Lindsey explains:

> In answer Jesus gave many general signs involving world conditions which he called 'birth pangs.' He said that these signs, such as religious apostasy, wars, national revolutions, earthquakes, famine, etc., would increase in frequency and intensity just like birth pangs before a child is born.—Page 52.

While the Watch Tower Society holds that this increase and intensification has been evident since 1914, Hal Lindsey argues that it has occurred since 1948, the starting point of his end-time "generation."

Seventh Day Adventist author Robert Pierson's book, *Good-bye, Planet Earth,* though not fixing on specific dates, adopts a similar stance as to the significance of our times. When speaking of war in this century, he speaks of it as "on a scale this world has never witnessed before," of "elements of destruction that boggle the human imagination"; when dealing with natural catastrophes, he describes nature as now "running wild all around us," of the earth's shaking and quaking "with increasing frequency and intensity"; when discussing hunger, he quotes predictions of "increasing famine, pestilence, the extermination of large numbers of people"—all presented as incontrovertible proof that "Jesus will come soon."—Pages 8, 15, 19–21, 23.

Dr. Billy Graham somewhat cautiously says that these signs are 'currently coming into focus' and will intensify in the near future. Commenting on the four horsemen of the Apocalypse—the symbols of war, famine, pestilence and death—he writes:

> At some time in the future—a time unknown to us—the terrible hooves of the four horsemen will finally trample across the stage of human history with an unprecedented intensity, bringing in their wake deception, war, hunger and death on a scale that staggers the imagination. . . .
>
> How near are the horsemen right now? I do not know! All I can say with certainty is that every sign points to one fact: the hoofbeats of the four horsemen are approaching, sounding louder and louder every day. . . . May God open our ears to hear and our eyes to see their warning before it is too late![4]

In a rather more flamboyant style, the Worldwide Church of God publication *Famine—Can We Survive?*, on pages 89 and 90, says:

> These crises of war, pestilence and FAMINE were predicted *long ago*. They were foretold centuries ago by the greatest newscaster who ever lived—JESUS CHRIST. Christ told his students to watch the signs of the times. . . .
>
> Jesus Christ, the world's greatest newscaster, was telling His students what would occur in OUR generation—the generation that would see these things come to pass (see [Matthew 24] verse 3). This fantastic forecast is being increasingly FULFILLED!

Faced with the fact that every age has had its share of wars, famines, pestilences, and so forth, these expositors thus hold, as does the Watch Tower Society, that it is the *increase* of these troubles that constitutes the sign of the end.

But was it really that aspect of the enumerated events upon which Jesus laid stress? With respect to wars, famines, pestilences and earthquakes, he did not tell his disciples that they should look for an increase of these afflictions.[5]

Nevertheless, the end-times expositors, either directly or by implication, take the position that Jesus *must* have had in mind an increase

---

4 Billy Graham, *Approaching Hoofbeats, The Four Horsemen of the Apocalypse*, 1983, pp. 74, 76. In this book the author holds that wars, famines, pestilences, and so forth, in earlier ages were only "precursors of the horsemen," and states that now "the shadows of all four horsemen can . . . be seen galloping throughout the world."—pages 9, 77.

5 While it is true that later Jesus spoke of increasing lawlessness, this apparently did not refer to the world in general, which was always lawless. Rather, it appears to refer to what would take place in the Christian congregation. Of course, it took a while for the foretold apostasy to reach the point of being revealed.

of the scourges he mentions. Otherwise these "signs" would not be signs, having nothing about them to make them distinctive. Many of these religious writers simply present their claims accompanied by descriptions—usually very dramatic—of modern-day calamities and troubles, without attempting to defend their position against any contrary evidence. The Watch Tower Society, by contrast, seems compelled to provide such defense and regularly endeavor to "shore up" confidence in their claims. Consequently they are quick to argue against any contrary evidence and do their utmost to prove that a unique increase in calamitous events had indeed taken place since 1914.[6] The publications of the Watch Tower Society virtually bristle with statements, quotations and statistics in support of their claim that wars, famines, pestilences and earthquakes *before* 1914 were mere trifles compared to their extent *after* that year. *The Watchtower* of February 1, 1985, page 15, states their position succinctly and unequivocally:

> True, there had been wars, food shortages, earthquakes, and pestilences down through the centuries of our Common Era until 1914. (Luke 21:11) Nevertheless, there had been nothing to compare with what has taken place since the Gentile Times ended in that momentous year.

A person seeking the truth, however, must ask himself: **How genuine is the startling picture of our times the various religious sources present when this picture is viewed against the background of mankind's past history? Are the statistical proofs they display genuinely trustworthy? Has the *full* evidence been brought to light, or have the views and interpretations of the writers influenced their selection of figures and quotations in a way that distorts the actual facts?**

A careful examination of their quotations and statistics may surprise millions of persons who, as a result of reading such publications, believe that world conditions dramatically mark their time as "special," a time uniquely focused on by Bible prophecy.

Is a thorough examination of the alleged "sign" proper?

Many may shrink back from such a critical investigation. Particularly among the millions affiliated with the Watch Tower organization,

6 See *Survival into a New Earth* (1984), pp. 22, 23.

many may feel that to do so would be to partake of the findings of "ridiculers" who would challenge the claims of Christ's "presence" as advocated by Jehovah's Witnesses. *The Watchtower* of July 15, 1979, page 13, categorizes any who refute its claims as lawless ones and false prophets, citing Second Peter, chapter three, verses 3 and 4, in support. *The Watchtower* of August 1, 1980, page 19, stated that the "ridiculers" could be found "within the Christian congregation" and spoke of them as "making light of the fulfillment of prophecies concerning Christ's 'presence.'"

Somewhat similarly, after discussing what he points to as signs of the final end, Adventist author Pierson's book, *Good-bye, Planet Earth,* has a subheading reading: **You Don't Believe It? Then You Are a Sign!** (Page 51) He, too, then quotes Peter's words about scoffers in the last days.

This would mean that anyone calling the end-times concepts of these sources into question is automatically classed among ungodly ones. Is this a fair and honest use of the text? Are the "ridiculers" described by the apostle Peter persons who firmly believe (as do we, the authors) that 'Jehovah's day will indeed come as a thief' and spell destruction to ungodly men and an evil system of things? Certainly not. As the context shows, the apostle rather describes persons who have utterly ceased to believe in the eventual—and certain—arrival of that day of divine judgment, *persons who question that it will ever come.*[7]

Our focusing a Scriptural and historical searchlight upon certain teachings dealing with claimed evidence marking our time, does not

---

7 The reader who is a Witness might well be impressed instead by the following quotation from the Watch Tower Society's book *Choosing the Best Way of Life* (1979), with which quotation the present writers heartily agree:

"In fulfillment of Peter's words, even today we hear the voice of ridiculers. (2 Peter 3:3,4) In effect they say, 'What reason is there to believe that the Son of God is going to execute the ungodly and reward his disciples? Why, nothing has changed since the time of creation. The original processes of life are continuing and give no indication of coming to a disastrous end in the near future. Men are marrying, and women are being given in marriage, babies are being born, and men continue to grow old and die.' Thus they imply that the Lord Jesus Christ never will come to execute judgment or that this event is so far off in the future that it is of no immediate concern." (Pp. 169, 170)

Such persons quite clearly were such as expect to see something unusual, striking, unprecedented in their day, as proof that the foretold event would indeed take place. Peter's words indicate that they would not see such, and because of not seeing it they would not exercise faith in the *certainty* of that day of judgment. In whatever time we live, as mortals, we all eventually face a very crucial end—the end of our lives. The quality of our personal relationship with God and his Son up until that time should ever be the matter of surpassing concern and importance to us.

reflect any doubt in the slightest as to the Bible's prophecies regarding Christ's "presence." On the contrary, we have seriously considered some often neglected words in Christ's great *parousía* prophecy, which we urge our readers to contemplate honestly also. Jesus foretold that "many" would mislead people in his name, claiming, **"The time is very near now."** True disciples should remain unimpressed, for Jesus, in the very same breath, added: **"Never follow men like that."**—Luke 21:8, J. B. Phillips translation.

Therefore for any Christian simply to shut his eyes and passively hold on to doctrines of religious authorities could be a serious, even fatal, error. In an article entitled "Fallacies Can Be Dangerous," the *Awake!* magazine of November 8, 1970, dealt with some fallacies found in popular ideas about such things as frostbite and quicksand, and then went on to say:

> But much more harm can result from clinging to careless and inaccurate religious ideas that run contrary to what the Bible says. Why so? Because it is not merely the present life that is endangered. Rather, everlasting life is involved. Truth and everlasting life are intimately connected. . . .Surely it is following the safe course to clear our minds of all fallacies!—Page 6.

Indeed, the "love of the truth" is essential for salvation and may at times require that we be willing to investigate and learn. (Compare Second Thessalonians 2:10.) If the reader decides to do so, he must, of course, keep an open mind. **"Having an open mind,"** the Watch Tower Society stated in the *Awake!* magazine of November 22, 1984, **"means to be receptive to new information and ideas. It means being willing to evaluate information without a biased attitude."**— pages 3, 4.

In presenting the information and data about calamities in history, the authors of this book have not, from considerations of space, been able to present all the material available. Nor have we gone into all the Bible texts that we feel might enhance the explanations presented. Nevertheless we are continuing our study and research and would welcome any constructive criticism, as well as other information relating to the subjects dealt with in this publication.

Consider now the evidence regarding famines, earthquakes, pestilence and war in our century as contrasted with the past. We believe the reader will find the facts to be quite different, at times shockingly different, from what many today claim.

CHAPTER 2

Famine—Is It Worse Today?

A VERY grim picture of earth's food situation comes to us through many writings dealing with the end-times. The writers understand Jesus' words "there will be famines," and the symbols in Revelation chapter six, as predicting global hunger of enormous and unparalleled proportions.

In 1982, best-selling author Hal Lindsey wrote in *The Promise* (page 198):

> Jesus predicted *a great outbreak of worldwide famine* on a scale never before known to man. Today the headlines of Time, Newsweek and the daily newspapers scream out the devastating facts that millions are dying of starvation right at this moment. And the forecast is that millions more will starve within the immediate years ahead . . .

In *Approaching Hoofbeats,* pages 151 and 153, Dr. Billy Graham states:

> Following the white and red horses, famine will prevail upon the earth. Millions will die of hunger. Millions more will suffer from malnutrition. . . . The black horse and rider are God's warning of the human suffering that lies ahead if man refuses to obey His commands.
>
> The black horse and his rider thunder in our direction. The hoofbeats of warning are the cries of children dying of starvation and disease.

Seventh Day Adventist writer Robert Pierson warns:

> . . . in at least thirty-two countries of earth today, . . . according to some estimates, seven hundred million (over three times the population of the United States of America) are facing starvation right now. . . .
>
> Speaking of the signs of His second advent Jesus said, 'There will be famines . . . everywhere.' . . .
>
> Another unmistakable sign of the times in which we live. Jesus is coming soon!—*Good-bye, Planet Earth,* pages 22, 24.

A Worldwide Church of God publication, *The Black Horse Famine* (1976), on page 48, makes these notable claims:

> There have always been famines, but there have never been famines the likes of which the world is currently experiencing. Usually famines in the past came in conjunction with droughts, wars and other natural or man-made disturbances. . . . Today worldwide famine is built into the *structure* of world society. Famine is now a way of life for millions of people. . . .
>
> Today's famines also differ in both nature and size from those of the past. Never before did multiple hundreds of millions of people suffer from hunger and malnutrition at any given period in history as they do today.

It is undeniable that, for some areas of the earth, the situation is genuinely grim. It is equally undeniable that "millions are dying of starvation right at this moment" and that millions of "children are dying of starvation." The question is, **is this situation unique to our times or to this twentieth century? Is it unusual—sufficiently distinctive to be pointed to as constituting a divine sign of imminent disaster?**

The earlier-quoted authors present what they view as ominous evidence of a predicted worldwide famine, either already here or very near. The Watch Tower Society is equally as explicit as the Worldwide Church of God, repeatedly announcing in its publications that a time of famine unparalleled in human history has definitely arrived. The claim is made, in fact, that such time of unmatched hunger for mankind has seen dramatic fulfillment since the second decade of this century.

What is the truth of the matter?

How many are really starving today?

There seems to be considerable confusion as to just how many people in the world are actually starving today. In the Watch Tower publication *Happiness—How to Find It* (1980) a news report is quoted as saying that, "At least <u>one out of eight</u> people on earth is still afflicted by some form of malnutrition." (Page 149) On the very same page, however, another news report is quoted as saying that "<u>more than one billion people</u> won't get enough to eat this year."[1] That would be one

---

1   As shown by *The Watchtower* of April 15, 1983, page 7, this statement was cited from the *Vancouver Sun,* which in turn claims it is an estimate by FAO, the United Nations Food and Agriculture Organization. See also the Watch Tower Society's book *Reasoning from*

out of every four persons on earth. An earlier publication, *From Paradise Lost to Paradise Regained* (1958), cited a United Nations food expert, Josué de Castro, to the effect that *two thirds of the human race* suffer from malnutrition or, as the Watch Tower Society "explains" the term, "slow starvation". According to de Castro, another expert, W. P. Forrest, put the figure at *85 percent of the population of the globe.* From the last-mentioned statements the Watch Tower Society drew the conclusion that "Since 1914 food shortages or famines have affected twice as many people as in the 900 years before," and "Never before the year 1914 was the whole earth short of food."[2]

What is the truth behind such conflicting statements? How many are *really* starving or "short of food" today: "one out of eight" (12.5 percent), "more than one billion" (25 percent), "two thirds of the human race" (67 percent), "85 percent", or "the whole earth" (100 percent)?

Famine and malnutrition—a distinction

Discussing the wide range of opinion among experts on the extent of hunger, Dr. Pandurang V. Sukhatme notes: **"The first and basic difficulty arises from lack of a precise definition of hunger."**[3] Up till modern times hunger and famine simply meant *starvation due to lack of food.* Thus the *Encyclopaedia of the Social Sciences* defines famine as "a state of extreme hunger suffered by the population of a region as a result of the failure of the accustomed food supply."[4]

Modern science, however, has broadened the concept of "hunger" to include also the so-called "hidden hunger" or *malnutrition,* which refers to *a lack of one or more essential nutrients in the diet such as various kinds of amino acids, mineral salts, and vitamins.* This "hidden hunger" was, quite naturally, little known in earlier centuries due to lack of knowledge of these essential nutrients, although such "hidden hunger" was even more widespread in the past than it is today, as this study will demonstrate.

---

the Scriptures (1985), page 235, where the same claim is repeated. The FAO, however, never said that one billion people were *starving,* which may be the impression the average reader would draw from this carelessly formulated newspaper report.

2 *From Paradise Lost to Paradise Regained* (1958), pp. 181, 182.

3 Pandurang V. Sukhatme, *Feeding India's Growing Millions* (London, 1965), p. 1. Other difficulties, says Sukhatme, are lack of a dietary standard and the limitations of available statistics on food consumption. (P. 2)

4 Frank A. Southard, Jr., in his article on "Famine" in the *Encyclopedia of Social Sciences*, Vol. 6 (New York, 1931), p. 85.

When modern food experts talk about hunger today, then, it is generally in this broader sense. Josué de Castro, quoted by the Watch Tower Society as saying that two-thirds of the human race suffer from malnutrition, uses "hunger" in this sense, as Lord Boyd Orr, the first Director of FAO (United Nations Food and Agriculture Organization), explains in the foreword to de Castro's book *Geography of Hunger:*

> The term 'hunger' used by the author needs to be defined. In the past it was used to mean lack of food to satisfy appetite and the number of deaths from hunger limited to emaciated people, who died from sheer starvation as in famine. The author, however, uses it in the modern sense as lack of any of the forty or so food constituents needed to maintain health. The lack of any of these causes premature death though not necessarily from emaciation due to lack of any kind of food that can be eaten.

Showing the effect this adjusted definition of hunger has on estimates of the world's hungry, he adds:

> If hunger be used in this sense then according to the best pre-war estimates two-thirds of the population of the world are hungry. A recent American Committee put the number as high as 85 per cent.[5]

Thus it is necessary to distinguish clearly between famine and hunger in the old (and still common) sense, and this modern concept of malnutrition.[6] So how many today are actually *starving,* and how many are *malnourished?*

The extent of starvation and malnutrition today

More recent and more careful investigations of the extent of hunger today have shown that the earlier, pre-war estimate that two-thirds of mankind suffer from malnutrition was erroneous. Dr. P. V. Sukhatme, for instance, after a very thorough investigation of the extent of hun-

---

5   Lord Boyd Orr in the foreword to *Geography of Hunger,* by Josué de Castro (London, 1952), pp. 5,6. A revised and enlarged edition of this book was published in 1973 and translated into English in 1977 as *The Geopolitics of Hunger.* This edition will be used in the following references.

6   M. K. Bennett, in the *International Encyclopedia of the Social Sciences* (ed. by David L. Sills, 1968), points out: "Shortage of a particular vitamin or mineral in a population, evidenced perhaps by uncommonly heavy incidence of scurvy, beriberi, pellagra, rickets, or impaired vision, *is not famine,* although in recent decades the word has been applied to such shortages." (Vol. 5, p. 322) Strictly, *malnutrition* should also be distinguished from *undernutrition,* defined as "inadequacy in calorie intake" (Sukhatme, p. 2). Famine, in turn "is to be distinguished from the more or less constant undernourishment of chronically poverty stricken districts." (Southard, p. 85)

ger in India, concluded that about 50 percent of the population in India suffer from undernourishment or malnutrition or both.[7]

If this holds true of India, until recently one of the most hunger-stricken countries in the world, the proportion of malnourished people in the world as a whole must, of course, be much lower, hence, considerably less than 50 percent.

Probably the most authoritative investigation of the extent of hunger today is that published before the World Food Conference in Rome in 1974.[8] The investigation showed that between 460 and 900 million in the world suffered from various degrees of malnutrition or undernutrition, that is, *12.5 to 25 percent of mankind.* Half of these were *children,* of whom about 10 million suffered from *serious* undernourishment or *starvation.*

The same estimates that indicate some one billion suffering from malnutrition or undernourishment also show that, of these, no more than *c. 40 million are actually starving.* This is *less than one percent of mankind!*[9]

The question, then, is this: When Jesus in his introductory words of warning said that, besides wars and earthquakes, "there shall be famines . . . in diverse places" (Matthew 24:7), did he then think of famine in the old, common sense—recurring and acute starvation catastrophes in various places? Or did he think of hunger in the modern sense, that is, chronic undernourishment or malnutrition due to inadequate calorie intake and/or lack of one or more essential nutrients in the diet?

7 Sukhatme, p. 75. Since Sukhatme's investigation twenty years ago the food situation in India has markedly improved.
8 The United Nations document *Assessment of the World Food Situation,* Item 8 of the provisional Agenda (of the World Food Conf. 1974), E/Conf, 65/3. More recently, FAO, on the basis of the Fourth World Food Survey (1977), has estimated that 455 million people in the developing countries (excluding China) suffer from malnutrition and/or undernutrition.
9 Swedish food experts Lasse and Lisa Berg in *Mat och makt* ("Food and Power"), (Avesta, Sweden, 1978), pp. 20–25. The *Awake!* magazine of October 22, 1984, indirectly agreed with these figures by quoting *The Unesco Courier* as saying that "Chronic hunger remains a problem for tens of millions of people," while "Nearly 500 million human beings, stagnating in poverty, are under daily threat of famine." (P. 6) Thus *hundreds* of millions are *threatened* by famine (that is, malnourished), but *tens* of millions are actually suffering it. Moreover, the estimates of between 500 million and one billion malnourished/undernourished are probably serious exaggerations. They have recently been criticized by a number of leading food experts, who would like to lower the figure to 240 million or less. See the well-known food expert D. Gale Johnson in *The Resourceful Earth,* edited by Julian L. Simon and Herman Kahn (London, 1984), pp. 76, 77.)

The answer seems obvious. The Greek word translated "famine", *limós,* refers to famine in the old sense: starvation due to lack of food. It is also noteworthy that the word is used in the *plural* number, *limoí* ("famines"). This does not indicate some chronic condition of under-nourishment, but indicates acute catastrophes of famine "in diverse places".

Applying the Bible term to the state of chronic undernutrition and malnutrition prevailing in some parts of the world today, as the Watch Tower Society does, and limiting this application to the period since 1914, not only conflicts with the natural understanding of Jesus' statement. It is also in conflict with the fact that the greater part of mankind has evidently suffered from malnutrition and undernutrition since time immemorial, and did so at the very time Jesus uttered his prophecy.

Have we, then, seen more and worse actual famines today than humanity ever saw in the past? Does raw hunger—or for that matter even "hidden hunger"—now gnaw at the vitals of mankind as never before? In the following discussion these questions will be answered first by a review of the history of famines in different parts of the world. Then we will take a closer look at malnutrition, and especially child mortality due to malnutrition or undernourishment, as compared with this problem in the past.

"The greatest famine of all history"—before or after 1914?

For decades the Watch Tower Society has claimed that the greatest famine and the worst food shortages in human history took place shortly after World War I:

> **The worst food shortages in human history followed on the heels of World War I.**—*The Watchtower,* October 15, 1975, page 634.
>
> **. . . in the wake of World War I came the greatest famine of all history.**—*"Let Your Kingdom Come",* 1981, page 122; see also *You Can Live Forever in Paradise on Earth,* 1982, page 150.

Which famines or food shortages followed in the wake of World War I? *The Watchtower* of April 15, 1983, explains:

> **In 1921, famine brought death to some 5 million people in the U.S.S.R. In 1929, famine caused an estimated 3 million deaths in China. In the 1930's, 5 million died of hunger in the U.S.S.R.** (Page 5)

Were these, however, the worst famines in all history? No, they were not. In the very same issue of the *Watchtower* the author, who evidently had done some research on the subject, felt compelled to contradict all earlier statements to that effect and admit:

> . . . it is true that history is full of accounts of famine from away back in the days of Abraham and Joseph up to the greatest recorded famine of all time, the one that struck China between 1878 and 1879. (Genesis 12:10; 41:54) Estimates of the number of Chinese who died in that famine vary from 9 to 13 million.—*The Watchtower*, April 15, 1983, page 3.

This admission is all the more interesting because the Watch Tower Society's publications had claimed for years that the biggest famine *in China* had occurred *after* World War I! Alluding to the drought in northern China in 1920–1921 the book *From Paradise Lost to Paradise Regained* (1958) stated: **"Shortly after World War I China had the biggest famine it ever had—15,000 died every day and 30,000,000 were affected."**[10] The 15,000 a day may seem impressive at first glance—until it is learned that the situation was soon relieved by government and private philanthropic efforts. According to the best obtainable information half a million (500,000) perished in the famine.[11] Although this is a frightening figure, the death toll in many other Chinese famines *previous to* 1914 was much higher, as will be shown in what follows.

Consequently, the "greatest famine" and "worst food shortages" in human history *did not* follow "on the heels of World War I", as the Watch Tower Society for decades had been telling the readers of its publications. Neither did China have its "biggest famine" "shortly after World War I". The greatest, biggest, and worst famines or food shortages all belonged to the past centuries—and they still do.

However, even if actual famines have not increased *in individual size* since 1914, it might be claimed that they have increased *in overall numbers* since that date. This is indicated by the author of the same *Watchtower* article cited above:

> Have we seen more such food shortages than have previous generations? We cannot say for certain because statistics are incomplete. But this century has had its share of natural calamities and has suffered more from

---

10   P. 181. This claim has been repeated many times since. See for instance *"Let Your Kingdom Come"* (1981), page 122, and *You Can Live Forever in Paradise on Earth* (1982), page 150.

11   Ping-ti Ho, *Studies on the Population of China, 1368–1953* (Cambridge, Massachusetts, 1959), p. 233; Walter H. Mallory, *China: Land of Famine* (New York, 1926), p. 2.

war than any other generation in history. Hence, it may be that overall there *have* been more food shortages than ever before.[12]

In this statement the *Watchtower* writer makes another surprising admission not found in earlier publications of the Society. He admits that it cannot be said *for certain* that famines have increased in numbers, only that this *may* be the case! If there is no definite proof that famines have increased *in size* or *in numbers* since 1914, how, then, can it be claimed that they are a "sign" of anything?

But the author, despite his caution, did not present the full truth about past famines. Even if it is true that statistics are incomplete, there is enough information preserved to demonstrate that the number of famines has *decreased* in our century compared with earlier centuries! This will become apparent in the following survey of past famines in China, India, Europe, and other parts of the world.

The study of hunger and famines

Of the three calamities, wars, famines and pestilences, famines have been the least studied subject. As de Castro noted, very little had been written about hunger until the end of World War II: **"For each study of the problems of hunger there were a thousand publications on the problem of war."**[13]

The reason why scholars seemed to avoid the subject was not that hunger was a small problem in the past. Quite the opposite was the case! The extent and destructiveness of famines in the past actually may have been too terrifying to invite scholars to take a closer look at them. The "human waste that has resulted from hunger is considerably greater than that produced by wars and epidemics combined."[14] It has rightly been said that history "will never be understood until a terrible book has been written—the History of Hunger." If such a book were written, observed E. P. Prentice, "a new light would be shed on the history . . . of the whole world—because *in all ages, and in all parts of the world, men have suffered from hunger.*"[15]

12 *The Watchtower*, April 15, 1983, p. 6.
13 Josué de Castro, *The Geopolitics of Hunger* (New York and London, 1977), p. 50.
14 Ibid., p. 50.
15 Ibid., p. 401 (quoting from E. Parmelee Prentice, *Hunger and History*, New York 1939). B. M. Bhatia, too, stresses the worldwide extent of famine in the past: "Before the industrial and commercial revolutions occurred in Europe, famine was a natural calamity from which no part of the world was completely immune."—*Famines in India*, 2nd edition (London, 1967), p. 1.

The first careful investigation of famines was done by Cornelius Walford of the Royal Historical Society in England, who published two lengthy articles on the subject in the *Journal of the Statistical Society* in 1878 and 1879.[16] In the first article Walford included a list of over 350 major famines in various parts of the world from A.D. 6 to A.D. 1878.[17]

Since then other studies have appeared, usually limited to certain areas or countries and covering different time periods. In 1892 Dr. Alwin Schultz published a table of famines in Germany during the years 1300–1499.[18] A lengthy study of famines in Europe from 700 to 1317 A.D. was published by Fritz Curschmann in 1900.[19] And Léopold Delisle published a list of famines in France in 1903, covering the period 1053–1414 A.D.[20] More recently, works on famines in China, India, and other parts of the world have appeared, which studies have been consulted for the information presented in the next sections.

China, "land of famine"

China, the home of nearly a quarter of the inhabitants on earth, is—and seems to have been for most of the past 2,000 years—the most populous part of the world.

This country has so often been visited by destructive famines that it came to be known throughout the world as "the land of famine".[21] As was demonstrated by a study completed in the 1920s, the country had suffered almost *a famine a year* in the past 2,000 years:

> **The food problem is an ancient one in China; from the earliest times famines have been an ever recurring scourge. A study recently completed by the Student Agricultural Society of the University of Nanking brought**

16 Cornelius Walford, "The Famines of the World: Past and Present," *Journal of the Statistical Society,* Vol. XLI, 1878, pp. 433–534, and Vol. XLII, 1879, pp. 79–275.

17 Walford (1878), pp. 434–449. The list also includes a few famines from the pre-Christian era.

18 Dr. Alwin Schultz, *Deutsches Leben im XIV. und XV. Jahrhundert,* (Vienna, 1892), pp. 639–651.

19 Fritz Curschmann, "Hungersnöte im Mittelalter," *Leipziger Studien aus dem Gebiet der Geschichte,* ed. by Buchholz, Lamprecht, Marcks, and Seeliger (Leipzig, 1900), pp. 1–217.

20 Léopold Delisle, *Études sur la Condition de la Classe Agricole* (Paris, 1903), pp. 627–648.

21 Ping-ti Ho, p. 227. "Until the revolution of 1949," says de Castro, "this huge country was the quintessential region of hunger." (P. 258)

to light the surprising and significant fact that between the years 108 B.C. and 1911 A.D. there were 1828 famines, or one nearly every year in some one of the provinces. Untold millions have died of starvation."[22]

The most terrible of these famines resulted from the periodic great droughts: **"Out of the thousand years from 620 to 1620, 610 were drought years in one province or another and 203 of these were years of serious famines."**[23] At least fifteen of these famines were so serious that the Chinese resorted to cannibalism.[24] In many of these famines millions of people must have died. Figures, however, are usually partly or wholly missing. During the four years between 1333 and 1337, for instance, Chinese records report that **"4,000,000 people perished from starvation in the neighbourhood of Kiang alone,"** this last word indicating that millions of others died in other areas.[25]

From the past few centuries better information is available. A number of very destructive famines afflicted China during the past century. **"The four famines of 1810, 1811, 1846 and 1849 are said to have taken a toll of not less than 45,000,000 lives."**[26] Of these "that of 1849 is said to have cost nearly 14 million lives".[27] Between 1854 and 1864 "another 20 million are believed to have perished".[28] Then, in 1876–1879, came the great famine referred to by *The Watchtower* quoted earlier as "the greatest recorded famine of all time", in which from nine to thirteen million human beings perished.[29]

The statement that it was the "greatest" of all famines is, however, not quite accurate. Mallory, writing in 1926, more correctly describes it as the "worst famine that has occurred in China within the memory of the present inhabitants."[30] Some earlier famines are known to have been even more deadly, for example that in China in 1849 (nearly 14 million dying), or the one that struck India in 1769–1770 (which may have claimed tens of millions of lives).

Towards the close of the already hunger-plagued nineteenth cen-

22 Walter H. Mallory, *China: Land of Famine* (New York, 1926), p. 1.

23 de Castro, pp. 271, 272.

24 Ibid., p. 272.

25 Ralph A. Graves, "Fearful Famines of the Past," *The National Geographic Magazine*, July 1917, Washington D.C., p. 89.

26 Graves, p. 89.

27 E. J. Hobsbawm, *The Age of Capital 1848–1875* (London, 1975), p. 133. See also Maurice Bruce, *The Shaping of the Modern World 1870–1939* (London, 1958, p. 801.)

28 Hobsbawm, page 133.

29 *The Watchtower*, April 15, 1983, p. 3. The situation in some areas was so desperate that cannibalism was reported "again and again". (Ping-ti Ho, p. 231)

30 Mallory, p. 29.

CANNIBALISM—A COMMON FEATURE DURING THE GREAT CHINESE FAMINE OF 1876–1879

BODIES LIE DEAD ON THE ROAD, AND THE LIVING STRIVE
TOGETHER FOR THEIR FLESH.

The superior man in ordinary times, while he eats cooked flesh, has his shambles and kitchen away from his hall; but in this year of famine, men eat one another. Letters from the country tell us that if a body lie unburied, the starving surround it, ready to rush on it with their knives, and cut off the flesh for food. The dead died because they could get no food, and the living seek now to prolong their lives by eating the dead. Would you have them die rather? What will not famine compel men to do?

Illustration published in *The Famine in China* (Committee of the China Famine Relief Fund, London: C. Kegan Paul and Co., 1878). (Republished in P. R. Bohr, *Famine in China and the Missionary,* Cambridge, 1972, after page 20.)

tury, yet another severe famine occurred in China in the years 1892–1894, claiming approximately one million additional victims.[31]

Thus, the nineteenth century was one of disastrous hunger for China, since during that century, according to de Castro's estimate, **"some one hundred million individuals starved to death"!**[32]

How many of those today who read books with exciting titles and striking statements about signs of the end-times are aware of these hard facts of history? As for the millions of Jehovah's Witnesses around the world, it is doubtful if even a handful of them are acquainted with the factual evidence on this subject.

What then can be said of China in our twentieth century? Has it experienced an increase in famines, either in size or number (frequency)? Is hunger there greater since 1914 than before? The record shows a very interesting development.

The first severe famine in China following 1914 took place in 1920–21, as has been mentioned. Since the number perishing came to half a million, it obviously came nowhere near to being China's greatest famine. Next was the great famine of 1928–29, causing more than three million deaths.[33] Neither of these two famines came close to the size of some of the great famines of the nineteenth century which we have discussed.

During the 1930's and the 1940's, China, under the leadership of Chiang Kai-shek, attempted to raise the living standards of the Chinese people, aided by loans from the Western powers. Despite these efforts, the situation did not improve much until after the Communist revolution under Mao Tse-tung had won in 1949. After that the new government took energetic measures to increase agricultural production in order to bring an end to starvation. The struggle turned out to be remarkably successful:

> In the space of seven years, China almost doubled its grain yield, averaging an annual increase of about 8 percent that astonished the entire world. . . . This tremendous increase in production and the lower costs that resulted from rising rates of productivity improved the standards of diets and *freed the Chinese people from the clutch of famine.* . . . Through

31 Ping-ti Ho, p. 233.
32 de Castro, p. 53.
33 Ping-ti Ho, p. 233; *The Watchtower,* April 15, 1983, p. 5.

organized and effective political action, the new China within ten years solved its greatest problem: the feeding of its 700 million inhabitants.[34]

The victory was not complete, however. A series of exceptionally severe droughts in 1960 and 1961—right in the middle of the unfortunate economic experiment called "the great leap forward"—forced China to import great quantities of grain from the Western countries. It has long been known that this crisis caused enormous suffering and a severe famine. But not until 1984, when the Chinese released the results of the 1964 census, could the real extent of the disaster be estimated by demographic experts. Estimates of the number of deaths due to famine, malnutrition and child mortality during the four years 1958–61 vary from 8 to 30 million.[35]

This famine, then, was fully comparable to some of the worst famines in the past. Yet it constitutes one dark spot in an otherwise bright or brightening picture. And, it may be noted, it would still not make the Chinese food situation anywhere near as critical for the twentieth century as it was during the disastrous nineteenth century.

Aside from the temporary setbacks listed, the food situation in

---

34 de Castro, pp. 298, 306.
35 Ibid., pp. 306–308; Lester Brown, *State of the World* (New York, 1984), p. 188; *Population and Development Review*, Vol. 7, No. 1 (March 1981), pp. 85–97; Vol. 8, No. 2 (June 1982), pp. 277, 278; Vol. 10, No. 4 (December 1984), pp. 613–645; *Scientific American*, December 1985, p. 194. The *Guinness 1983 Book of World Records* (Bantam Books, 21st U.S. edition, p. 465) erroneously dated this famine in 1969–71 instead of 1959–61. (Personal correspondence.) It should be noted that the estimates of the number of deaths (8–30 million) in this famine are not based on contemporary eyewitness reports, but are demographic estimates made more than 20 years after the disaster. These estimates are based on the Chinese censuses of 1953, 1964 and 1982, of which the first two (1953 and 1964) are said to be of doubtful or defective quality and therefore "of limited usefulness for demographic analysis." (J. D. Durand, "Historical Estimates of World Population," *Population and Development Review*, Vol. 3, No. 3, September 1977, pp. 254, 255, 260–264; J. S. Aird, "Population Studies and Population Policy in China," Ibid., Vol. 8, No. 2, pp. 272–278; "Population Trends, Population Policy and Population Studies in China," Ibid., Vol. 7, No. 1, P. 91.)

If the recent estimates of the number of deaths in the famine of 1959–61 indicate the true magnitude of this disaster, it seems curious that a crisis of such severity would not only have gone unmentioned by contemporary Chinese leaders, but also have passed unnoticed by trained Western observers, who visited China during the catastrophe. Thus Marshal Montgomery, who made a long visit to China during 1961—at what would have been the height of the crisis—in an interview with the *Times* of London stated that "he had seen no hunger in China, that the population seemed well nourished, and that only certain products were rationed as a result of an exceptionally bad year for agriculture." (de Castro, pp. 306, 307)

China has steadily improved. In 1973, world food expert de Castro wrote:

> Since 1962, despite a population increase of about 2 percent a year, agriculture has expanded at an annual rate of 4 percent, and has been able to keep pace well enough to banish the specter of famine completely.[36]

Thus China, the old "land of famine", no longer deserves that designation. Having been visited by famines almost annually for thousands of years, this country has in this century—for the first time in its long history—gradually attained a remarkable freedom from the scourge of famine. The population has grown to over one billion people, but forceful measures are now being taken to limit this growth. The claim that famines have increased since 1914 clearly does not hold true for this quarter part of all mankind. On the contrary, famine in this land has decreased, virtually disappeared, in this until recently the most hunger-plagued part of the world!

Famines in India

Next to China, India was and still is the most populous country in the world. If Pakistan and Bangladesh, which up to 1947 were parts of India, were included its present population would be close to 900 million, or about one fifth of the population on earth. Next to China, India has also experienced more massive famines than any other country.

> India has suffered from famines since time immemorial. Though a connected and complete account of all the famines that occurred in the pre-British period of Indian history is lacking, the available evidence suggests that in the earlier times a *major* famine occurred once in every 50 years.[37]

The ancient records tell about devastating famines, now and then accompanied by cannibalism among the starving victims. Whole provinces are said to have been depopulated in 1022 and 1052 A.D. **"In 1555, and again in 1596, violent famine throughout northwest India resulted in scenes of cannibalism, according to contem-**

---

36 de Castro, p. 308. Since de Castro wrote this in 1973, progress has continued. Swedish food experts Lasse and Lisa Berg, in 1978, wrote that China, in three decades, has "eradicated starvation and probably also undernourishment." (*Mat och makt*, Avesta, Sweden, 1978, p. 170)

37 B.M. Bhatia, *Famines in India*, second edition (London, 1967), p. 7.

porary chroniclers."[38] In 1630 a devastating drought "afflicted the province of Gujarat and whole centers were depopulated."[39]

Perhaps the greatest famine on record was the catastrophe of 1769–1770, during which, according to some estimates, one third of the Indian population perished. In Bengal alone, fully ten million perished, and possibly several tens of millions died in all India.[40]

The frequency of famines in India seems to have increased after the British colonization began in 1756. From 1765 to 1858 the country experienced twelve famines and four severe scarcities. Another six major famines occurred during the twenty years from 1860 to 1880. Of the forty-nine years from 1860 to 1908, *twenty were years of famine or scarcity.*[41] Several of these famines caused millions of deaths each. **"The famines of the early 1800's, according to Andre Philip, killed off half the inhabitants of Madras, Mysore and Hyderabad."**[42] The famine of 1865–66 took close to three million lives, and that of 1876–78 over five million.[43] The nineteenth century closed with two of the most disastrous famines of the century: over five million perished in the famine of 1896–98, and another 3.25 million in the years 1899–1900.[44]

What we are interested in knowing is whether this twentieth century has seen any increase in the number of famines in India, and particularly so since 1914. The answer will certainly come as a surprise to some: **"There was no major famine in the country after 1908 till the fateful Bengal tragedy of 1943,"** Dr. Bhatia, the leading expert on Indian famines, points out.[45]

Thus, during nearly three decades immediately following upon World War I—in the period when the Watch Tower Society's "composite sign" required more famines than ever—the vast, hunger-stricken peninsula of India did not contribute one single famine to this "sign"! Why not? Bhatia explains:

---

38 Fernand Braudel, *Civilization and Capitalism 15th–18th Century: The Structures of Everyday Life* (London, 1981), p. 76. Speaking of the past history of China and India, Braudel notes that "Famines there seemed like the end of the world." (P. 76)

39 Graves, p. 87.

40 Walford (1878), p. 442; Graves, p. 88. *The Guinness 1983 Book of World Records* in a footnote accompanying its table (page 465) of the greatest catastrophes in the world mentions that the great Indian famine of 1770 took *several tens of millions of lives.* We have not been able to authenticate this statement, however.

41 Bhatia, pp. 7, 8, 58. Compare Walford (1878), pp. 442–449.

42 de Castro, p. 320.

43 Bhatia, pp. 68, 70, 74, 108.

44 Ibid., pp. 242, 261.

45 Ibid., p. vi.

> The famine of 1907–08 . . . proved to be a turning point in the long history of food and famine problem in India. Henceforth, drought ceased to be a problem of serious concern. Attention was turned, on the other hand, to price of food, availability of employment and the rate of wages.

Explaining what this meant as to famine in India, he explains:

> Famine no more meant mass starvation because of want of food; it came to imply, as in some other modern economies, high prices of foodgrains unaccompanied by a proportionate increase in wages resulting in reduced consumption of foodgrains on the part of the poor and, therefore, semistarvation. Famine was transformed into Food Problem, which ever since has continued to be with us.[46]

Consequently, over a period of thirty-five years, from 1908 to 1942, **"India experienced a number of scarcities but no major famine involving any considerable loss of life."**[47] The Bengal famine of 1943, therefore, came as a shock, and India was unprepared for it. Before the situation got under control, a million and a half poor and helpless people had starved to death.[48] Again in 1974, Bengal (by then separated from India as Bangladesh) experienced a famine in which several hundreds of thousands died from starvation, a famine that, according to observers, was brought about by political causes and could have been avoided.[49]

Of India itself in its present dimensions, Bhatia wrote in 1965: **"Over the last two decades we have succeeded in avoiding deaths from starvation in any part of the country."**[50] This was made possible by large imports of foodgrains and by international aid.

---

46 Ibid., p. 270. *The Watchtower* of April 15, 1983, quotes on page 6 George Borgström, an authority on world nutrition, as saying that food conditions in India became "unbearable" in the nineteenth and twentieth centuries. But as Dr. Bhatia, the leading authority on Indian famines, shows, this holds true for the nineteenth century, but not for the twentieth, when the situation has radically changed. Further, Borgström's statement that only ten million in India are "adequately fed" is also shown to be much in error by the careful investigation of Dr. Sukhatme, who concluded that 50 percent of the Indian population is adequately fed! (See information under the subheading "The extent of starvation and malnutrition today.") Borgström was one of the "doomsday prophets" of the 1960's who warned of a coming famine catastrophe. Some of these even predicted that many countries, headed by India, would experience widespread famines in the 1970's—a prediction that failed completely. (See for instance W. & P. Paddock, *Famine-1975!*, London, 1967, pp. 60,61. This book was quoted repeatedly in Watch Tower publications previous to 1975; not since.)

47 Bhatia, p. 309. In a footnote Bhatia adds: "From 1910 to 1940 there were 18 scarcities, but there was no loss of life due to starvation over the entire period." (P. 309)

48 Ibid., p. 310. One expert put the death figure as high as 3.5 million. (Bhatia, p. 324)

49 Berg and Berg, p. 112.

50 Bhatia, p. 342.

Since 1966, Indian leaders have struggled hard to free their country from dependence on international charity, and the situation has gradually improved. De Castro wrote in 1973:

> Because of technical and organizational measures, India's nutritional situation, until 1966 among the worst in the world, began to show signs of reaching a turning point. During the past two years farm production has increased at a rate of 8 percent, which is a real miracle.[51]

What of the situation today? India is still a very poor country; nonetheless the economic development has continued. In 1985, *Time* magazine could report:

> The most important gains have been made in food production. Fifteen years ago, India had to rely heavily on imported grain to feed its hungry millions and drought was regularly a life-or-death issue. The country is now self-sufficient in food. Since 1971, grain production has increased by 40%, largely as a result of the 'green revolution,' the scientific program of using high-yield seeds and extensive irrigation that began in the mid-1960s.[52]

As in China, the picture of famine in India, then, shows a notable development. Having been plagued by recurrent famines for most of its history, this vast and populous peninsula has made great strides toward freeing itself from severe famine over the course of this twentieth century. Great efforts are being made to control population expansion and to eliminate India's perennial problem of poverty.

In brief, malnourishment certainly exists in India. This is neither new or unusual to its history. What is new and unusual is the fact that, rather than worsening, the situation is definitely improving in our century.

Thus far our investigation has demonstrated that the two most populous and famine-plagued countries of the world, China and India, both show a striking *decrease* in the size and number of famines since 1914, quite contrary to the trend we should have found if the remarkable claims of various religious sources were correct! In both countries the 1800's were remarkably worse in famines than the 1900's have been. Let us turn our attention, then, to another great populous center on earth today—the third in order: Europe.

---

51 de Castro, pp. 341, 342.
52 *Time* magazine, January 14, 1985, p. 25. (Compare *Science* magazine, August 3, 1984.)

Europe's history of hunger

Europe (its border on the east reaching to the Soviet Union) covers an area a little vaster than the Indian peninsula but holds only slightly more than half as many inhabitants: 500 million. For more than a century famines have been practically unknown on the European continent. People today are usually well fed, often overfed, and even malnutrition is a very small problem in most countries of Europe compared with some other parts of the world. Most people live in fortunate ignorance of the continent's past dreadful history of famines. Perhaps they would count themselves even more fortunate if they knew something about it.

In stark contrast to present conditions, from the earliest times famine constantly visited the European continent, often killing multitudes of people and partly or wholly devastating large areas. A climax seems to have been reached during the Middle Ages. During the 600 years from the tenth century to the sixteenth, **"some 400 widespread famines racked the countries of the Continent and the British Isles."**[53] Many of these were so dreadful and had such demoralizing effects, that even in these Christianized countries people resorted to cannibalism. Throughout these centuries, says Bhatia, **"Britain and countries of Western Europe . . . were more frequently menaced by famines than any other part of the globe."**[54]

The situation improved somewhat from the seventeenth century onward, but local or widespread famines continued to cause tremendous havoc from time to time far into the nineteenth century.[55]

The impression that Europe, during these centuries, was kept in a near permanent state of hunger is fortified by a closer look at the state in the individual countries. Historian Fernand Braudel writes:

> **Any national calculation shows a sad story. France, by any standards a privileged country, is reckoned to have experienced 10 *general* famines during the tenth century; 26 in the eleventh; 2 in the twelfth; 4 in the fourteenth; 7 in the fifteenth; 13 in the sixteenth; 11 in the seventeenth and 16 in the eighteenth. While one cannot guarantee the accuracy of this eighteenth-century calculation, the only risk it runs is of over-optimism, because it omits the hundreds and hundreds of *local* famines. . . . The same could be said of any country in Europe.**[56]

53 de Castro, p. 398.
54 Bhatia, p. 2.
55 Southard, in the *Encyclopedia of the Social Sciences*, Vol. VI, says that 450 famines are known to have occurred in Europe from A.D. 1000 to A.D. 1855. (P. 85).
56 The great historian Fernand Braudel in *Civilization & Capitalism 15th–18th Century: The*

Mortality figures are usually missing in the ancient sources, the authors mostly restricting themselves to such general statements as, "great mortality", "endless multitudes died", "whole villages emptied", "the ground covered with dead bodies", and so on. In several cases it is stated that "one third of the population" in the country perished.[57] To convey to the reader some of the almost indescribable misery that prevailed in Europe during these food catastrophes, the following list presents a few examples from the hundreds of devastating famines that visited the continent during earlier centuries.[58] The list is accompanied by comments quoted from the ancient sources:

A.D.	Comments
192	*Ireland:* General scarcity, "so that lands and houses, territories and tribes, were emptied."
310	*England:* 40,000 perished.
450	*Italy:* "When parents ate their children."
695–700	*England, Ireland:* Famines and pestilences, "so that men ate each other."
836	*Wales:* "The ground covered with dead bodies of men and beasts."
879	*Universal* famine prevailed.
936	*Scotland:* After a comet, famine for four years, "till people began to devour one another."
963–964	*Ireland:* An intolerable famine, "so that parents sold their children for food."
1004–1005	*England:* "Such a famine prevailed as no man could remember." "This year was the greatest famine in England."[59]
1012	*England, Germany:* Endless multitudes died of famine.
1016	*Europe:* Awful famine throughout Europe.
1069	*England:* Widespread famine, "so that man, driven by hunger ate human, dog, and horse flesh."
1073	*England:* Famine, followed by mortality so fierce that the living could take no care of the sick, nor bury the dead.

Structures of Everyday Life (London, 1981), p. 74.
57 Fritz Curschmann, *Leipziger Studien aus dem Gebiet der Geschichte* (Leipzig, 1900), pp. 60–62.
58 Sources: Walford, pp. 434–449; Graves, p. 84; Braudel, p. 74; E. P. Prentice, *Food, War and the Future* (New York, London, 1944), p. 14; E. Le Roy Ladurie, *Times of Feast, Times of Famine* (London, 1972), pp. 68, 70; Prof. Eino Jutikkala, "The Great Finnish Famine in 1696–1697," *The Scandinavian Economic Review,* III, 1955, pp. 48–63. The Roman famines up to the time of Trajan (98–117 A.D.) have been examined by Kenneth Sperber Gapp in his doctorate *A History of the Roman Famines to Time Trajan*, Princeton University, 1934. Unfortunately, it has not been possible to acquire a copy of this thesis.
59 Some of the old chroniclers declare that during the long famine period from 1005 to 1016 fully *half* the population of the larger island perished! (Graves, p. 81.)

1116   *Ireland:* Great famine, "during which the people even ate each other."

1239   *England:* Great famine, "people ate their children."

1316   Europe: Universal dearth, and such a mortality, particularly of the poor, followed, that the living could scarcely bury the dead.

1347   *Italy:* A dreadful famine swept away by absolute starvation vast numbers of the inhabitants. Followed by pestilence.

1437   *France and other countries:* A great famine swept over France and many other countries, lasting for two years. "Multitudes in the large towns dying in heaps on dunghills."

1586–1589 *Ireland:* Great famine period, "when one did eat another for hunger."

1693   *France and neighboring countries:* "An apocalyptic medieval-type dearth which killed millions of people in France and the neighboring countries."

1696–1697 *Finland:* One of the most dreadful famines in the history of Europe. A quarter or up to a third of the country's population perished.

1709   *France:* About one million starved to death.

1846   *Ireland:* The whole potato crop rotted. A million people starved to death and still more fled the country to escape the same fate. *This was the last great famine in Europe.*

Upon reading such descriptions, one cannot but consider oneself fortunate to be living in the twentieth century. Where, in any part of Europe today, do we read of millions—or thousands or even hundreds—dying because of famine? Where today, even in famine-stricken areas, do we read about people "eating each other", "eating their children", or "selling their children for food"? It is true that certain areas on earth are still scourged by severe famines, but conditions have clearly improved. The progress made in storage methods and in communications has contributed much to this situation, and international aid via the United Nations, the Red Cross, and many other charity organizations can quickly reach the stricken areas on a scale that was completely unthinkable just a hundred years ago—provided that enough money is available.

As Bhatia points out, famine "was almost banished from Europe after 1850."[60] The last great famine in that part of the world was the Irish calamity of 1846–47.[61]

It is true that famine conditions threatened parts of Europe during

60 Bhatia, p. 2.
61 de Castro, pp. 400, 401.

THE LAST GREAT FAMINE IN EUROPE: IRELAND 1846–47

The Irish famine of 1846–47 reduced the peasantry to starvation and forced them to beg at the doors of the workhouses. Over one million starved to death and many more emigrated abroad. This, Europe's last severe famine, took place *some 140 years ago*. (Illustration from *Collier's Encyclopedia*, 1974 edition, Vol. 9, p. 553.)

and after World War II, especially in Poland and Holland, where tens of thousands faced starvation, and many actually died of hunger or undernourishment.[62] Relief measures initiated by the U.S.A., however, soon changed the situation. Supported by the American Marshall

62 Ibid., pp. 421–424.

Plan in 1947 **"the European economy recovered rapidly and the marks of hunger quickly diminished across the whole area. In a short time Europe had regained its pre-war nutritional level."**[63] Since then the continent for almost a whole generation has experienced a steadily increasing prosperity.

Our examination of famines in the three greatest population centers on earth, with a combined population of *more than half of mankind,* thus shows a most remarkable development: from having been the most famine-plagued areas on earth, our twentieth century has seen these centers gradually freed almost completely from the scourge of famine!

This phenomenal *decrease* of famines in these countries is more than enough to show that any claimed *increase* in famines in this century, or since 1914 in particular, simply has no foundation in fact. For the sake of completeness, however, a brief summary will also be given of the past and present food situation in the rest of the world. How much have Russia, Japan, Africa, America, and other areas contributed to the claimed "hunger sign"?

Famines in other parts of the world

Our search for the supposed increase of famines in our century has so far been fruitless, in spite of the fact that about half of mankind has been explored. Instead of *increases* in hunger we have found *tremendous decreases*. Turning now to the other half of mankind, we will be confronted by the same palpable trend in one area after the other: decreases instead of increases. Several vast and populous areas are completely freed from famines today. These include North America, the Soviet Union, Japan, Indonesia, the Philippines, and most countries in South West Asia west of Afghanistan.

These areas, with a combined population of about one billion people today, were scourged by numerous famines in the past centuries.

In *Russia,* for instance, hunger has always played a decisive role. **"Imperial Russia . . . suffered famine nearly every year."**[64] It is true that the country was stricken by some major famines in the two decades following upon World War I, one in 1921 in which between

63 Ibid., pp. 438–440.
64 Southard, p. 86.

1 and 3 million died, another in 1932–33 that killed five million.[65] These, however, were only the last in a long series of other great famines. **"Russia was scourged by major famines eleven times between 1845 and 1922."**[66] Among the most severe famines in the history of the country were the three of 1891, 1906, and 1911, all of them coming *before* 1914.[67] Since the 1940's, agricultural advances have steadily improved the food situation, and famine has ceased to menace the country.

As for *North America,* with the exception of certain American Indian communities, such as the Pueblo Indians, it seems that extensive famines have been absent from this vast area since the days of Columbus![68] In the U.S.A., even problems of malnutrition are largely limited to some pocket areas, mainly in the South. Food is notably abundant throughout the continent.

Japan is another country visited by periodic famines in the past. The victory over hunger began with the abolishment of feudalism in the 1860's, followed by agrarian reforms and the introduction of scientific agricultural methods. Long before World War II these advancements had **"put an end to famines that periodically decimated the population and left the survivors with lifelong signs of physical degeneration"**[69] Not only has famine disappeared but the rise in living standards and the improved diet, especially since the 1950's, have also freed Japan from malnutrition and undernourishment.[70]

South West Asia is yet another area with a famine-stricken past. **"The late 1860s and early 1870s saw an epidemic of hunger in the entire belt of countries stretching from India in the east to Spain in the west."**[71] Persia alone "lost between 1.5 to 2 million in the great famine of 1871–3."[72] Malnutrition and undernutrition still prevail in many of the countries in the region, but, with the exception of a serious famine in Afghanistan in the 1970's, the great famines that once afflicted this vast area are gone.[73]

---

65 Richard G. Robbins, Jr., *Famine in Russia 1891–1892* (New York and London, 1975), p. 172. The statement on page 5 in *The Watchtower,* April 15, 1983, that the famine in 1921 killed "some 5 million people" does not seem to be correct. "Reliable sources estimate that there were between 1 and 3 million victims of the disaster." (Robbins, Jr., p. 172.)

66 Southard, p. 86.

67 Graves, p. 89.

68 Graves, p. 90; Southard, p. 87.

69 de Castro, pp. 348–351.

70 Ibid., pp. 365, 366.

71 Hobsbawn (1975), p. 133.

72 Ibid., p. 133.

73 *Awake!,* February 8, 1973, p. 29. Death figures are not available.

None of this is to say that severe famines belong entirely to the past. At times acute famine conditions do develop in certain parts of the earth, particularly in Africa, and South America, the regions where malnutrition and undernutrition are also most widespread. Of the two areas, *Africa* is the most affected. In the early 1980's, three or four years of widespread droughts have hit the continent, affecting millions of people in 24 countries, with Ethiopia evidently being the country suffering most dramatically. Of the nearly 40 million people in the land, drought affected 6–7 million, and by the end of 1985 experts estimated that about one million had starved to death. Thousands of others died in the Sudan, Mozambique and other countries. However, international efforts by United Nation's organs (the UNDP and UNICEF), by the Red Cross and numerous other charity organizations succeeded in preventing a much greater catastrophe. Thus it is estimated that the food aid to Ethiopia in 1985 saved about five million people from starving to death. For most countries in Africa, the crisis is now over, but much aid is still needed in years ahead to prevent a recurring catastrophe.

Famines today usually generate widespread publicity. The simple fact is that much of this is due to famine's having become more and more of a rarity among mankind. Public interest today is aroused to the need in distant parts of the earth and many are moved to contribute to charity organizations and share in relief activities. In the past, newspapers could not equal the graphic impact of television-reporting of conditions in remote areas; inadequate means of communication sharply hindered extensive relief aid. The publicity given to recent famines in Africa has made them "official," known to the general public, in contrast to famines in earlier times. The effect has been to cause some to believe that the recent famines are the worst ever in Africa.

As an example, a series of droughts hit Africa in the early 1970's, afflicting Ethiopia and the countries bordering the Sahara Desert; the resulting famine caused about 100,000 deaths.[74] The *Awake!* magazine of July 22, 1974, called it **"the greatest 'natural' disaster in Africa's history."** (Page 6) Such statements, which often appear in different newspaper articles during catastrophes of various kinds, tell

---

74 *The Watchtower,* April 15, 1983, p. 6. Estimates vary; some set the death figure at 200,000 or more. John C. Caldwell, in his study of the Sahelian drought, concluded that death figures had been exaggerated. He stated that "the figures in the newspaper headlines were figments of the imagination and many apparently serious reports were little better." See *The Sabelian drought and its demographic implications* (Washington, D.C.: American Council on Education, Overseas Liaison Committee Paper No. 8, 1975), p. 26.

more about the ignorance of the authors of such articles—and of those quoting from them—than of the history of the country.

Numerous famines that ravaged Africa in the past were much greater than those that have scourged the continent in our century.

Because of the current prominence of the Ethiopian famine, it may be instructive to examine more closely some of its past famines.

In February 1984, representatives from many African countries met in Addis Ababa, Ethiopia, to discuss the climatic situation and drought in that continent. At the conference, the Ethiopian delegation released a document on these topics that included a table of occurrences of drought and famine in their country, covering the period from 253 B.C. to A.D. 1982.[75] Although the document points out that much data is lacking for the centuries previous to A.D. 1800, the table gives a terrifying picture of Ethiopia's past.

Many of the famines listed affected not only Ethiopia but also "Sudan, Egypt and [apparently] also the rest of Africa and the Sahelian region." (Page 14) Many of these famines undoubtedly claimed millions of lives but "Reports on human mortality are practically non-existent for the droughts of the period before the first half of the present century." (Page 25) For the nineteenth century the table reveals 9 major famines, five of which affected the whole of Ethiopia. Of one of these, the famine of 1888–92, the table states: **About ⅓ of the population perished."** (Page 16) By contrast, the recent famine in Ethiopia affected about 15 percent of the people and about 2.5 percent of the population died—far less than the 33 percent of the nineteenth-century famine victims. It should be kept in mind, of course, that the present population is considerably greater today than in the past. The seriousness of the present situation, as the Ethiopian document shows, owes to the fact that the intervals between recurrent droughts tend to become shorter and shorter, and soil erosion caused by human misuse (deforestation and over-grazing) aggravate the situation further.

Famine, then, is admittedly a current and serious problem in Africa. This is true. What is not true is the view that this is distinctive of our time. Africa has suffered from famines "since remote antiquity."[76] Best known are the famines of Egypt. A series of severe famines swept over Egypt from the tenth to the twelfth centuries,

---

75 A copy of the document was kindly forwarded to us by Anders Johansson, present at the conference as Africa correspondent for *Dagens Nyheter,* the largest morning newspaper of Sweden. Johansson is presently News Editor of this newspaper.

76 de Castro, p. 367.

when the Mohammedans ruled the country. The famine of 968 A.D. "swept away 600,000 people in the vicinity of Fustat."[77] Another more widespread and more disastrous famine came in 1025. A still more terrible famine began in 1064 and lasted for seven years. The desperate people finally resorted to cannibalism and human flesh was sold in the open market. The same suffering and degradation were induced by the dreadful famine in the years 1201 and 1202, when "the very graves of Egypt were ransacked for food."[78] Severe famines have also hit other countries in Africa. In the famines between 1861 to 1872 the Moslem population of Algeria "dropped by over 20 per cent." Morocco lost three million people—close to one-third of its population—in the famine of 1878–79. Numerous other famines have scourged Algeria, Tunisia, Morocco and other North African countries throughout the centuries, as shown by studies carried out by Dr. Charles Bois.[79]

In our century food conditions have actually improved in the very northernmost countries of Africa and in South Africa. They are not afflicted by famine, although the nutritional problem is still serious in some areas.[80]

Similarly, in *Latin America,* a high percentage of the population suffers from undernourishment and malnutrition, and several countries have a high child mortality. Again, however, this state is nothing new to that part of the world. **"It comes from the past,"** says de Castro, **"from the time of the earliest discovery of these lands."** And speaking of Central America he explains, **"The multideficient diet throughout Central America and the chronic starvation that results are in a sense an inheritance from the indigenous pre-Columbian culture, although the situation has since been aggravated in many respects by the shortsighted methods of colonial exploitation,"** which began in the sixteenth century.[81]

Famine and hunger have scourged Latin America "all through history," and famine conditions still develop in different areas.[82] Nothing seems to have changed basically, then, in these respects in our century.

---

77 Graves, p. 75.
78 Ibid., pp. 75, 77, 79.
79 Hobsbawn (1975), p. 133; *Revue pour l'Étude des Calamités,* No. 21 (Jan.–Dec. 1944), pp. 3–26; No. 26–27 (Jan. 1948–Dec. 1949), pp. 33–71; No. 28–29 (Jan. 1950–Dec. 1951), pp. 47–62. (This journal was published in Geneva, Switzerland.)
80 de Castro, pp. 374–376, 388, 389.
81 Ibid., pp. 142, 199.
82 Ibid., p. 139.

Our review of the famines in the world, past and present, ends here. The evidence brought to light during our investigation can lead to only one conclusion, namely, that on a world basis famines have *decreased,* and decreased *very conspicuously,* in this twentieth century, including the period since 1914.

This development should not really surprise us. Famines in the past were principally a consequence of primitive agricultural methods (which often brought on crop failures due to being more easily affected by changes in the weather) and a consequence of the primitive means of communication, which often made help from adjacent areas unattainable. The Industrial Revolution brought better farming implements, more resistant varieties of grains, and improved communications, and the food situation began to change:

> **Around 1800 A.D. a development started in Western Europe and North America that almost abolished famines and epidemics and also lowered the normal level of mortality, so that the remaining average length of life increased from the 30 years of that time to the 75 years of today.[83]**

Chronic malnutrition, however, still remains as the greatest hunger problem, as the great European demographer (population expert) Alfred Sauvy points out:

> **While acute and disastrous famine has almost disappeared, chronic malnutrition is still a problem in many parts of the world.[84]**

We are thus faced with the remaining question as to whether malnutrition and undernourishment are indeed more widespread today than in the past.

Malnutrition and child mortality in the past and today

As shown earlier, *about one percent* of mankind is *starving* today, very probably the lowest proportion is known history. A far greater

---

83 Danish demographer P. C. Matthiessen in *Befolkningsutvecklingen—orsak och verkan,* second edition (Lund, Sweden, 1972), p. 35. (Translated from the Swedish edition).

84 Jan Lenica and Alfred Sauvy, *Population Explosion, Abundance or Famine* (New York, 1962). The quotation is taken from the Swedish edition (*Befolkningsproblem,* Stockholm, 1965, p. 44.)

number, however, perhaps as much as *25 percent,* are *malnourished* or *undernourished* or both.[85]

About half of these are children. The majority of those who die from malnutrition or diseases indirectly caused by malnutrition or undernutrition are children under six years of age.

In discussing the ride of the black horse of Revelation, symbolizing hunger, Dr. Graham draws attention to the plight of children, saying that **"the hoofbeats of warning are the cries of children dying of starvation and disease,"** and he cites a Mennonite Central Committee report which estimates that **"twelve million infants die of the effects of malnutrition every year in the developing countries."** (*Approaching Hoofbeats,* pages 153, 154) The picture is certainly a heart-rending, deeply disturbing one. There is no question about that. What may rightly be questioned, however, is whether the situation is unique to our times.

The Watch Tower Society clearly endeavors to bolster its "famine-sign" by the aid of child mortality figures, using these to counteract the evidence of surpassing hunger in the past:

> **A report from the United Nations Children's Fund estimates that 17 million of the world's children died from hunger and disease in 1981.** *That is more than the estimated deaths during the terrible Chinese famine of the years 1878–9.*[86]

But comparing *child mortality* in all the world in 1981 with the *great famine in China in 1878–79*—if done with the goal of distinguishing our time as preeminently hunger-stricken—is at best a sign of ignorance, at worst a sign of dishonesty. Why? Because, although certainly not as clearly identified as today, malnutrition, with resultant child mortality, definitely co-existed right along with famine in the past.[87] And just as with famine, malnutrition was evidently not a smaller problem in past centuries. The evidence is that it was greater.

This is indicated by the undeniable fact that *mortality at all ages,*

---

85 As explained earlier (in footnote 6), *undernutrition* refers to the *quantity* of food eaten, while *malnutrition* has to do with the *quality* of the diet. About half of the malnourished, perhaps 10–15 percent of mankind, are also undernourished. Starvation is an extreme form of undernutrition, and famine is widespread starvation.

86 *The Watchtower* of April 15, 1983, p. 7. Child mortality seems to have declined somewhat in 1982. The *1983 UNICEF Annual Report* shows that close to 15 million (40,000 a day) children died or were disabled that year due to malnutrition and hunger-related diseases such as diarrhea. (Pp. 3, 28)

87 Even today malnutrition is, in the majority of the cases "invisible", even to mothers of malnourished children. Hence the term "hidden hunger".

and particularly child mortality has steadily declined during the whole twentieth century in almost every country![88]

Swedish demographer Professor Erland Hofsten estimates that infant mortality in earlier centuries was as high as 40–50 percent in many countries, possibly even higher in some areas![89]

In Sweden, where running statistics have been kept of child mortality since 1749, the child mortality rate was 20–25 percent from 1749 to 1814, but then it began to decline. By 1985 it had been reduced to 0.7 percent![90] A similar development has occurred in many other countries, especially in Europe and North America.

Progress has been slower in the developing countries, but there, too, a palpable improvement has taken place, especially since the end of World War II:

> **Practically everywhere in the poor countries mortality has declined sharply since the War. . . . mortality has declined at all ages.** *The decline of infant mortality has been particularly significant.*[91]

True, large numbers of children still die of malnutrition in many poorer areas of the earth. But infant mortality in the developing countries has *declined* during this century from 40–50 percent to only 9 percent on the average in 1983, although in a few countries it remains as high as 20 percent.[92] Modern medicines, improved diet and better hygiene have pushed back death and more than doubled the length of life in the whole Western world, and a similar development is now in progress also in the developing countries, even though it is somewhat slower.[93]

---

88 This is also indirectly admitted in the *Awake!* of August 8, 1983, where the population "explosion" is *partly* explained in the following way: "It is due in part to a worldwide decline in the death rate as a result of improved medical care and economic and social conditions. Consequently, fewer babies are dying and more people are living longer." (P. 4)

89 Erland Hofsten, *Världens befolkning* ("World Population", Upsala, Sweden, 1970), pp. 94–96.

90 According to information regularly released by *Statistiska Centralbyrån* ("The Statistical Central Office") in Sweden.

91 Erland Hofsten, *Demografins grunder* ("Basics of Demography", Lund, Sweden, 1982), p. 139.

92 Hofsten, *Världens befolkning*, p. 96; *1985 World Population Data Sheet*, published by the Population Reference Bureau, Inc., Washington, D. C.

93 In China, for instance, infant mortality declined from c. 15 percent in 1950 to 3.8 percent in 1983. (Roy Prosterman, *The Decline in Hunger-Related Deaths*, 1984, p. 16; *The 1985 World Population Data Sheet*.)

The *1983 UNICEF Annual Report* says that, "Between the mid-1940s and the early

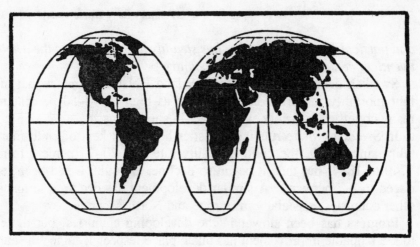

In 1900, *every nation on earth* had an infant mortality rate of over 50 per 1,000 live births.

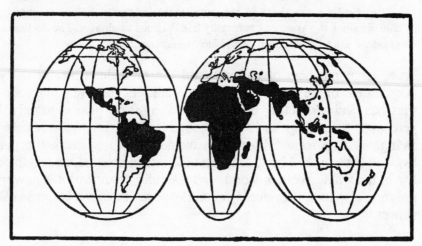

By 1983, *84 nations* had lowered their infant mortality rate below 50 per 1,000 live births.

Authorities regard the infant mortality rate to be the best indicator of overall social and economic well-being. When the rate has fallen to 5 percent (= 50 deaths per 1,000 live births) or below, this indicates that that country "is *meeting basic human needs,* including food, shelter, clothing, safe drinking water and sanitation." The fact that in 1900 all nations had an infant mortality rate surpassing 5 percent is a strong indicator of the lack of proper nutrition then prevailing. That 84 nations, by 1983, had lowered this rate below 5 percent, is an equally strong indicator that within their borders hunger had ceased to be a basic, society-wide issue. (Roy L. Prosterman, *The Decline in Hunger-Related Deaths,* San Francisco 1984, pp. 1, 4; *Ending Hunger: An Idea Whose Time Has Come,* published by the Hunger Project in 1985, p. 384; *1985 World Population Data Sheet,* published by the Population Reference Bureau, Inc., Washington, D.C. in 1985.)

Consequently, those who would employ child mortality figures in an attempt to "prove" that our generation has seen more famine and malnutrition than earlier centuries can only do so by ignoring all the contrary evidence. How many millions of children died annually in earlier centuries due to malnutrition and hunger-related diseases no one can say with certainty, as global estimates of the annual death rate were never made. But in view of the fact that *a four-fold or even five-fold decline* in child mortality has taken place in many of the developing countries, and up to *a twenty-fold decline* in numerous countries in the Western world, it is easy to realize that in earlier centuries many millions of children died every year from hunger and hunger-related diseases—in spite of the fact that the population of the world was much smaller in those days!

Undoubtedly this exceptional decline in infant and child mortality has saved hundreds of millions of lives in the developing countries alone. Professor D. Gale Johnson states:

> Those of us who decry the high rates of population growth in the developing countries should not forget that the increases in these rates have been due entirely to reductions in death rates and not at all to an increase in birth rates. There has been an enormous reduction in human suffering that has gone largely unrecognized—the pain and grief of hundreds of millions of parents that have been avoided by the reduction in infant and child mortality.[94]

In a world where 99 percent of mankind do not starve, and 75 percent are not even malnourished, it is not often realized that this situation is something *new and unique* in human history, and that in the past poverty and want were so universal that most people regarded them as matters of course, conditions that were inevitable, and therefore seldom questioned or even talked about. The book *Hunger and History* states:

> Feasts could well be occasions of happy memory, but of daily want was so little said that a world which regards hunger as a wrong from which no person in civilized countries should suffer, finds it somewhat difficult to understand that want and hunger were the lasting conditions under which previous generations lived. . . . It is hard for persons living under modern

---

1970's there was a 50 per cent reduction in child death rates in many low-income countries," although the rate of progress has slowed since then. (P. 7)

94 D. Gale Johnson, *World Food Problems and Prospects* (Washington, D.C., 1975), p. 19.

conditions to realize even inadequately what life was when the population pressed upon food supply during those ages <u>when want was universal</u>.[95]

Is a future famine catastrophe unavoidable?

Faced with the hard evidence that famine and hunger were unquestionably greater in past centuries than today, those who write material designed to excite a sense of impending doom often resort to the discussion, not of what *has* happened or *is* happening, but of what *might* happen.

It is not difficult to find statements by prominent persons pointing to some future tragedy as likely. In the book *The Late Great Planet Earth* (pages 101, 102), J. Bruce Giffing, Chairman of the Genetics Department at Ohio State University, is quoted as stating in 1969 that **"Unless mankind acts immediately, there will be a worldwide famine in 1985, and the extinction of man within 75 years."** Evidently mankind 'acted' in time, for 1985 saw nothing remotely resembling a worldwide famine.

Similarly, *The Watchtower* of April 15, 1983, points to the rapidly increasing world population today, "that strains the world's long-term capacity to feed itself," and quotes food expert E. R. Duncan as saying that "this situation is <u>unique</u> in human history." Did Duncan, however, conclude that population will inevitably outstrip food production, causing large-scale famines within the next few decades? No, while acknowledging the possibility, he finds no reasons for believing it will necessarily come. **"Indeed, this may eventually be true, but recent history shows that while the situation is precarious it is not disastrous except in a few cases."**[96] In the long run, he believes that population "will be stabilized at a manageable level."[97]

Many other authorities agree, pointing to the fact that the rapid

95 E. P. Prentice, *Hunger and History*, pp. 10, 137. French historian Fernand Braudel summarizes the world's food situation in the past in this way: "Famine recurred so insistently for centuries on end that it became incorporated into man's biological regime and built into his daily life. Dearth and penury were continual, and familiar even in Europe, despite its privileged position." (*Civilization & Capitalism 15th–18th Century*, p. 73) Like Prentice, Braudel emphasizes that "chronic under-nourishment" prevailed all over the world in the past. (P. 91) N. W. Pirie, one of England's best known scientists, agrees: "It seems likely that malnutrition permanently or during certain times of the year has been the usual condition of mankind and that it was regarded as normal."—*Food Resources Conventional and Novel*, 1969. (Quoted from the Swedish edition, published in Stockholm, 1970, p. 32)

96 E. R. Duncan (editor), *World Food Problems* (Ames, Iowa, 1977), p. 3.

97 Ibid, p. xi.

population increases that started in the 1940's reached a climax in the 1960's with an annual growth rate of around 2.0 percent, but then began to decline. Today the global growth rate is 1.7 percent, and energetic efforts are being made in many countries to limit the growth further.[98] If these efforts turn out to be successful, the "population bomb" can be disarmed before it explodes in a world catastrophe.

Equally as important, food production has so far kept pace with the population increases. **"Worldwide the period from 1950 to 1971 saw a doubling of cereal grain production, while population increased by only half that amount,"** Duncan notes.[99] And according to FAO (United Nations Food and Agriculture Organization), there is still no lack of food in the world. On the contrary, in the world as a whole there has been a growing *surplus* of food in recent years.[100] The *1983 UNICEF Annual Report* states that **"food production exceeded population growth in 1982, and, with the exception of Africa south of Sahara, increased harvests were recorded for all developing regions."** (Page 6) If this is so, why do we yet see tens of millions starving today, and hundreds of millions, possibly over a billion persons, are malnourished or undernourished?

As Edouard Saouma, the present Director of FAO, explained at the World Food Conference held in Rome in October, 1983, these hundreds of millions are malnourished or starving, simply *because they are poor.* They cannot afford to buy the food that actually exists. And what is worse: This poverty in the underdeveloped countries is kept up by strong economic and political interests in the developed countries, who are unwilling to share their abundance.[101]

---

98 The fact is that leading experts now believe that the global population crisis is essentially over. "The population bomb is being defused," said *New Scientist* magazine of August 9, 1984. "Almost unnoticed, in the past 10 years the annual growth in the world's population has shrunk from 2 per cent to 1.7 per cent. . . . The United Nations now predicts that the world's population, currently around 4.7 billion, will reach only 6.1 billion by 2000 (20 per cent less than some past estimates) and will stabilize at around 10 billion sometime around the end of the next century." (P. 12) See also *New Scientist* of August 16, 1984, p. 8, and *Awake!* of April 8, 1984, p. 29.

99 Duncan, p. 23.

100 *1982 FAO Production Yearbook* (Rome, 1983), pp. 5, 9, 75, 76, 97–101, 261, 262.

101 As James P. Grant, the present Execution Director of UNICEF, explains on page 2 of the *1982 UNICEF Annual Report,* with only $6.5 billion a year over the next 15 years "it would be possible to break the back of large-scale hunger and malnutrition." Further new techniques developed during the last few years "could reduce disabilities and deaths among children in most developing countries . . . by at least half before the end of this century." These techniques, says, Grant, "are even less costly than we had thought." (*1983 UNICEF Annual Report,* pp. 3, 4)

WHAT LEADING AUTHORITIES SAY ABOUT HUNGER TODAY COMPARED WITH THE PAST

"For the first time ever, a society is possible in which poverty can be abolished and with it, misery and hunger. The eradication of hunger is no longer a utopian scheme; it is a perfectly available objective."—Josué de Castro in *The Geopolitics of Hunger* (New York, 1977), pp. 447, 448.

"In every age and in every land people have starved, . . . yet the fact seems to be that man, on the average, is steadily achieving a better diet. . . . certainly the people today are, on the average, somewhat better fed than they were 100 years ago."—*The Biology of Human Starvation* by A. Keys, J. Bozek, A. Henschel, O. Michelsen and H. Longstreet Taylor (St. Paul, 1950), pp. 3, 12.

"A world which regards hunger as a wrong . . . finds it somewhat difficult to understand that want and hunger were the lasting conditions under which previous generations lived. . . . It is hard for persons living under modern conditions to realize even inadequately what life was . . . during those long ages when want was universal."—E. Parmalee Prentice, *Hunger and History. The Influence of Hunger on Human History* (Caldwell, Idaho, 1951), pp. 10, 137.

"Famine over the centuries has been a frequent phenomenon and has tended to be regarded as a more or less normal calamity. . . . But there is every indication that the incidence [in earlier times] was considerably greater than it is today in nearly all inhabited areas of the world."—Bruce F. Johnston in his article on "Famine" in *Colliers Encyclopedia*, Editorial Director William D. Halsey, Vol. 9 (New York, 1979), pp. 552, 553.

"We might be inclined to deduce from the pictorial evidence of famine that we have seen recently on television, in newspapers, and in magazines that the world is more prone to famine now than it used to be. But the evidence is clearly to the contrary. . . . There has been a rather substantial reduction in the incidence of famine during the past century."—Food expert Professor D. Gale Johnson, *World Food Problems and Prospects* (Washington, D. C., 1975), p. 17.

"Consumption of food per person in the world is up over the last 30 years. . . . Famine deaths have decreased in the past century even in absolute terms, let alone relative to population. World food prices have been trending lower for decades and centuries . . . and there is strong reason to believe that this trend will continue."—Julian L. Simon and Herman Kahn in *The Resourceful Earth* (London, 1984), p. 16.

Neither population increase nor food production, then, is the real problem. It is a well-known fact that the resources of the earth could well feed a world population many times greater than that living on earth today. And what is more: For the first time in history mankind has at its disposal the means for exploiting these resources to that extent. As de Castro observes:

> **The knowledge that man now possesses, if intelligently applied, would provide humanity with enough food of the necessary quality to insure its nutritional balance for many years to come, even if the population were to double, quadruple, or increase tenfold.**[102]

Whether mankind will make use of these possibilities to put an end to famine and malnutrition or not, is, of course, unpredictable. Anything can happen in the next few decades, and we make no attempt to speculate or to prophesy. Basically, the problem is one of *love for one's neighbour.* How do we as Christians react on hearing and reading about the existing millions of poor and hungry people? If our interest in them is limited to the question: Are they numerous enough to constitute one of the features of a supposed "composite sign" of the end?—would that not indicate that there is something fundamentally wrong with our "Christianity"? If our interest in such hungry ones goes no further than that, would we not then run the risk of being placed among those to whom our Lord Jesus Christ will say on the "day of judgment": **"I was hungry and you gave me nothing to eat. . . ."**?—Matthew chapter twenty-five, verse 42, NIV.

---

102 de Castro, p. 466. "It is no accident," said *New Scientist* of August 9, 1984, "that it is in Africa where farming methods are least developed, that famine persists." (P. 15) Yet it would be possible for many countries in Africa to increase considerably their food production *with the use of the present primitive methods.* FAO (UN's Food and Agriculture Organization) says that "only half of the world's potential land is under cultivation today." This includes many parts of Africa, where in 11 countries, "including Zaire, Zambia, Angola and the Ivory Coast, the people could, using current methods, feed five times their current populations. The Congo could feed 20 times its population and Gabon 100 times. Overall, Africa could, with primitive methods, feed 2.7 times its current population, says the FAO." (Ibid., p. 15)

CHAPTER 3

Earthquakes and Historical Facts

WHAT ARE the facts about earthquakes in our time? Is our planet Earth shaking with greater frequency and intensity than ever before in human history?

As we have seen, in *The Late Great Planet Earth*, Hal Lindsey listed this as one of the signs marking the time for Christ's setting up his Kingdom. (Pages 52, 53) Again in *The Promise*, he states that Jesus **"warned that earthquakes would increase in frequency and intensity as this old earth prepared for its final cataclysm."** (Page 198) This piece of the prophetic "jigsaw puzzle" is supposed to have come into place in our day.

In his book *Good-bye Planet Earth* (1976), Seventh Day Adventist author Robert H. Pierson has a subheading **"A Shaking, Quaking Planet."** Under it he states:

> **With increasing frequency and intensity Mother Earth has been shaking and quaking. Hundreds of thousands of people have lost their lives. Multiplied thousands more will perish in greater earth spasms ahead. Never since the days of Noah has the world been so badly battered.**
>
> **Again God is speaking to us—He is seeking to tell us that our time is short. His Son, Jesus Christ, will return soon. Nature's voice speaks through the floods, the storms, the earthquakes.** (Pages 21, 22)

He then quotes Jesus' words at Luke chapter twenty-one, verse 11, as evidence of this.

The most remarkable and detailed claims in this regard, however, are those made by the Governing Body of Jehovah's Witnesses and their Watch Tower Society. Maintaining that Christ's statement regarding "great earthquakes" (Luke chapter 21, verse 11) has seen its true fulfillment only since 1914, the Watch Tower Society claims that we have experienced an enormous increase in such earthquakes since that year:

The frequency of major earthquakes has increased about *20 times* what it was on an average during the two thousand years before 1914.—*Survival into a New Earth* (1984), page 23.

This is a fantastic claim. It is really possible to prove such a statement? How much is actually known about earthquake activity in the past? Are ancient records on earthquakes complete enough to allow for reliable comparisons with our century? And what is meant by a "great" earthquake? What determines its 'greatness'?

To be able to assess accurately the claims of the Watch Tower Society, we must first seek an answer to these questions.

Recording earthquake activity

The Greek word for "shaking" and (when it applies to the earth) "earthquake" is *seismós*. The science of earthquakes, therefore, is called *seismology*.

Seismology is a very young branch of science. **"Not . . . until the early 1850s did the first true seismologist, as we would recognize the term, appear on the scene. He was an Irishman, Robert Mallet."**[1] After him came *John Milne*, called "the father of seismology."[2] In 1880 he invented the first proper *seismograph*, and from the end of the last century a fairly accurate recording of earthquakes has been possible.[3]

Consequently seismologists are able to present a complete list of the great earthquakes that have occurred on earth from 1903 onward.[4] With further improvement of the seismograph an increasing number of countries have adopted its use. But not until the end of the 1950's did this observation network reach a global scale.[5] Since then it has

---

1 Peter Verney, *The Earthquake Handbook*, New York and London 1979, p. 47. There is no general consensus about this. Professor N. N. Ambraseys, for instance, considers John Michell (1724–93) 'the first true seismologist.' (Ambraseys, *Engineering Seismology*, University of London, Inaugural lecture 18 Nov. 1975, p. 54.)

2 Verney, p. 51. Others would term him the 'father of *English* seismology' only, recognizing that other, contemporary scientists in other countries, too, made important contributions to the early development of seismology. (See the discussion by Dr. August Sieberg in *Geologische, physikalische un angewandte Erdbebenkunde*, Jena 1923, pp. 2, 373.)

3 Verney, pp. 53, 54; B. Booth & F. Fitch, *Earthshock*, London 1979, p. 89.

4 G. A. Eiby, *Earthquakes*, London 1968, p. 191. This holds true only of earthquakes measuring 7.9 and above on the Richter scale.

5 Markus Båth, *Introduction to Seismology*, 2nd ed., Basel, Boston, Stuttgart 1979, pp. 27, 262–266.

been possible to record and measure all earthquakes, small and major, all over the globe.

It is not an easy matter to compare the *complete* list of great earthquakes recorded in our century by modern seismologists with that of past centuries. This is because of the comparatively scanty and incomplete information available from earlier centuries. Historical sources become more and more sparse the farther back in time we go. Even of modern records, seismologist A. W. Lee in 1939 wrote:

> The statistics are complete enough to give a fair representation of the distribution of the earthquakes which now occur, but, since they extend over less than half a century, are insufficient for showing whether there has been any secular change in the frequency.[6]

Another factor that considerably limits our knowledge of ancient earthquakes is that most earthquakes take place *outside Europe,* the source of most of our information for the greater part of history from the first century to the "Age of Discovery" in the fifteenth century. *The Encyclopedia Americana* tells us that:

> Roughly 80 percent of the seismic energy of the world is released in a belt which girdles the Pacific Ocean. A secondary belt, starting in the Mediterranean area and running easterly across Asia, is the scene of earthquakes which represent over 15 percent of the seismic energy of the world.[7]

"Western Europe," writes Verney, "might be considered almost a stable zone by comparison with the hectic earthquake history of the Andes or elsewhere on the Ring of Fire [the Pacific Ocean belt]."[8]

As the historical source material for past centuries is, with a few important exceptions, limited to Europe and the Mediterranean area, it is easily realized what this means. What do we, for instance, know about the "hectic earthquake" activity in North, Middle and South America *before Columbus?* John Milne points out: **"The records before the Christian era, and prior to the year 1700, are practically confined to occurrences in Southern Europe, China and Japan."[9]** In our own century, the majority of the most destructive earthquakes

---

6 J. Milne & A. W. Lee, *Earthquakes and Other Earth Movements,* 7th ed., London 1939, pp. 134, 135.

7 *The Encyclopedia Americana,* 1966, under "Earthquake," p. 496.

8 Verney, p. 75.

9 *Report of the Eightieth Meeting of the British Association for the Advancement of Science, Portsmouth: 1911, Aug. 31–Sept. 7* (London 1912), p. 649.

THE EARTHQUAKE BELTS OF THE EARTH

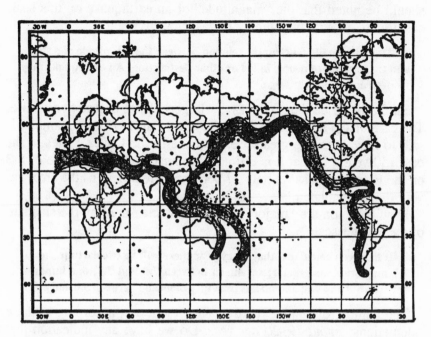

Seismic map showing the two earthquake belts of the world. (From R. A. Daly, Our Mobile Earth, New York & London 1926, p. 6.)

have occurred in areas *outside* Europe and in most cases in areas from which no historical records of past occurrences are available for comparison. The Watch Tower Society, either by choice or otherwise, *takes not a single one of these vital factors into consideration when making its remarkable claim.*

What constitutes a "great" earthquake?

According to Luke's rendering of Jesus' words to his disciples there would be "great earthquakes." (Luke 21:11) What is meant by a "great" earthquake?

Modern seismologists measure the size of an earthquake according to certain scales. The one in common use today is the so-called *Richter scale,* devised by C. F. Richter in 1935. This scale measures *the total amount of energy* released in seismic waves during an earthquake. Earthquakes measuring 7.0 or more on the scale are termed "major," while those measuring 8.0 and over are termed "great."[10] It should be noted that the "magnitude" of an earthquake on this scale has little to do with the number of casualties:

> There is usually no clear correlation between the magnitude of a shock and the number of people killed or other destruction. An earthquake may be destructive but not large.[11]

Similarly an earthquake may be large but not destructive of life. The earthquake in Owens Valley, California, in 1872, for example, is said to have been the greatest earthquake in the United States in the past 150 years, in that it is estimated to have had a magnitude of 8.3 on the Richter scale. Yet only 27 persons were killed, as the area was very thinly populated.[12]

How common are "major" earthquakes, measured by the standard of the Richter scale?

> It has been calculated that every year there will be two earthquakes of 7.7 magnitude or greater; seventeen between 7.0 and 7.7; one hundred between 6.0 and 7.0; and no less than fifty thousand between 3.0 and 4.0.[13]

The number of "major" earthquakes, then, are, according to these calculations, *about 19–20 per year.* Do we have any indication that the "major" (7.0 and more in magnitude) and "great" (8.0 and more) earthquakes have increased in number and magnitude during the period it has been possible to measure them instrumentally, that is, since the end of the last century onward?

If we were to believe a recent claim by the Worldwide Church of God, an increasingly vocal organization proclaiming the speedy end of the age, the answer would be 'Yes.' On page 7 of the April, 1986, issue of its monthly *The Good News of the World Tomorrow,* Norman L. Shoaf, a spokesman of the movement, confidently asserted:

> Did you know that from 1901 to 1944, during more than four decades, only three earthquakes measured magnitude 7 or over? . . . Then, in just 10 years from 1945 to 1954, the number leaped to 21 quakes measuring 7

---

10 Booth & Fitch, p. 90; C. F. Richter, *Natural History,* December 1969, p. 44.
11 Båth, p. 137.
12 Verney, p. 96. The earthquake in San Francisco in 1906, that killed about 700 people, also had a magnitude of 8.3. (The three earthquakes in New Madrid, Missouri, in 1811–12 were greater than these two, with estimated magnitudes of 8.6, 8.5 and 8.7, respectively.)
13 Verney, p. 72. *The Encyclopedia Americana,* 1966 ed., under "Earthquake," page 496, states that, "If all shocks down to the very smallest are included, it is likely that the total may be well over a million." The great majority of these shocks are, of course, not noticed by man, being recorded only with the aid of instruments.

or over. From then on, large earthquakes have increased dramatically. From 1955 to 1964—in just one decade—87 earthquakes measured 7 or over; from 1965 to 1974, 136; from 1975 to 1984, 133.

It would be a charitable understatement to say that this claim is simply nonsensical. When confronted with this claim, Professor Seweryn J. Duda, a renowned seismologist at the University of Hamburg, West Germany, wrote that "In the time 1901–1944 about 1000 (one thousand) earthquakes with magnitude 7 or over have taken place worldwide." In fact, his letter to the authors dated July 7, 1986, contradicted the entire statement of the Worldwide Church of God. See Appendix A for the complete text of his letter.

The simple fact, then, is that no such unique increases have been observed, either since 1914 or at any other subsequent point of this century. Actually, the evidence produced by modern seismologists indicates *the contrary*.

Charles F. Richter, former President of the Seismological Society of America and the originator of the "Richter scale," made reference to this evidence in an article published in the December 1969 issue of *Natural History* magazine:

> One notices with some amusement that certain religious groups have picked this rather unfortunate time to insist that the number of earthquakes is increasing. In part they are misled by the increasing number of small earthquakes that are being catalogued and listed by newer, more sensitive stations throughout the world. It is worth remarking that the number of great [that is, 8.0 and over on the Richter scale] earthquakes from 1896 to 1906 (about twenty-five) was greater than in any ten-year interval since.[14]

Parts of this statement were quoted disapprovingly on page 72 of *The Watchtower* of February 1, 1974—without the reader being informed that it came from a leading authority on seismology. Jesus was not speaking of any "ten-year interval," said *The Watchtower,* but of a whole "generation."

Dr. Richter's statement, however, was aimed at demonstrating that the claimed *increase* in the earthquake activity during our century finds no support in the recorded seismological data during the period

---

14 *Natural History,* Dec. 1969, p. 44. In his *Elementary Seismology* (San Francisco 1958, page 357) Richter similarly states that "There is no escape from the conclusion that the greatest shallow [that is, near the surface] shocks were more frequent before 1918 than afterward."

of *instrumentally* measured seismicity, which covers the period from 1896, or more particularly from 1903 onward.

Still, his statement was made back in 1969. What, then, of this claim found on page 30 of the book *The 1980's—Countdown to Armageddon,* by Hal Lindsey?

> **The 1970's experienced the largest increase in the number of quakes known to history. In fact, the dramatic increase in quakes in 1976 led many scientists to say we are entering a period of great seismic disturbances.**

This statement has no more basis in fact that do those of the Watch Tower Society and the Worldwide Church of God. More recent statistics published by other seismologists, who have carefully and objectively examined the matter, not only confirm the accuracy of Dr. Richter's statement, but show that it continued to be true into the 1970's.

In 1965 the well-known seismologist Seweryn J. Duda published a catalog of the major earthquakes for the period 1897–1964. In 1979 this catalog was updated to include the period 1965–1977 in an article written by the same author jointly with professor Markus Båth, another seismologist of worldwide repute. Their very thorough study shows that during this eighty-year period (1897–1977) about twenty (19.94 to be exact) major earthquakes occurred annually. Any change in the *number* of earthquakes with a magnitude of 7.0 and above on the Richter scale could not be demonstrated for the period after 1914, compared to the period before that date. As to the *magnitude* of the quakes, on the other hand, their study revealed that the first twenty years of our century (1900–1920) had about *twice as great* an energy release per year as the whole period thereafter up to 1977![15]

15 S. J. Duda, "Secular seismic energy release in the circum-Pacific belt," *Tectonophysics,* 2 (1965), pp. 409–52; Markus Båth and S. J. Duda, "Some aspects of global seismicity," *Tectonophysics,* 54 (1979), pp. T1–T8. Newspapers often present grossly misleading data on earthquakes. Richter (1958, p. 5) points out that "the popular press" can be used "only with caution." However, *The Watchtower* of May 15, 1984, p. 25, referred to an article published in *The New York Times* that termed 1983 "A Year of Earthquakes," because of a claimed "rash of lethal earthquakes" that year. To prove this *The Watchtower* reproduced a list of 9 quakes from a period of 3 months, all of which were said to be "major earthquakes, reckoned on the Richter scale." A closer look at the list, however, shows that only 3 of the 9 earthquakes are "major," having a magnitude of 7.0 or more. As Professor Markus Båth points out (personal letter, dated October 3, 1984), this is *not above, but below the normal:* "The information from *The New York Times* is completely misleading. With 3 earthquakes of a magnitude of 7 or more during 3 months, the number of such quakes would be 12 in a year. This is clearly below the average, which is 20 quakes a year

The table on page 54, published in 1912 (for the years 1899 to 1909), gives some idea of the high seismicity recorded in the period previous to 1914. For the period before the beginning of our century reliable instrumental data are missing, as was pointed out earlier.

What is the conclusion to be drawn from this very careful study of the period from which reliable instrumental recordings are available? It is this: No marked change in the *number* of major earthquakes may be demonstrated during the period from 1897 to 1977. On the other hand, the study shows the frequence of the *greatest* earthquakes to have been considerably higher in the first twenty years of this period than in the sixty years that followed!

Efforts to Overcome the Evidence

It goes without saying that, on being confronted with these scientific statistics, the Watch Tower Society takes no great delight in the measurements of the seismologists. The Society's tendency has been to reject them altogether when making statistical comparisons on earthquake activity before and after 1914, supplying instead a definition of their own making as to what is meant by a "great" earthquake. We read:

> **What is it that makes an earthquake 'great'? Is it not its effect on lives and property? But modern earthquake students tend to consider an earthquake 'great' only if it rates high on the Richter scale, which rates 'magnitude,' the power or force a quake releases.**[16]

---

with a magnitude of 7 or more. The statement in the newspaper points to a quake activity that is below the normal!" Nor was 1983 "A Year of Earthquakes" measured by *death figures*. According to information available from the *World Data Center A for Solid Earth Geophysics* (see later, footnote 19), only 2,328 persons died in earthquakes during 1983, which is far below the average.

Even 1976 did not see the 'dramatic increase in quakes' claimed by Hal Lindsey, despite the great earthquake in China that year. Professor Markus Båth, in his *Introduction to Seismology*, says: "The year 1976 deserves a special comment. Numerous earthquake disasters occurred throughout the year, with maximum number of casualties in China. . . . On the other hand, looking at 1976 from a purely seismological point of view, there were not more or stronger earthquakes this year than in average." (P. 151) Commenting on the period after 1976, Professor Båth, in a private letter, adds: "The years after 1976 until now [1985], at least, have shown a clear decline in the seismic activity of the earth, both with respect to the number of great earthquakes (high magnitudes, over 7.0) and the number of quake victims. But this is, of course, just an example of an occasional variation that has always occurred." (Private letter Båth-Jonsson, dated August 21, 1985.)

16 *The Watchtower*, February 1, 1974, p. 72.

Megaseismic Frequency.

Between 1899 and 1909 the number of very large earthquakes recorded was not less than 976. Many of these were recorded at stations all over the world, others over the whole of the Northern Hemisphere, and none of them disturbed an area less than that of Europe and Asia.

The numbers recorded in successive months were as follow:—

Year	J.	F.	M.	A.	M.	J.	J.	A.	S.	O.	N.	D.	Total.
1899	9	5	9	4	3	6	7	7	12	4	7	4	75
1900	7	3	3	2	3	4	2	4	5	6	5	3	47
1901	7	4	8	4	4	3	0	8	6	6	11	6	67
1902	12	7	9	8	4	2	4	11	8	3	6	3	77
1903	10	11	7	4	8	8	5	5	8	9	6	10	91
1904	4	2	8	9	5	8	6	8	7	6	5	6	74
1905	7	11	10	7	6	8	11	3	7	6	5	5	86
1906	14	18	20	11	4	9	5	22	12	10	8	7	140
1907	8	4	9	6	12	9	7	7	5	10	10	7	94
1908	4	6	11	5	8	4	4	12	9	8	13	6	90
1909	9	10	11	14	11	14	8	13	13	15	8	9	135
	91	81	103	74	68	75	59	100	92	83	84	66	976
		275			217			251			233		

Winter months . . 508 ⎱ 976
Summer months . . 468 ⎰

Seismologist F. M. Walker in *Report of the Eighteenth Meeting of the British Association for the Advancement of Science,* London 1912, pages 38 and 39. The expression "very large," here has no reference to the Richter scale, which was not in use at that time.

The Watch Tower Society, thus, prefers to measure the magnitude of an earthquake in *the number of deaths* caused. It states:

One way to prove clearly that the generation since 1914 is unusual as far as earthquakes are concerned is to consider how many deaths they have caused.[17]

Some reflection will soon reveal why the Watch Tower Society would prefer this method of reckoning the 'greatness' of earthquakes. It contains several flaws of which most persons are unaware, and the claims of the Society *depend* on that fact for their appearance of au-

17 *The Watchtower,* February 1, 1974, p. 73.

thenticity. When the false premises upon which the Society bases its arguments are clearly seen, however, their statistics lose their impressiveness. Consider:

First, as was pointed out earlier, data on earthquakes and death figures are much sparser from past centuries due to the fragmentary historical sources, which moreover, previous to the year 1700, "are practically confined to occurrences in Southern Europe, China and Japan." So the idea that completely accurate comparisons can be made between modern-day and historic earthquake death figures is simply not true.

Second, the rapid population growth and urbanization in our century has very reasonably increased the number of deaths in great earthquakes, particularly when these have hit densely populated areas. An increase in the number of deaths, then, would not be a valid indicator of an increase in the number of "great earthquakes." We may also rightly ask: Did Jesus, in referring to "great earthquakes," actually speak of an increase either in the number of quakes or the number of victims? His simple statement was that, along with war, famine and pestilence, "there will be great earthquakes." Anything beyond that is human assumption, a reading into his words more than they actually say.

Despite their choice of death figures in preference to seismological measurements, when it suits their argumentation the Watch Tower Society does not hesitate to quote statements about earthquakes that are based on the Richter scale—without telling their readers that they are doing so. For example, the very same issue of the *Watchtower* (February 1, 1974) quoted above presents a long string of statements on earthquakes occurring since 1914, the statements said to be taken from "highly respected reference works" (though no references are given):

> China (1920), 'one of the most appalling catastrophes in history.' Japan (1923), 'the worst disaster in [Japan's] history.' Pakistan (1935), 'one of the greatest earthquakes of history.' El Salvador (1951), the most destructive quake in El Salvador's history.' Egypt (1955), 'Egypt experienced the worst earthquake in its history.' Afghanistan (1956), 'believed to be the worst in the history of the country.' Chile (1960), 'no earthquake in history has ever had a greater range than this.' Alaska (1964), 'the largest earthquake ever recorded in North America.' Peru (1970), 'the worst natural disaster on record in the Western Hemisphere.'[18]

18 *The Watchtower*, February 1, 1974, p. 74.

But the reader is not informed that expressions such as "largest," "worst," "greatest," and so forth in these statements in several cases do *not* refer to the number of deaths in these earthquakes, and at least in some cases clearly refer to the Richter scale which this same article has said should not be the means of measuring earthquake "greatness"!

Thus the earthquake in Alaska in 1964—"the largest earthquake ever recorded in North America"—took only 114 (some sources say 131) lives, although it had a very great magnitude of 8.5 on the Richter scale![19]

The phrase "the largest . . . ever recorded" further limits the time of comparison to the period during which earthquakes have been measured *instrumentally,* that is, from the end of the last century onward. Some of the earthquakes included were not "great" on any count, neither according to Richter's scale, nor in the number of lives lost. What is called the "most destructive quake in El Salvador's history" had a magnitude of only 6.5 and took 400 lives (according to another source 1,100 lives), while the claimed "worst earthquake in [Egypt's] history" had a magnitude of 6.3 and took just 18 lives![20]

Several of the statements quoted are certainly not scientific descriptions. They rather reflect sensation-rousing newspaper headlines created during the immediate impact of the catastrophe. Although some of the earthquakes mentioned (China 1920, Japan 1923, Pakistan 1935, and Peru 1970) were indeed very great and claimed thousands of lives, most seismologists would certainly be hesitant to term *any* of them the "worst" or "greatest" in the history of the country in question.

Quite recently the Watch Tower Society has come up with a new definition of a "great" earthquake. According to the *Awake!* magazine of October 22, 1984, its latest statistical calculations are now said to include earthquakes that meet at least *one* of the following qualifications:

Magnitude .... **7.5 or more on the Richter scale**
Deaths .... **100 or more**
Damage .... **$5 million (U.S.) or more in property destroyed.—Page 6.**

---

19 Booth & Fitch, p. 80; Robert A. Ganse and John B. Nelson, *Catalog of Significant Earthquakes 2000 B.C. – 1979,* Boulder, Colorado 1981, p. 63 (Report SE-27 of the *World Data Center A for Solid Earth Geophysics*).

20 Ganse & Nelson, pp. 56, 58. The earthquake in Afghanistan in 1956 claimed 220 lives according to some tables, 2,000 according to others.

These standards for measuring "greatness" are also used in the 1985 Watch Tower Society publication *Reasoning from the Scriptures*, page 236.

Surprisingly, the Richter scale, previously rejected, has now been introduced to play an important role in their statistics. On a closer look at their calculations, the reason soon becomes apparent. While seismologists properly make comparisons based on the Richter scale only for the period during which earthquakes have been measured *instrumentally*, that is, by seismograph since the end of the last century, the Watch Tower Society elects to include *the past 2000 years* in its comparisons! This allows for a very biased comparison. How so?

While it is true that seismologists have *estimated* magnitudes for many great earthquakes of the past, for the bulk of destructive earthquakes before A.D. 1900 such estimates are missing.[21] All these destructive earthquakes obviously would fail to meet the first criterion set up by the Watch Tower Society—no matter how great in magnitude they actually may have been![22] And if they do not meet at least one of the other two criteria, they are conveniently excluded from the calculations altogether!

As to the second criterion, it has already been pointed out that death figures are often missing in ancient records, especially if the losses amounted to only some hundreds or less. In fact, many severe earthquakes that involved relatively few fatalities may have been completely ignored in the early records. This can only mean that countless "qualified" earthquakes in the past have been excluded by the Society's arbitrarily set standards of comparison!

The same holds true for damage, the third criterion set up by the Watch Tower Society. Damages are far better known for modern earthquakes than for the earlier ones.[23] Besides that, since there are manifold more buildings nowadays—and larger and more sophisticated

---

21 The estimates of this kind that do exist seem to have been generally included in the catalog prepared by Ganse and Nelson. (See earlier footnote 19.)

22 In this connection it is noteworthy that *The Watchtower*, February 1, 1974, p. 72, states that "some of the earthquakes with the highest magnitude ratings . . . are under the oceans" and that such "have had virtually no effect on men." Speaking of "potentially damaging earthquakes" (3.8 and over), seismologist J. H. Latter, in the *Advancement of Science* (June 1969, page 365) even says that "the overwhelming majority occur beneath the sea or far from inhabited regions." As such quakes in most cases would pass unnoticed before the time of instrumental registration, it is clear that the Society's magnitude criterion could grossly distort the real facts about earthquake frequency.

23 Although Ganse and Nelson have tried to estimate such damages for past earthquakes in their catalog, the damages for numerous earthquakes are stated to be "unknown."

ones at that—a comparison of the sort carried out by the Watch Tower Society of necessity must clearly do injustice to any comparison with the past. This is stressed by N. N. Ambraseys, who is professor of Engineering Seismology at Imperial College of Science and Technology in London. He says that,

> . . . the exact repetition of an old earthquake at the present day will differ not only in the type of structures damaged but also in the degree of damage. In some cases modern structures will be more severely damaged than old buildings. A distant large earthquake ten centuries ago would have caused practically no damage in Istanbul, Ankara or Jerusalem; the same earthquake today would cause damage to a large number of long-period structures in these cities.[24]

Quite naturally, many earthquakes in earlier times, although involving substantial damage, would fail to meet the Watch Tower Society's purely arbitrary criterion of "$5 million or more in property destroyed."

Obviously the new criteria for "great earthquakes" suggested by the Watch Tower Society are designed to *qualify* the largest number possible of the earthquakes *after* 1914 and to *exclude* as many as possible from the time *previous* to that year. We are not at all surprised to find that calculations based on such slanted and biased reasoning would *appear* to show an enormous increase of "great" earthquakes in our century compared to earlier times. The *Awake!* article just quoted concluded:

> Since 1914 the yearly average of reported earthquakes has soared. There are 11 times the number that there were, on an average, annually during the 1,000 years before that date. And 20 times the annual average for the 2,000 years preceding 1914.[25]

The present world seismological situation does not actually lend itself to such statistical comparison with that of the past two millenia. This is because, as demonstrated earlier, available data on earthquakes

---

24 N. N. Ambraseys, "Value of Historical Records of Earthquakes," *Nature*, Vol. 232, August 6, 1971, p. 379.

25 *Awake!* Oct. 22, 1984, p. 6. Note the wording "reported earthquakes." It indicates that the Society knows that written records of great quakes in the past are incomplete. However, the unsuspecting reader is not likely to notice this distinction. The Society obviously wants him to conclude that there *actually* has been a *tremendous* increase of earthquakes since 1914. Thus the Society's book *Survival into a New Earth* (1984) does not hesitate to state that the frequency of major earthquakes "has increased about 20 times what it was on an average during the two thousand years before 1914." (p. 23)

are much sparser from earlier centuries. In fact, for *whole continents* data are completely lacking for the greater part of the past two millenia, and especially previous to the year 1700. Similarly, it has only been in this century that tremors occurring in oceanic beds or uninhabited regions could be recorded, yet it is in such regions that the vast majority of high magnitude quakes occur.

It should also be observed that the method of comparison used in the earlier-quoted calculation contains another fraudulent element, not easily recognized by the unsuspecting reader. By extending the pre-1914 period of comparison thousands of years back in time to include the long ages of poor reporting of earthquakes, the Watch Tower Society naturally gets a very low *overall* annual average, even for later centuries when reporting actually increased. This conceals the large number of severe earthquakes known from the latest centuries, leveling them out with the aid of earlier centuries when reporting was poor. It is further concealed that this method does not point to 1914 any more than to any other date within the last 200–300 years. The choice of 1914 as the seismic "turning point" is thus wholly arbitrary. It would be equally possible to use the identical method to choose, for example, 1789, when the French Revolution started, or 1939, when World War II began and obtain similar results. Whatever date during the last 200–300 years picked as a watershed would get the full advantage of modern reporting following it, giving an apparent great increase in the annual average.

It is safe to say that any scientist who would slant and manipulate statistical data in this way in a scholarly journal would be quickly exposed as a fraud. In a religious paper, however, read by millions of unsuspecting people who feel that it might be a sin to question their leaders, such calculations easily pass as if they were firmly established facts.

When foretelling "great earthquakes" Jesus, quite evidently did not have in mind any modern standard, such as magnitudes on the Richter scale or a certain minimum of fatalities or damages calculated according to modern money standards. The Watch Tower Society's use of such standards does not appeal to us, as it should be natural for Christians first of all to turn to the Bible for clarification. True, we do find that an earthquake damaging "a tenth of" a city and killing "seven thousand persons" is termed "great" at Revelation chapter eleven, verse thirteen. However, the two earthquakes described as "great" at Matthew chapter twenty-eight, verse two, and Acts chapter sixteen, verse twenty-six, are not shown to have caused any appreciable damage, let alone any loss of life. Yet the Society accepts both of these as proof that there was a "first-century fulfillment of Jesus' words" regarding great earthquakes![26]

From the Scriptures themselves, then, it is only reasonable to conclude that Jesus spoke of "great earthquakes" in a general sense, of tremors affecting—with greater or lesser severity—people, property and landscape. He could not reasonably have had in mind statistics of average numbers of annual deaths before and after certain dates! Nonetheless, since such figures play a very major role in the Society's calculations, we will now proceed to a closer look at its statistics.

How to "prove" by statistics

In an article entitled "Can Statistics Mislead You?" the *Awake!* magazine of January 22, 1984, said on page 25:

> Figures don't lie, we are told. But be on guard. Honestly used, they can be very informative and useful. However, statistics can also be presented in a way that misleads you.

The examples presented below will show that this warning has a pertinence that its writer probably did not realize.

According to *Awake!*, February 22, 1961, page 7, the estimated number of annual deaths in earthquakes before 1914 was 5,000.

But in 1974 the Watch Tower Society lowered that figure. *The Watchtower* of February 1 that year cited a statement in the *1971 Nature/Science Annual*, according to which "more than three million people (possibly four million)" have died in earthquakes during the past 1,000 years. Estimating that at least 900,000 of these had died since 1914, the Society presented the following impressive statistics (page 73):

Earthquake deaths each year
Before 1914:   3,000
Since 1914:   15,000

These same statistics were published again in *Awake!*, January 8, 1977 (pages 15, 16). However, the book *Happiness How to Find It,*

---

26 *The Watchtower*, May 15, 1983, p. 5. In *Awake!*, August 8, 1968, p. 30, the Society emphasized that an earthquake in the latter part of June that year "claiming the lives of 16 persons and injuring 100 others" fulfilled "Scripture prophecies," although no magnitude rating or property value was considered. We agree that this earthquake met Jesus' prophecy, even if the Society should now reject it in the light of their latest criteria. There have been innumerable such earthquakes since Jesus spoke his words about them.

published in 1980, managed to "improve" the figures considerably, as the table on page 149 shows:

Earthquake deaths
Up to 1914   1,800 a year
Since 1914   25,300 a year

That the number of annual deaths could be increased in four years (from 1974 to 1980) to such an extent—from 15,000 to 25,000 a year—is relatively simple to explain:

In 1976 China was hit by the greatest killer earthquake in this century. Western newspapers, misled by a premature report from Hong Kong, first put the death toll of the quake at 650,000 or more (some even said 800,000). If this figure is divided by the number of years that had then passed since 1914 (62 years, from 1915 to 1976 inclusive), we get an average—from just this one earthquake—of close to 10,500 deaths a year. Thus a single great earthquake may create impressive statistics for a whole generation! If we were to take in place of this earthquake the great earthquake in China in 1556 which is listed as claiming about 830,000 victims, and then divide that death figure by the same number of years (62), we would get an average of about 13,400 deaths a year from that one earthquake alone.[27] (Adding other disastrous earthquakes from that century would, obviously, increase substantially the number of annual deaths during that sixteenth century.)

The Watch Tower Society, however, by its method of employing statistics, not only increased the annual death rate after 1914 from 15,000 to 25,300. They also succeeded in *reducing* the number of annual deaths *before 1914* from 3,000 a year (according to their statistics of 1974) to just 1,800 a year (according to their statistics of 1980)! This is perplexing indeed. How did they arrive at this new figure?

The answer is that the latest (and lower) statistics were not based upon the estimated 3–4 million victims of earthquakes during the past

27 This quake is usually said to have claimed more lives than any other recorded earthquake in history. However, it may have been surpassed in this respect by the earthquake that hit Upper Egypt and/or Syria on July 5, 1201, which, according to some ancient records, cost about 1,100,000 lives. If this figure were divided by a period of 62 years, we would obtain an annual average of 17,740. This would be a higher figure than the correct figure for the 20th century, 15,700, as shown in this section. See S. Alsinawi and H. A. A. Ghalith, "Historical Seismicity of Iraq," *Proceedings of the First Arab Seismological Seminar,* Seismological Unit of Scientific Research, Baghdad, Iraq, December 1978; also Ganse and Nelson, p. 6.

1,000 years, as were the earlier Society statistics, but upon *a much smaller figure*, 1,973,000 victims during a period of 1,059 years. The extraordinary feature about this is that this new figure is not some estimate made by any modern seismologist—it is a figure which the Watch Tower Society itself has created by adding up the number of deaths *in only 24 major earthquakes, selected from among literally thousands of destructive quakes that took place in the 1,059 years before 1914!*

The new figure first appeared in the *Awake!* magazine of February 22, 1977, page 11. In connection with a list of 43 earthquakes from the period of 1915–1976, it stated:

> Interestingly, for a period of 1,059 years (856 to 1914 C.E.), reliable sources list only 24 major earthquakes, with 1,972,952 fatalities. But compare that with the accompanying partial list citing 43 instances of earthquakes, in which 1,579,209 persons died during just the 62 years from 1915 to 1976 C.E.. . . . The dramatic upsurge in earthquake activity since 1914 helps to prove that we are now living in the time of Jesus' presence.

The statement that 'reliable sources list only 24 major earthquakes for the 1,059 years from 856 to 1914' is so far from the truth that it is almost impossible to understand how anyone with even an elementary knowledge of the subject could make such a statement. *The fact is that reliable sources list literally thousands of destructive earthquakes during this period!* (The evidence of this will be discussed in the last section of this chapter.) And this is by no means the end of the matter. The writer of the *Awake!* article takes those 24 pre-1914 earthquakes and seeks to make a comparison between them and earthquakes in the 62 years following 1914. But whereas the 24 earlier earthquakes were all *major* catastrophes, they are now compared with a modern list that includes both great *and small* disasters (some have death figures of 52, 65, 115, 131, and so on).

This unequal method of comparison is either the result of sheer carelessness or of deliberate bias and manipulation of fact. And, to further add to the distorted picture, the writer describes his post-1914 list as "partial," thus implying that the 24 major earthquakes allotted to the 1,059 years *before* 1914 is a *complete* number! With this the statement becomes so foreign to fact as to be almost comical.[28]

Yet it is upon absurd figures of this kind that the Watch Tower So-

---

28 The author of the Society's textbook *You Can Live Forever in Paradise on Earth* (1982), clearly presents these 24 quakes as a *complete* list of *major* quakes by saying that "from the year 856 C.E. to 1914, there were only 24 major earthquakes." (P. 151)

ciety has built up its figures of the average number of annual deaths before and after 1914 in its publications.[29]

The tendency is apparent. In the statistics of the Watch Tower Society, whereas the number of annual deaths *after 1914* has been raised, the average number of annual deaths *previous to 1914* has been steadily shrinking, as follows:

> *Annual earthquake deaths before 1914*
> Society statistics of 1961: 5,000 per year
> Society statistics of 1974: 3,000 per year
> Society statistics of 1980: 1,800 per year

If this trend were to continue at the same rate for another 20 years, the annual death figure previous to 1914 would be reduced to *zero* in the statistics of the Watch Tower Society!

How many people have actually died in earthquakes in past history? Due to the incomplete source material no one can say with definite certainty and estimates vary. **"It has been estimated that over seven million people have lost their lives in earthquakes,"** wrote Verney.[30] Another source states that probably ten million have died in earthquakes since the time of Christ.[31] An outstanding seismologist, Professor Båth, however, says:

> **It has been estimated that during historical time 50 to 80 (according to one estimate 74) million people have lost their lives in earthquakes or their immediate aftereffects, such as fires, landslides, tsunamis, etc.**[32]

It is obvious, then, that estimates of annual deaths in earthquakes in the past will be as divergent as the guesses of the total death number upon which they are based. Population growth is an important factor.

---

29 *Happiness How to Find It*, 1980, p. 149; the same impressive statistics were again published in *The Watchtower* of May 15, 1983, p. 7 (chart III).

30 Verney, p. 7. Seismologist J. H. Latter estimates that "a minimum of five million people have died as a result of earthquakes, and half a million as a result of volcanic eruptions, since A.D. 1000." But he adds: **It is probable that the maximum figures are between two and three times higher than this,**" that is, 10–15 million since A.D. 1000. This would mean a maximum of 1.5 million per century on the average. (*Advancement of Science*, June 1969, p. 362)

31 *New York Times*, August 20, 1950. Compare *Awake!* December 22, 1960, p. 14.

32 Bath, p. 137. The *Time* magazine of September 1, 1975, similarly stated: "During recorded history, earthquakes—and the floods, fires and landslides they have triggered—are estimated to have taken as many as 74 million lives."

Since about half of the world's population lives in the earthquake belts of the earth, it would certainly not be surprising if the number of deaths in earthquakes kept pace with the population growth in those areas. This would not constitute proof, however, that earthquakes have increased either in numbers or severity.

Along with their figures for pre-1914 earthquakes and their shifting death statistics, the Watch Tower Society has published lists of earthquakes with death figures from the year 1914 onward. Interestingly, the death figures in these lists also seem to change from one list to next, and they differ with authoritative reports in several instances. A comparison between the two latest lists—published in the *Awake!* of February 22, 1977, page 11, and in *The Watchtower* of May 15, 1983, page 7—gives the following result:

Earthquakes:	Death figures according to Awake! 2/22/1977	Death figures according to Watchtower 5/15/1983:
1920, China	180,000	200,000
1939 Turkey	23,000	30,000
1950, India	1,500	20,000
1962, Iran	10,000	12,230
1972, Nicaragua	6,000	10,000
1976, China	655,235	800,000
Total:	875,735	1,072,230

As can be seen, the death figures have been raised in the latest list by a total of nearly 200,000! This does not mean that the figures have been deliberately falsified. Lists showing deaths in earthquakes, published in different works, often vary. But the Watch Tower Society's listings reveal a clear tendency to choose always the *highest*, not the most *reliable*, figures in these works, evidently in an attempt to present the earthquakes of the twentieth century as being as "great" as possible, while the tendency to *reduce* the numbers and size of the earthquakes *before* 1914 is equally apparent. This is not an honest, objective use of data.

Actually, the most authoritative works often present much lower figures than those given by the Watch Tower Society in both of their post-1914 lists quoted above. The 1920 earthquake in China, which the Society lists as claiming 180,000 or 200,000 lives, according to the *Encyclopedia Americana* claimed about 100,000 victims.[33] Likewise the great earthquake in China in 1976, which the latest list of the Society shows as causing 800,000 deaths, in reality claimed 242,000 lives according to the figures released by the Chinese authorities![34] This lower figure is now generally believed by seismologists to be the correct one.[35] Inasmuch as the latest estimate of annual deaths in earthquakes since 1914 published by the Society is based upon figures that include a death toll of 650,000 for this quake, the correction mentioned here reduces the actual death figure of the Society by as much as one third![36]

The varying figures to be found in different works clearly demonstrate what a hazardous task it is to try to make any comparisons between earthquakes before and after 1914 *based on death figures*. It also demonstrates how easy it is to create a seemingly very impressive and convincing, *but completely misleading,* statistical picture, simply by choosing only those figures that best support a preconceived view from among the many different lists that have been published. To do this reflects, at best, shallow research and irresponsible journalism; at worst, deliberate deception.

33 *Encyclopedia Americana,* 1966, "Earthquake," page 498. Båth (page 141) has the same figure, 100,000, in his list. The earthquake in Japan 1923, which according to the Society's list took 143,000 lives, killed 95,000 according to the *Encyclopedia Americana*. But as shown by C. F. Richter (*Elementary Seismology,* page 562), who gives the death figure as 99,331, an additional number of 43,476 were reported as missing. The total death toll, then, was probably about 143,000. In one case the *Encyclopedia Americana* has a considerably higher figure than *The Watchtower*. This is the 1939 earthquake in Turkey, which the encyclopedia claims to have taken about 100,000 lives, while *The Watchtower,* like Båth, Ganse & Nelson, and other seismologists, sets the death figure at 30,000.

34 A report from Hong Kong first erroneously set the death figure at 655,237, from which the Western estimates of 650,000–800,000 were derived. When finally, the Chinese authorities, who at first kept all information about the catastrophe secret, released information about the earthquake, they put the death total at 242,000. ("Chinese Seismological Society Report on July 28, 1976 Event," Dalian Meeting 1979 Xinhua News Agency. Compare Ganse & Nelson, p. 70, 148, ref. 61.) The *Dallas Times Herald* of Sept. 3, 1983, summarized the new information as follows: "Officials now put the Tangshan death toll at 148,000 with another 81,000 seriously injured. In a deadly triangle anchored by Tangshan, Peking and Tianjin, nearly 100,000 other people died, increasing the official death total to 242,000. Western estimates placed the death toll as high as 800,000."

35 Professor Båth, in a personal letter dated October 3, 1984, explains: "A recent example [of exaggerations] is the China earthquake 27/7, 1976 (page 149 in my 'introduction'), for which Hongkong (!) gave a much too high a figure immediately after the quake. Long afterwards (too late, in fact, to be included in my book) an official Chinese report gave the number of victims as 242,000, which now is regarded as the correct figure."

36 Professor Båth, in his letter of October 3, 1984, points out that the annual deaths in earthquakes during the twentieth century are 15,700 on the average (as against the Society's 25,300).

How to "prove" with quotations

The seismic activity in the earth's crust is not quite constant. The activity seems to have had varying cycles during different periods in the past, with periods of greater activity and periods of lesser activity. The evidence is, however, that in a longer perspective the activity has been stable. The above-mentioned fluctuations, then, are only minor variations in the overall pattern. Some popular writers feel that the earth is now going through one of the periods of increased activity. "There are now indications that the planet Earth is moving into an era of increasing earthquake activity," writes Verney.[37]

But it is doubtful if any seismologists would agree with this. True, *The Watchtower* of May 15, 1983, claims that seismologist Keiiti Aki "speaks of 'the apparent surge in intensity and frequency of major earthquakes during the last one hundred years,' though stating that the period from 1500 through 1700 was as active." (Page 6) It is difficult to see how such a statement can be helpful to the Watch Tower Society since it embraces "the last one hundred years," rather than the much shorter period following 1914.

However, the true significance of Professor Aki's statement was obviously glossed over by the Watch Tower Society. In his letter to the Watch Tower Society, Professor Aki *did not* indicate that there had been a *real* or *actual* increase in the earthquake activity during the last one hundred years. His full statement was:

> **The apparent surge in intensity and frequency of major earthquakes during the last one hundred years is, in all probability, due to improved recording of earthquakes and the increased vulnerability of human society to earthquake damage.** (Letter from Keiiti Aki to the Watch Tower Society, dated 30 September 1982. A copy of this letter is reproduced in Appendix A.)

From that letter it is clear that the *Watchtower* magazine misused the information supplied to them. Professor Aki's letter to the Watch Tower Society shows that when referring to "the apparent surge in intensity and frequency of major earthquakes" he clearly used the term "apparent" in the sense of a *seeming* surge, not in the sense of that which is evident or noticeable. For he stated in the same sentence that

---

37 Verney, page 7. The *Awake!* of April 8, 1981, also quoted Robert I. Tilling, chief of the U.S. Geological Survey's office of Geochemistry and Geophysics, as saying that there are "some suggestions that both volcanoes and earthquakes worldwide are on the increase." Professor Markus Båth, however, who is a leading authority on earthquake activity, comments that "Tilling's statement is wrong. No increase in the seismic activity of the earth has occurred." (Personal letter of October 3, 1984)

such "apparent" surge was "in all probability, due to the improved recording of earthquakes and the increased vulnerability of human society to earthquake damages." The Watch Tower Society saw fit to drop this portion, thereby giving to the quoted phrase a meaning that it does not have.

The true standpoint of Professor Aki is that there has been no increase at all in earthquake activity in our century, and that the seismicity of the earth has been stationary for milleniums. In a private letter to the authors, dated September 5, 1985, Professor Aki explains:

> **I feel strongly that the seismicity has been stationary for thousands of years. I was trying to convince Jehovah's Witnesses about the stationarity of the seismicity, using the data obtained in China for the period 1500 through 1700, but they put only weak emphasis in the published statement.** (For the entirety of this letter, see Appendix A.)

Obviously, then, *The Watchtower* quoted Professor Aki in a way that concealed his true position and views. As Professor Aki, on being confronted with the Watch Tower Society's use of his letter, remarked, "it is clear that they quoted the part they wanted, eliminating my main message," namely that the seismicity has been essentially stable, with *no* increase. (Letter from Keiiti Aki to the authors, dated June 16, 1986.)

Regrettably, it must be said that this method of "proving" a case is in no way exceptional in the publications of this movement, as the following additional examples demonstrate.

In September 1950 the *Scientific American* magazine published a brief news item on earthquake activity. Parts of this have been quoted in Watch Tower publications, time and again, for about twenty years, as the *principal* proof of their claim that great earthquakes have increased in numbers since 1914. The sentences cited by the Watch Tower Society are:

> **Major quakes used to occur in clusters, each period of activity being followed by a rest period. . . . But the periods of activity became progressively shorter and closer together. Since 1948 the pattern has entered a new phase with approximately one great quake a year.**[38]

---

38 *Scientific American,* September 1950, p. 48. The quotation may be found, for example, in *Awake!,* March 8, 1956, pp. 7,8; *Awake!,* December 22, 1960, pp. 14,15; *The Watchtower,* 1961, p. 628; *Awake!,* October 8, 1965, p. 16; and in *Aid,* 1971, p. 478. In each case, the quotation was the sole evidence of an increase in the earthquake activity since 1914!

Earthquake Patterns

WILL seismologists someday be able to predict earthquakes? Workers at the California Institute of Technology seem to have taken a step-in that direction. They have found evidence that earthquakes throughout the world follow a rough pattern of recurrence and are related to a world-wide stress system.

Investigators at the Institute's Seismological Laboratory studied the 48 great earthquakes that have occurred all over the world since 1904, when reliable instrumental observations began. The study was limited to the highly destructive shallow quakes, which take place less than 45 miles below the earth's surface. All these quakes fell into a pattern "as orderly and regular as the cutting edge of a saw."

Major quakes used to occur in clusters, each period of activity being followed by a rest period. Thus there was violent activity between 1904 and 1907 and then quiescence for 10 years, except for two quakes in 1911 and 1912. Four more active periods, separated by quiet intervals, occurred between 1917 and 1948. But the periods of activity became progressively shorter and closer together. Since 1948 the pattern has entered a new phase, with approximately one great quake a year. Instead of accumulating over a period of years, strain in the earth's crust now seems to find release as fast as it is generated.

The nature of the "global force" that controls this orderly pattern is unknown. One speculation is that periodic increases in the earth's rate of spin due to slight changes in the tidal forces of the sun and moon may enlarge the earth, opening its seams sufficiently to release the accumulated tensions.

Scientific American, September 1950, page 48.

These sentences, isolated from their context, strongly convey the impression of an *increase* in the number of major earthquakes in our century, and especially since 1948. A careful examination of the whole news item, however, gives quite another impression. For the reader's benefit, we present the news item above in its entirety.

Does the news item actually claim that major earthquakes have increased in number since 1948? Does it say they have been more violent or destructive since that date? No, it does not. It refers to a study of a special type of great earthquakes, "the highly destructive shallow quakes, which take place less than 45 miles below the earth's surface." Forty-eight quakes of this kind had occurred between 1904 and 1950, that is, *about one such quake a year, on the average.* But while they earlier used to occur in clusters, followed by a rest period, the pattern entered a new phase in 1948, "with approximately one great quake [that is, of 8.0 magnitude or more] a year." Thus the *average* number of earthquakes was still the same.

To illustrate, if in a ten-year period a cluster of four great earthquakes occurred in the first year, another cluster of three in the sixth year, and a third cluster of three in the tenth, with the intervening years being years of quiet, the total number would be ten great earthquakes in the ten-year period. This would be the same as if there had been one great earthquake each year during the ten-year period. The total number would be the same in either case.

The *Scientific American* news item itself clearly shows that *no increase in either the total number or size of earthquakes had occurred.* Only by quoting two or three sentences out of context was it possible to create the opposite impression.

According to the study of seismologists Båth and Duda, mentioned earlier, about 20 major (7.0 or more in magnitude) earthquakes a year have occurred from 1897 to 1977. No marked change in that pattern could be demonstrated for this whole period, except that the frequency of the greatest earthquakes was almost twice as great before 1920, compared to the whole period thereafter up to 1977. The "new phase" mentioned in the *Scientific American* of September 1950, then, must have been a comparatively trivial episode in the larger pattern.[39]

In spite of this, the sentences quoted out of context by the Watch Tower Society have been used, time and again, in an attempt to "prove" that earthquake activity entered a new and *more violent* phase in 1948, and that this phase *has persisted* since. In the long run, of course, the *Scientific American* item of September 1950 could not be dusted off every time this need to be "proved."[40]

39 It should also be observed that the "new phase" had appeared for at most parts of three years, from 1948 to 1950, when the information was published. The information could not show, of course, whether the "new phase" would continue *after* 1950. Certainly this would be a slender thread of evidence upon which to build such startling claims.

40 There is evidence that it was realized that the *Scientific American* article of 1950 had begun to take on a somewhat outdated look, one in need of renewal. The Watch Tower Society's Bible dictionary *Aid to Bible Understanding,* published in 1971, thus made use of this quote in an unusual way, one that gave a further false appearance, as is shown in the following quotation: "Jesus foretold earthquakes in great number and magnitude as a feature of the sign of his second presence. (Matt. 24:3, 7, 8; Mark 13:4, 8) Since 1914 C.E., and especially since 1948, there has been an increase in the number of earthquakes, especially of major ones. Before 1948, they occurred in clusters, with a rest period in between, but since then there has been a major quake almost annually, in addition to a great number of smaller ones.—See *The Encyclopedia Americana,* Annals, 1965–1967, under 'Earthquakes.'" (*Aid to Bible Understanding,* p. 178.) The sentences from the *Scientific American* are almost literally repeated in this dictionary, but instead of referring to that magazine (by then some twenty years old) as the source, *The Encyclopedia Americana,* Annuals of 1965–1967, is referred to, evidently in order to give this "proof" a more current look and to indicate that the 1948–50 phase still persisted. The problem is, however, that this encyclopedia has nothing whatever to say about such a "new phase" from 1948, or of any increase in earthquake activity in our century! The unsuspicious and loyal reader of the Watch Tower publications takes it for granted that the new source cited confirms the statement about such an increase. It is most unlikely that he will check the source to find out that he has been misled. This way of substantiating claims is far from honest, especially as the statements are presented as the sole proof of the claimed post-1914 increase in earthquakes.

NUMBER OF GREAT "SHALLOW QUAKES," 1897–1977

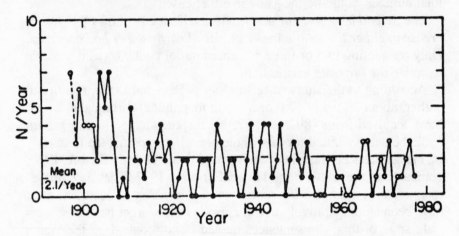

This figure shows the annual number of *great shallow quakes* of 1897–1977, measuring 7.8 or above on the Richter scale. These are usually the most destructive quakes, especially when they hit densely inhabited areas. The great earthquake that struck Mexico City on September 19, 1985, belongs to this category. About 2.1 quakes of this type occur each year on the average. No increase in the number of such quakes has been observed in our century. As regards those who would designate 1914 a turning point, the fact is that the number was highest in the pre-1914 period! (K. Abe & H. Kanamori in *Tectonophysics*, Vol. 62, 1980, p. 196.)

A new "evidence" advanced

By 1978 the statement in *Scientific American* magazine had been used for about twenty years as the Watch Tower Society's *principal* or *only* neutral "proof" of the claimed increase in earthquake activity since 1914. In 1978, however, another "evidence" began to be quoted, one that has served as virtually the only "neutral" source of proof since then. A closer scrutiny of the source and dependability of this new evidence will give us yet another interesting lesson in the Society's art of "proving" by the aid of quotations.

The erroneous statement presented in 1977 that "reliable sources list only 24 major earthquakes" from A.D. 856 to 1914 would soon become useful to the Watch Tower Society in another, most unexpected way. The year after that claim was published, in the Italian journal *Il Piccolo,* of October 8, 1978, a writer, Geo Malagoli, presented the following views:

Our generation lives in a dangerous period of high seismic activity, as statistics show. In fact, during a period of 1,059 years (from 856 to 1914) reliable sources list only 24 major earthquakes causing 1,973,000 deaths. However, if we compare this figure to the partially complete list of recent disasters, we find that 1,600,000 persons have died in only 63 years, as a result of 43 earthquakes which occurred from 1915 to 1978. The dramatic increase further goes to emphasize another accepted fact—our generation is an unfortunate one in many ways. (Quoted from *The Watchtower,* May 15, 1983, page 6.)

By stating that fatality figures indicate that ours is a "period of high seismic activity," Geo Malagoli reveals that he is definitely not a seismologist.[41] He is clearly a reader of the *Awake!* magazine, however. A careful comparison will show that his statement is practically a word-for-word repetition of the same statement published by the Watch Tower Society one and a half years earlier. (See page 62.)

It is quite evident that the source of Malagoli's "information" was the *Awake!* magazine of February 22, 1977, quoted earlier. The slight differences are easy to explain. He has rounded off the figures: 1,972,952 to 1,973,000, and 1,579,209 to 1,600,000. As one year had passed since the figures were originally published in *Awake!,* he has also raised the 62 years (from 1915 to 1977) to 63 years (1915–1978). But aside from this, all details are identical. And from now on this Geo Malagoli began to appear in the Watch Tower publications, time and again, every time the subject of earthquakes was brought up for discussion—elevated to the position of a neutral, impartial earthquake authority!

Malagoli's statement in *Il Piccolo* was first picked up and cited under the heading of "Insight on the News" in *The Watchtower* of June 15, 1979 (page 11), without the reader being informed that Malagoli had in turn borrowed his information from the *Awake!* magazine. Next year—in 1980—Malagoli and his statement appeared again, this time in the book *Happiness How to Find It,* where he is quoted on page 148 as *the sole "evidence"* presented of the claimed increase in earthquake activity since 1914. A few months later, in the *Awake!* of October 8, 1980, Malagoli is again quoted as the one and only source of evidence:

41 High seismic activity is not necessarily translated into high death figures. As Båth (quoted above, see footnote 11) points out, "There is usually no clear correlation between the magnitude of a shock and the number of killed people or other destruction." Only if the seismic activity is manifested in densely populated areas can there be high death figures. Seismologists, therefore, measure seismic activity by instruments, not by fatality reports.

Has the frequency of earthquakes really increased? The Italian magazine *Il Piccolo* observed: 'Our generation lives in a dangerous period of high seismic activity, as statistics show.' And then it produced figures for the past thousand years to prove it. (Page 20, 21)

And of course they avoided mentioning the fact that the 'figures produced' were —originally—produced by the Watch Tower Society itself.

In 1981 Malagoli was quoted in the Society's book *"Let Your Kingdom Come"* on page 113, and in 1982 "his" figures were referred to three times: in the *Awake!* of April 8, page 13, in *The Watchtower* of April 15, page 9, and in the new study book *You Can Live Forever in Paradise on Earth,* page 151. Each time Malagoli's figures were the only "evidence" offered as to increased earthquake activity. In the special discussion of earthquake activity published in *The Watchtower* of May 15, 1983, Malagoli was finally brought up again as the principal witness (aside from the Watch Tower Society's own misleading statistics) to the claimed increase in the earthquake activity since 1914. Incredible as it may seem, this time his statement was used to "disprove" what an authentic earthquake authority, Keiiti Aki, states, namely, that the period from 1500 through 1700 was as active as the past 100 years!

Thus we find that the Watch Tower Society's principal, yes, its sole seemingly "neutral" and "impartial" proof that earthquake activity has increased since 1914 is an Italian writer, who—undoubtedly in good faith—borrowed his "information" right out of the *Awake!* magazine. That "information" on seismic activity in the past is, in turn, completely erroneous and has nothing to do with actual historical evidence. The fact that the Society, time and again, has presented this false information—seemingly taken from a neutral source—in order to "prove" its interpretation of the "sign" since 1914, should induce every honest reader of its publications to ask if this Society is genuinely deserving of his or her confidence in its remarkable claims.

Quotations taken out of context and given a different, slanted meaning, biased selection of figures and data, misuse of and even fabrication of statistics that are then presented as though coming from an outside, neutral source—these are the methods employed by the Watch Tower publications to support the claim that the number of earthquakes and of quake victims has soared since 1914. How is it that persons considered as devout and respectable men resort to such methods?

An article entitled "Fraud in Science," published in the *Awake!* of May 22, 1984, pointed out that dedicated scientists such as Ptolemy, Galileo, Mendel, Newton and others sometimes resorted to manipulation of figures, data selection and even fabrication of data in order to support their theories. The article then says that, **"conscientious and honorable though a scientist, or anyone, may be in other things, when his own reputation or interest is at stake, he can become quite dogmatic, irrational, even reckless, or take a short-cut."** (Page 6) Emphasizing that **"science, too, has its skeletons in the closet,"** the article concludes:

> **Their occasional exposure ought to make us realize that though science and scientists are often put on a pedestal, their place on it should be carefully reevaluated.** (Page 8)

We ask: When such "skeletons" are also found in the "closet" of a religious organization, should not this induce a similar reevaluation of the exalted position which that organization claims for itself?

Earthquakes in the light of history

What are, then, the actual facts about earthquakes in the past? If, as seismologists clearly demonstrate, *thousands* of destructive earthquakes took place during the period from 856 to 1914, how is it possible for anyone to state that "there were only 24 major earthquakes" during that period? One possibility is that such a listing was found under the entry "Earthquake" in a reference work of one kind or another. Encyclopedias and other reference works often present tables with a brief selection of major earthquakes of the past. *But in no case have we ever found any such list that claims to be complete.* On the contrary, one is usually informed in one way or another that the list presented is incomplete. Thus seismologists Frank Press and Raymond Siever, on page 651 of their popular textbook *Earth* (San Francisco 1974) list 32 (note!) earthquakes from 856 to 1914 under the heading **"Some** of the world's worst earthquakes (in lives lost)." Clearly, only a writer grossly ignorant of the facts could honestly claim that pre-1914 history recognizes only 24 major earthquakes! Only such a writer would also be able to pen the following statement on page 18 of the *Awake!* of May 8, 1974:

> **Further, the great earthquakes of the past were generally isolated events occurring years, even centuries, apart. There were not many of them in a single generation.**

In a remarkably similar statement, Hal Lindsey's book *The 1980's—Countdown to Armageddon* (1981), on page 29 says:

> There have been many great earthquakes throughout history, but, according to surprisingly well-kept records, in the past they did not occur very frequently. The 20th century, however, has experienced an unprecedented increase in the frequency of these calamities. In fact, the number of earthquakes per decade has roughly doubled in each of the 10-year periods since 1950.

Although lacking even the slightest foundation in fact, such statements could be the hasty impression obtained by someone whose main, perhaps only, information about earthquakes in history has been brief looks at tables containing partial selections of major earthquakes.

As has been shown, the earthquake catalogs carefully worked out by seismologists list a vastly greater number of major earthquakes for the period 856–1914. For this reason the Watch Tower Society has felt it necessary to try to undermine confidence in these catalogs. The *Awake!* magazine of May 8, 1974, stated:

> Nor do all historical records about 'great' earthquakes of the past inspire confidence in their reliability. That was the view of noted cataloger John Milne. 'In these catalogues,' we read in the 1939 edition of his book *Earthquakes and Other Earth Movements* (revised and rewritten by A. W. Lee), 'there are uncertainties in the dates, or even the years, for many of the ancient earthquakes. There are numerous inaccurate or obscure references in the original writings.' (Page 18)

With this quotation, taken out of context, the Watch Tower Society dismisses all the catalogs of thousands of earthquakes in the past, carefully compiled by modern specialists. Was it really the view of John Milne and A. W. Lee that these catalogs could be ignored, because the ancient documents often contained "inaccurate or obscure references," and because "there are uncertainties in the date, or even the years," for many of the quakes? Milne's statement *seen in its context* gives the reader quite a different impression:

> The information available for examination of the distribution of earthquakes in different parts of the world throughout historic times has been collected in many catalogues. The older catalogues, which were prepared from reports found in the histories of various countries, are necessarily incomplete, and do not give a fair representation of the distribution of seismic phenomena over the entire globe. In these catalogues there are

uncertainties in the dates, or even the years, for many of the ancient earthquakes. There are numerous inaccurate or obscure references in the original writings, and the dates are frequently given according to some little known system of reckoning. The entries for these ancient shocks refer, for the most part, to widespread disasters.[42]

Read in its entirety and in its context, Milne's (and Lee's) estimation of the catalogs presents a quite different meaning. What they in fact point out is that, since the *older* catalogs are *incomplete,* the real number of ancient earthquakes was actually *larger,* and that these catalogs, therefore, do not give a fair representation of the full scope of the situation as regards earlier seismic activity. The uncertainties regarding certain dates or years, they say, are owing to the fact that the dates are frequently given according to some system of reckoning that is little known today. This in no way says, then, that the ancient sources were careless and thus unreliable in this respect, an impression created by the Watch Tower Society by taking the statement out of its context and interrupting the quotation in the middle of a sentence. Nor does the observation that the descriptions of the ancient earthquakes sometimes contain "inaccurate or obscure references" constitute a denial that these earthquakes did indeed take place.

Turning to one of the learned classical writers of antiquity, we obtain an interesting illustration of this incompleteness of existing catalogs of earthquakes of the past. Shortly before his death in A.D. 65, the famous Roman writer Seneca stated that frequent earthquakes had long been a characteristic of the ancient world:

> How often have cities in Asia, how often in Achaia, been laid low by a single shock of earthquake! How many towns in Syria, how many in Macedonia, have been swallowed up! How often has this kind of devastation laid Cyprus in ruins! How often has Paphos collapsed! Not infrequently are tidings brought to us of the utter destruction of entire cities. (*Seneca Ad Lucilium Epistulae Morales,* translated by Richard M. Gummere, Vol. II, London & New York, 1920, p. 437.)

No existing earthquake catalog would claim to embrace all the disastrous shocks presupposed by this statement. In fact, only a very small number of earthquakes before A.D. 65 have been specifically identified. But it would certainly be a mistake to infer from this that earthquake catastrophes "did not occur very frequently" in the past,

---

42 John Milne & A.W. Lee, *Earthquakes and Other Earth Movements,* seventh edition, London 1939, p. 134.

as author Lindsey states and the Watch Tower's *Awake!* magazine implies. Seneca's personal testimony is that as far back as the first century they did occur with notable frequency. That few if any specifics are known today about these destructive quakes certainly does not mean that they did not take place.

That modern earthquake catalogs, far from exaggerating the number of shocks in the past, actually list only a small minority of them, has been noted by several seismologists. In 1971, for example, seismologist N. N. Ambraseys at Imperial College of Science and Technology, London, reported that he had identified about 2,200 "larger shocks" in the Eastern Mediterranean alone between A.D. 10 and 1699. Having started a fresh and painstaking examination of contemporary source material and recent archaeological evidence from that area of notable seismicity, he stated:

> The total number of all earthquakes, large and small, identified so far for the period AD 10 to 1699, is just over 3,000, or about twenty times the number of genuine earthquakes listed for the same period in modern catalogues.[43]

Professor Ambraseys has not yet published a documented study of these findings, but the series of catastrophic earthquakes that befell the Eastern Roman Empire in A.D. 447—the year of Attila the Hun's second invasion—are probably among the 2,200 larger shocks mentioned above. We learn of them through historian E. A. Thompson, who states the following in his book *A History of Attila and the Huns* (Oxford, England, 1948), on page 91:

> As the Hun squadrons prepared to move, a disaster of the first magnitude befell the Romans. The series of earthquakes which shattered the Eastern Empire for four months beginning on 26 January 447 were, in the belief of Evagrius, the worst in its history. Entire villages were swallowed up and countless disasters occurred both on land and sea. Thrace, the Hellespont, and the Cyclades all suffered. For three or four days after the earthquakes began, the rain poured from the sky, we are told, in rivers of water. Hillocks were levelled with the ground. Countless buildings were thrown down in Constantinople, and, worst of all, a stretch of the massive walls of Anthemius, including no less than fifty-seven towers, fell to the ground.

43 N. N. Ambraseys in *Nature*, August 6, 1971, pp. 375, 376.

Yet these disastrous shocks of 447 A.D. *are not included in any of the earthquake catalogs the authors of this present work have had access to.*

It is only since the middle of the last century that seismologists have intensively studied records of earthquakes in the past. Robert Mallet, "the first true seismologist," not only examined the older catalogs compiled by his predecessors, but he also searched through libraries all over Europe, looking for records of ancient earthquakes. Finally, in the *Reports of the British Association* for the years 1852–54, he published a catalog of nearly *seven thousand earthquakes,* dating from 1606 B.C. to A.D. 1850![44] As Milne and Lee pointed out, these entries "refer, for the most part, to widespread disasters," that is, *great and destructive* earthquakes.

But this was just a beginning. When John Milne, "the father of seismology," arrived in Tokyo in 1875, "it was to find records of over two thousand earthquakes in the Japanese archives."[45] In Japan a running list of destructive earthquakes had been kept for a period of more than two thousand years! Soon also similar records were discovered in China. The Chinese records go back to 1100 B.C. and "are fairly complete from around 780 BC, the period of the Chou dynasty in north China."[46]

Within a short time several seismologists started working out careful catalogs of quakes in different countries. Thus Davison's *History of British Earthquakes* lists 1,191 shocks from A.D. 974 to 1924 in England alone—a country far removed from the earthquake belts of the earth.[47] In Italy, Mario Baratta, in his *I Terremoti d'Italia,* published in 1901, gives accounts of 1,364 earthquakes which have shaken Italy from A.D. 1 to 1898.[48] Similar catalogs list earthquakes in Austria, Russia, China, Japan and so on.[49]

The greatest earthquake collector among modern seismologists, however, was a Frenchman, Count F. Montessus de Ballore. From

---

44 Milne/Lee, p. 2; Verney, p. 50. To his catalog, Mallet added a bibliography of about seven thousand books and pamphlets.
45 Verney, p. 76.
46 Milne/Lee, p. 135. Booth/Fitch, p. 76.
47 Milne/Lee, p. 135.
48 Milne (1911; see footnote 9 above), p. 655.
49 Milne (1911), pp. 655–658. Wong Wen-Hao's list for China, compiled from historical records, includes 3,394 earthquakes from 1767 B.C. to 1896 A.D.!—*Comptes Rendus Congrès Géol. Interntl. XIII,* Belgium 1922, fasc. 2, Liege 1925. pp. 1161–1197.

1885 to 1922 he devoted all his time to studying and cataloging earthquakes. **"His greatest work, however, was never published. This is a monumental catalogue of the earthquakes in all parts of the world since the earliest historic times, and contains information about 171,434 earthquakes"**! The manuscript is stored in the library of the Geographical Society in Paris, where it occupies 26 metres (over 84 feet) of bookshelves.[50]

John Milne, too, spent several years in compiling his catalog of earthquakes from all over the world. Limiting his study to *destructive* earthquakes only, he lists *4,151 destructive earthquakes* between the years A.D. 7 to A.D. 1899.[51] The entries before A.D. 1700, which "are practically confined to occurrences in Southern Europe, China, and Japan," are, for logical reasons, sparser.[52] Milne was admirably strict in handling his sources. He states:

> **Not only have certain small earthquakes been omitted, but whenever the information on which the accounts of larger ones have been based has been of doubtful character, these also have been rejected.[53]**

Milne indicated the intensity of the earthquakes he listed according to the scale I, II and III, with III referring to the most destructive earthquakes, "those which destroyed towns and devastated districts," cracking walls, shattering old buildings, and so forth "up to a distance of 100 miles" from the center. During the last century alone (the nineteenth), when the records are most complete, about 370 earthquakes of class III are listed. When compared with such documented evidence the Watch Tower Society's reference to only 24 major earthquakes from 856 to 1914 A.D. becomes virtually ludicrous.

As a matter of fact, the Watch Tower Society in effect has now recognized this. In the summer of 1985 they published a statement acknowledging that there had been 856 severe earthquakes during the 2000 years preceding 1914. (See *Reasoning from the Scriptures,* 1985, page 236.) Although this is a step in the right direction, this figure also is a far cry from the actual truth. The arguments based on this new figure actually are as deceptive as those based on the earlier figures. (See the accompanying box on page 79.)

When it comes to the *number of deaths* in different earthquakes in the past, the ancient records are often silent or give very scanty infor-

---

50 Milne/Lee, pp. 137, 138.
51 Milne (1911), pp. 649–740. Milne/Lee, p. 138.
52 Milne (1911), p. 649.
53 Milne (1911). p. 651.

FROM 24 TO 856 EARTHQUAKES

In its textbook *You Can Live Forever in Paradise on Earth* (1982), the Watch Tower Society claimed that "from the year 856 C.E. to 1914, there were only 24 major earthquakes." (Page 151)

Obviously leaving that claim behind, three years later the textbook *Reasoning from the Scriptures* (1985) offers a vastly greater number of earth-

> **With data obtained from the National Geophysical Data Center in Boulder, Colorado, supplemented by a number of standard reference works, a tabulation was made in 1984 that included only earthquakes that measured 7.5 or more on the Richter scale, or that resulted in destruction of five million dollars (U.S.) or more in property, or that caused 100 or more deaths. It was calculated that there had been 856 of such earthquakes during the 2,000 years before 1914. The same tabulation showed that in *just 69 years* following 1914 there were 605 of such quakes. That means that, in comparison with the previous 2,000 years, the average per year has been 20 times as great since 1914.**

Did the Data Center in Boulder really support the claim?

Terming this statement a "misuse of the statistics" seismologist Wilbur A. Rinehart at the National Geophysical Data Center in Boulder, Colorado, stated that "there has been no significant increase in the numbers of earthquakes during this or any other century." (For his complete reply to our questions, see Appendix A.)

What about the "20 times increase"?

Writing about the limited area of the Eastern Mediterranean basin, the renowned seismologist N. N. Ambraseys stated in 1971:

> **The total number of all earthquakes, large and small, identified so far for the period AD 10 to 1699, is just over 3,000, or about twenty times the number of genuine earthquakes listed for the same period in modern catalogues. . . . for the larger shocks, about 2,200 in all, the homogeneity of the material can be proved to be satisfactory for the whole period.**—*Nature* magazine, August 6, 1971, pp. 375, 376.

These findings of themselves totally nullify the Watch Tower Society's claims.

What leading seismologists comment

The Watch Tower Society's statement about a 20-fold increase in earthquakes since 1914 was also sent to a number of leading seismologists around the world. All of them rejected the claim and none of them thought that our century is in any way unique with respect to the number of great earthquakes. A number of the answers received are reproduced in the Appendix (Appendix A).

mation. The *Awake!* issue of July 8, 1982, on page 16, claimed that, "From the time Jesus gave his prophecy until 1914, history records five earthquakes that each took 100,000 lives or more," while "In the period since 1914 at least <u>four more</u> such superearthquakes have occurred."

Just to demonstrate how erroneous such a statement is, the following table presents 24 such "superearthquakes" from the period A.D. 532 to 1914. Perhaps as many as *seven* of these (there are quite naturally some uncertainties) occurred in the eighteenth century alone.[54]

	Location	Deaths
A.D. 532	Syria	130,000
678	Syria	170,000
856	Iran: Qumis Damghan	200,000
893	India: Daipul	180,000
893	Iran: Ardabil	150,000
1138	Egypt, Syria	230,000
1139	Iran: Gansana	100,000
1201	Upper Egypt, Syria	1,100,000
1290	China: Chihli	100,000
1556	China	830,000
1641	Iran: Dehkwargan, Tabriz	300,000
1662	China	300,000
1669	Sicily (Etna eruption)	100,000
1693	Sicily: Catania and Naples	100,000
1703	Japan (tsunami)	100,000
1721	Iran: Tabriz	100,000
1730	China: Chihli	100,000
1730	Japan: Hokkaido	137,000
1731	China: Peking	100,000
1737	India: Calcutta	300,000
1780	Iran: Tabriz	100,000
1850	China	300–400,000
1876	Bay of Bengal (tsunami)	215,000
1908	Italy: Messina/Reggio	110,000

54 Robert A. Ganse and John B. Nelson, *Catalog of Significant Earthquakes 2000 B.C. – 1979*, Boulder, Colorado, 1981, pp. 3–33. (Report SE-27 of the World Data Center A for Solid Earth Geophysics.) On the Messina/Reggio quake, see A. Imamura, *Theoretical and Applied Seismology*, Tokyo 1937, pp. 140, 202, 204, which says that some 83,000 died in Messina and c. 20,000 in Reggio. Other sources used are: N. N. Ambraseys in *Revue pour l'étude des calamités*, No. 37, Geneve, December 1961, p. 18f; J. H. Latter, "Natural Disasters," *Advancement of Science*, June 1969, pp. 363, 370; N. N. Ambraseys & C. P. Melville, *A History of Persian Earthquakes*, Cambridge 1982; R. A. Daly, *Our Mobile Earth*, New York & London 1926; A. T. Wilson, "Earthquakes in Persia," *Bulletin*

Comparing this information with the statement of the *Awake!* writer earlier-quoted, it becomes painfully evident how remarkably superficial the research of the Watch Tower publications is, how utterly irresponsible the claims made actually are.

In many cases great numbers of deaths have been caused by accompanying results or consequences of earthquake activity, such as tsunamis, volcanic eruptions, landslides, fires, and similar factors. But this holds equally true for some of the "superearthquakes" occurring *after* 1914. The 100,000 that died in the earthquake in China in 1920, for example, were killed primarily by a landslide triggered by the quake. The earthquake in Japan in 1923 caused a fire storm that killed 38,000 of the 143,000 victims. It should also be added that the table above certainly does not claim to list all "superearthquakes" before 1914.

In view of the population increase it might seem only reasonable to expect that more people have died in earthquakes during our century than during earlier centuries.[55] The following challenge on page 19 of the *Awake!* magazine of May 8, 1974, would therefore seem rather safe to make:

> **All together, over 900,000 persons have died in earthquakes since 1914! Can any single 'generation' equal that terrible record? Jesus' prophecies about earthquakes apply now.**

Although this number has subsequently increased by a few hundred thousands in the years that have passed since that statement was pub-

---

of the School of Oriental Studies, London Institution, Vol. VI (1930–32); Dr. A. Sieberg in *Handbuch der Geophysik* (ed. Prof. B. Gutenberg), Vol. IV, Leipzig 1932; and James Cornell, *The Great International Disaster Book,* New York 1979. Death figures vary, and in several cases some sources give considerably higher figures than shown in our table. Thus the New Catalog of *Strong Earthquakes in the U.S.S.R. from Ancient Times through 1977* (Report SE-31 of the World Data Center A, July 1982) gives 200,000–300,000 deaths for the earthquake in Gansana, Iran, in 1139. Cornell (page 153) sets the death figure for the 1693 quake in Sicily at 153,000, and Sieberg (in Gutenberg, p. 854) has 150,000 for the Japanese earthquake in 1703. For the two earthquakes that hit Tabriz in Iran in 1721 and 1780, estimates range up to 250,000 and 205,000 respectively. (Ambraseys/Melville, pp. 54, 184, 186) Two other relatively recent quakes that may have been "superearthquakes" are the earthquake in Japan in 1855, which may have claimed 106,000 lives (Sieberg in Gutenberg, p. 854), and the earthquake in Kangra, India, in 1905, of which Cornell (p. 139) says that "some other reports claim nearly 370,000 people were killed in Central India when several villages were completely destroyed." Neither of these has been included in the table.

55 Professor Båth points out that "the coastal areas are most often visited by quakes, and that these areas always have been those most densely populated." Thus, "one cannot reckon with the total population on earth as a clue for earlier times" when estimating the total number of earthquake victims in the past. (Personal letter of October 3, 1984.)

lished in the *Awake!* magazine, we will nonetheless take up the gauntlet presented by the Watch Tower's challenge.

As the historical entries before A.D. 1700 "are practically confined to occurrences in Southern Europe, China and Japan" (Milne), we choose the generation from 1714 onward and compare it with the generation after 1914. The table in the *Awake!* of February 22, 1977, covering the period 1915–1976, has been updated to include the years up to 1983 inclusive. A correction of the figure for the great earthquake in China in 1976 has been made at the bottom of the table, with a reference to a later statement in *Awake!*. (See page 83.)

The results show that the total death figure in earthquakes from 1915 to 1983 amounts to 1,210,597, which is an annual average of 17,545.

The accompanying table (on the left side) listing 43 major earthquakes from 1715 to 1783 shows a total of 1,373,845 deaths, which is about 163,000 more, giving an annual average of 19,911!

To prove that 1914 was a real seismic "turning point" *The Watchtower* of May 15, 1983, made reference to 50 destructive earthquakes during the 68 years between 1914 and 1982. (Page 7) We have therefore prepared a table for the 68 years *preceding* 1914 (1847–1914) showing a partial list of 50 destructive earthquakes compiled from reliable sources. It demonstrates very conclusively that 1914 cannot have been the conspicuous turning point the Watch Tower Society claims it was.

Of course, no such tables are complete. For a number of great earthquakes from the 18th century onward, no death figures are known, the contemporary records simply giving the information that "many" were killed in them. Even if death figures were to be added to all three tables by including more earthquakes from the three periods involved, the comparison still would only demonstrate that the generation of 1914 is in no way unique as far as earthquakes are concerned.[56] (See page 84.)

We have seen, one by one, the different claims of the Watch Tower Society demolished by historical facts—that the period A.D. 856–

---

56 Sources used for the table on the 18th century earthquakes include: the catalog by Ganse & Nelson; Milne (1911), pp. 686–698; Robert Giffen in the *Journal of the Statistical Society*. Vol. XLI, London 1878, pp. 442–444; Charles Davison, *Great Earthquakes*, London 1936; Akitune Imamura, *Theoretical and Applied Seismology*, Tokyo 1937; Richter (1958); Båth (1979), page 139; Booth & Fitch, p. 78; and *Encyclopedia Americana: Annals*, 1965–67, page 498. If the fact that the population on earth today is six-fold as great as that of the 18th century (c. 750 million in 1770), and the number of earthquake victims is seen as a ratio of the total population, the 18th century far surpasses the 20th!

A COMPARISON OF EARTHQUAKE VICTIMS
1715–1783:   1915–1983:

(See *Awake!* February 22, 1977)

Year	Location	Deaths	Year	Location	Deaths
1715	Algeria	20,000	1915	Italy	29,970
1717	Algeria	20,000	1920	China	180,000
1718	China	43,000	1923	Japan	143,000
1719	Asia Minor	1,000	1927	China	200,000
1721	Iran	100,000	1932	China	70,000
1724	Peru (tsunami)	18,000	1933	U.S.A.	115
1725	Peru	1,500	1935	India (Pakistan)	60,000
1725	China	556	1939	Chile	30,000
1726	Italy	6,000	1939	Turkey	23,000
1727	Iran	77,000	1946	Turkey	1,300
1730	Italy	200	1946	Japan	2,000
1730	China	100,000	1948	Japan	5,131
1730	Japan	137,000	1949	Ecuador	6,000
1731	China	100,000	1950	India	1,500
1732	Italy	1,940	1953	Turkey	1,200
1736	China	260	1953	Greece	424
1737	India	300,000	1954	Algeria	1,657
1739	China	50,000	1956	Afghanistan	2,000
1746	Peru	4,800	1957	Iran (Northern)	2,500
1749	Spain	5,000	1957	Iran (Western)	2,000
1750	Greece	2,000	1960	Chile	5,700
1751	Japan	2,000	1960	Morocco	12,000
1751	China	900	1962	Iran	10,000
1752	Syria	20,000	1963	Yugoslavia	1,100
1754	Egypt	40,000	1964	Alaska	131
1755	China	270	1966	Turkey	2,529
1755	Iran	1,200	1968	Iran	11,588
1755	Portugal	60,000	1970	Turkey	1,086
1755	Morocco	12,000	1970	Peru	66,794
1757	Italy	10,000	1971	U.S.A.	65
1759	Syria	30,000	1972	Iran	5,057
1763	China	1,000	1972	Nicaragua	6,000
1765	China	1,189	1973	Mexico (Western)	52
1766	Japan	1,335	1973	Mexico (Central)	700
1771	Japan (tsunami)	11,700	1974	Pakistan	5,200
1773	Guatemala	20,000	1975	China	200
1774	Newfoundland	300	1975	Turkey	2,312
1778	Iran (Kashan)	8,000	1976	Guatemala	23,000
1780	Iran (Tabriz)	100,000	1976	Italy	900
1780	Iran (Khurasan)	3,000	1976	Bali	600
1783	Italy (Calabria)	60,000	1976	China	242,000*
1783	Italy (Palmi)	1,504	1976	Philippines	3,373
1783	Italy (Monteleone)	1,191	1976	Turkey	3,790
			1977–1983 addition:		44,623+
Total 1715–1783:		1,373,845	**Total 1915–1983:**		1,210,597
Annual average:		19,911	Annual average:		17,545

*See page 65, footnote 34; compare *Awake!* July 8, 1982, p. 13.

+Ganse & Nelson list a death figure of 44,623 for this period.

DID 1914 REALLY BRING A CHANGE?

Year	Place	Deaths	Year	Place	Deaths
1847	Japan	34,000	1882	Italy	2,313
1850	China	300–400,000	1883	Italy	1,990
1851	Iran	2,000	1883	Greece, Asia Minor	15,000
1851	Italy	14,000	1883	Java	36,400
1853	Iran (Shiraz)	12,000	1885	India	3,000
1853	Iran (Isfahan)	10,000	1887	France	1,000
1854	Japan	34,000	1887	China	2,000
1854	El Salvador	1,000	1891	Japan	7,283
1855	Japan	6,757	1893	Western Turkmenia	18,000
1856	Java	3,000	1896	Japan	27,122
1857	Italy	10,000	1897	India (Assam)	1,542
1857	Italy	12,000	1902	Guatemala	2,000
1859	Ecuador	5,000	1902	Turkestan	4,562
1859	Turkey	15,000	1903	Turkey	6,000
1861	Argentina	7,000	1905	India (Kangra)	19,000
1863	Philippines	10,000	1905	Italy	2,500
1868	Peru	40,000	1906	Colombia	1,000
1868	Ecuador, Colombia	70,000	1906	Formosa	1,300
1872	Asia Minor	1,800	1906	Chile	20,000
1875	Venezuela, Colombia	16,000	1907	Jamaica	1,400
1876	Bay of Bengal	215,000	1907	Central Asia	12,000
1879	Iran	2,000	1908	Italy	110,000
1879	China	10,430	1909	Iran	6–8,000
1880	Greece (Chios)	4,000	1910	Costa Rica	1,750
1881	Asia Minor	8,866	1912	Marmara Sea coast	1,958
Total victims for 68 years previous to 1914:					1,148,973–1,250,973
Annual average:					17,149–18,671

SOURCES: Båth: *Introduction to Seismology* (1979); Richter: *Elementary Seismology* (1958); Imamura: *Theoretical and Applied Seismology* (1937); Ganse-Nelson: *Catalog of Significant Earthquakes* (1981); Ambraseys: *Earthquake Hazard and Vulnerability* (1981); Ambraseys-Melville: *A History of Persian Earthquakes* (1982); Latter: Natural Disasters (*Advancement of Science*, June 1969); Press-Siever: *Earth* (1974); *Handbuch der Geophysik* (ed. Prof. B Gutenberg), Band IV (Berlin 1932).

1914 saw only 24 major earthquakes, that the great earthquakes of the past occurred "years, even centuries, apart," that history records only five "superearthquakes" from the time of Christ to 1914, and that no single generation before 1914 can equal the one following that year with respect to earthquake victims. Is it really possible that the writers of the Watch Tower publications are so ignorant of past earthquakes— or are they trying to conceal the truth about them from their readers? We prefer to believe that they *primarily* have been ignorant of the facts. But if so, it is extremely remarkable that an organization claiming to have been authorized by Jesus Christ to interpret the signs of the time for people of our days, seems to take so little interest in verifying how its interpretations and statistics tally with historical reality.

Finally, what do the seismologists themselves say as to the overall picture? Have they found any marked difference between the frequency of earthquakes since 1914 compared with earlier centuries? Seismologists J. Milne and A. W. Lee declared that **"there is no indication that seismic activity has increased or diminished appreciably throughout historic times."**[57] And professor Markus Båth agrees: **"For earlier centuries we do not have the same reliable statistics, but there are no indications at all of any increase in the activity in the course of time."**[58]

As the ancient records become more and more sparse and incomplete the farther back in time we go, it is only natural that we have more and better information from the latest centuries than from the earlier ones. There is, however, one exception: Japan. As was shown earlier, the Japanese have kept a running record of destructive earthquakes in that country (with its frequent seismic activity) reaching back to well before the birth of Christ. According to Milne's catalog the number of *destructive* earthquakes in Japan recorded during each century from the ninth to the nineteenth are:

Century	No. of destructive earthquakes in Japan
9th	40
10th	17
11th	20
12th	18
13th	16
14th	19
15th	36
16th	17
17th	26
18th	31
19th	27

57 Milne/Lee, page 155.
58 Professor Båth, private letter dated June 17, 1983. See also Richter as quoted earlier, *Natural History*, December 1969, page 44, and Appendix A.

WHAT LEADING SEISMOLOGISTS SAY ABOUT EARTHQUAKES TODAY AND IN THE PAST

"There is no indication that seismic activity has increased or diminished appreciably throughout historic time."—Seismologists J. Milne and A. W. Lee, *Earthquakes and Other Earth Movements*, seventh edition (London, 1939), p. 155.

"Certain religious groups have picked this rather unfortunate time to insist that the number of earthquakes is increasing. In part they are misled by the increasing number of small earthquakes that are being catalogued and listed by newer, more sensitive stations throughout the world. It is worth remarking that the number of great earthquakes from 1896 to 1906 was greater than in any ten-year interval since."—Professor Charles Richter in *National History,* December 1969, p. 44.

"For earlier centuries we do not have the same reliable statistics, but there are no indications at all of any increase in the activity in the course of time."—Professor Markus Båth, private letter dated June 17, 1983.

"I certainly would agree with both Professors Båth and Richter in their assessment that there has been no significant increase in the number of earthquakes during this or any other century."—Wilbur A. Rinehart, seismologist at the World Data Center A, Boulder, Colorado. Private letter dated August 8, 1985.

An expert on the seismicity of the Mediterranean area, one of the earth's major earthquake regions, says:
"Most certainly, there has been no increase in the seismic activity of the Mediterranean during this century. Quite the contrary, in the Eastern Mediterranean the activity of this century has been abnormally low when compared with that of the 10th–12th and 18th centuries."—Professor N. N. Ambraseys, private letter dated August 9, 1985.

"I feel strongly that the seismicity has been stationary for thousands of years. . . . Excellent geological evidence for the stationarity has been obtained by Prof. Kerry Sieh of Caltech, for the San Andreas fault."—Seismologist Keiiti Aki, professor at the Department of Geological Sciences, University of Southern California, Los Angeles. Private letter dated September 5, 1985.

"There are indications that worldwide seismic activity—if expressed in terms of earthquakes with magnitude 7 or over—has decreased steadily in the time from the beginning of the 20th century until now."—Seweryn J. Duda, Professor of Geophysics, University of Hamburg. Private letter dated July 7, 1986.

(The private letters quoted above are reproduced in their entirety in the Appendix.)

In our own century about 20 earthquakes of some importance had occurred in Japan up to 1983, pointing to a final total of perhaps 25–30 for the *whole* present century.[59] Evaluating these figures, Milne and Lee reported that **"the data support the conclusion that during historic times the amount of seismic activity has not changed to any appreciable extent."**[60]

Consequently, there is no evidence whatsoever in support of the claim made by various religious sources, including the Worldwide Church of God, a Seventh Day Adventist author, and notably by the Watch Tower Society, that earthquake activity is markedly different in our century compared with earlier centuries. All information available points to the contrary. The shifting, twisting, uncoordinated claims of the Watch Tower Society and their juggling of facts and figures in an effort to prove that an increase has occurred have been revealed above as fraudulent—hopefully not deliberately so, but as a result of remarkably poor research, superfical analysis and wishful thinking.

59 Compare the table by Milne/Lee (pp. 232–235), Eiby (pp. 191–195), Båth (pp. 114–117), and the statements by Verney (p. 77). Also Ganse & Nelson.
60 Milne/Lee, p. 156.

CHAPTER 4

Pestilences—Past and Present

PICTURES OFTEN have a deeper impact on our minds than words. Unproven or erroneous statements may seem more convincing and true if they are accompanied by dramatic and impressive illustrations.

The front cover of the November 22, 1983, issue of the *Awake!* magazine, for example, has a picture showing people attempting to escape from a terrible sea wave that covers almost the whole page. The bold words across the page proclaim that mankind today is being "DELUGED BY EPIDEMICS." The illustration is a skillful presentation of the claim of the Watch Tower Society that mankind since 1914 has seen a tremendous *increase* of pestilences or epidemics. Is this true? Does the picture give a correct presentation of the actual facts?

In similar vein, another end-times expositor, Hal Lindsey, states:

> Jesus said that *plagues would sweep the world* prior to his return. For years now, scientists have felt that the great plagues that used to threaten mankind were virtually under control. But in just the past few years great epidemics have killed millions and even though vaccines are available against some of them, there's no way to innoculate the world's masses.[1]

Thus, while acknowledging that a change has come with regard to "the great plagues that used to threaten mankind," author Lindsey, who holds that since 1948 mankind has entered a divinely marked period, at least implies that there is evidence today of 'plagues sweeping the world.'

We may ask, then, what are the "great epidemics" of this century? To what extent have they "deluged" mankind or "swept the world,"

---

1 *The Promise* (1982), page 198.

Awake!

NOVEMBER 22, 1983

DELUGED BY EPIDEMICS

THERE IS A WAY OUT

since 1914, or 1948 or any other supposed 'prophetically marked date' of our time?

The greatest plague of our century was the so-called *Spanish influenza* that swept swiftly over the world in the years 1918–1919, killing between 15 and 25 million people.

The Watch Tower Society, however, goes much farther and claims that this was the greatest plague, not only of our century, but *in the whole history of mankind*. The text book *You Can Live Forever in Paradise on Earth* (1982), for instance, says on page 151:

> **Right after World War I more people died of the Spanish flu than had died of any disease epidemic in the history of mankind.**[2]

In proof of this claim the Watch Tower Society has sometimes quoted an American magazine, *The Saturday Evening Post* of September 26, 1959, in which a writer stated that **"No recorded pestilence before or since has equaled the 1918–1919 death toll in total numbers."**[3]

Such a statement, however, only reveals that the journalist had done very little research on the great, devastating plagues of the past.

It suffices here to remind of the Black Death, the great plague that visited mankind time and again from the fourteenth century onward, and which claimed between 25 and 40 million lives *in Europe alone* in its first attack during the three years from December 1347 to December 1350. The Spanish flu of 1918–1919, on the other hand, took only 2–3 million lives in Europe, and this in spite of the fact that the population of Europe at that time had quadrupled since 1347![4]

Along with the Black Death, several pestilences in the past have influenced human history more profoundly than the Spanish flu, as will become evident in the discussion that follows.

What other pestilences, then, have "deluged" mankind since 1914? Having mentioned the Spanish flu, the earlier-mentioned text book of the Watch Tower Society goes on to say:

> **Yet pestilence and disease continue to rage. Millions die each year from heart trouble and cancer. Venereal disease is spreading rapidly. Other**

2 See also similar statements in *Awake!*, March 8, 1971, page 3, and in *The Watchtower* of April 15, 1982, page 9.

3 See *The Watchtower* of 1961, page 128, and *The Watchtower* of October 15, 1975, page 634.

4 *Awake!*, July 22, 1956, pp. 22–24; *Awake!*, March 8, 1971, p. 6.

terrible diseases, such as malaria, snail fever and river blindness, occur in country after country, especially in Asia, Africa and Latin America.[5]

It is true that such diseases are widespread in some areas. What we are interested to know, however, is: Is there anything new or different about this situation? Have these diseases *increased* during our twentieth century? Has mankind experienced *more* and *greater* pestilences in this century than in any other period of human history?

What about other plagues that killed millions of people in the past, such as smallpox, the bubonic plague and cholera?

And what about heart trouble and cancer? Are such diseases really "pestilences" in the sense the Bible writer Luke uses this word at Luke 21:11?

Evidently, before we take a closer look at the dreadful history of pestilences, there is another question that first needs answering: What *is* a pestilence?

The meaning of "pestilence"

In his gospel account Mark does not mention pestilences among the calamities of which Jesus spoke, but Luke (and possibly also Matthew, according to some manuscripts) does:

> . . . there shall be great earthquakes, and in divers places famines and pestilences.—Luke 21:11, ASV.

The Greek word translated "pestilences" in this verse is *loimoí,* the plural of *loimós*. According to W. E. Vine this word means "a pestilence, any deadly *infectious* malady."[6] The word is used at only one other place in the New Testament, at Acts chapter twenty-four, verse 5, where the Jewish leaders accuse the apostle Paul before governor Felix, saying:

> For we have found this man a pestilent fellow [Greek: *loimós*], and a mover of insurrections among all the Jews throughout the world, and a ringleader of the sect of the Nazarenes. (ASV)

---

5 *You Can Live Forever in Paradise on Earth* (1982), p. 151.

6 *Vine's Expository Dictionary of New Testament Words,* unabridged edition, MacDonald Publishing Company (McLean, Virginia), p. 862. *Loimós,* therefore, is commonly rendered "pestilence" (see *King James Version, American Standard Version, New International Version,* and *Goodspeed*), or "plague" (see *The Jerusalem Bible* and *The New English Bible*).

Although the word *loimós* is used metaphorically in this text, it is clear that the allusion is not merely to a disease of whatever sort, but to an *infectious* disease, a pestilence. In the eyes of these Jewish leaders Paul was a dangerous threat, an infectious subversive whose teachings were being spread throughout the Roman world like an epidemic disease, causing risings among the Jews everywhere.

The well-known Bible commentator Albert Barnes, who is cited in *The Watchtower* of May 1, 1983 on page 3, also stresses the *loimoí* at Luke 21:11 refers to "raging, epidemic diseases."[7]

The word *loimós,* then, was confined to deadly, epidemic diseases or pestilences. Interestingly, the Watch Tower Society in its Bible dictionary *Aid to Bible Understanding* defines "pestilence" as **"Any rapidly spreading infectious disease capable of attaining epidemic proportions and of causing death."** (Page 1295) This definition gives the meaning of *loimós* in an excellent way. When talking of diseases in a more general way, the Greeks had other words, such as *nósos.* This term is used, for example, at Matthew 4:23, where it is stated that Jesus was healing "all manner of *disease*" (*nósos*). The same verse also mentions "all manner of *sickness*," which translates the Greek word *malakía.* A third term for disease was *asthéneia,* meaning "weakness." This word is used of Lazarus' illness at John chapter eleven, verses 1–6.

The reason for this linguistic digression is this: the Watch Tower Society, in its attempts to prove that pestilences have been increasing since 1914, counts *heart trouble* and *cancer* among the pestilences supposedly fulfilling Jesus' words at Luke chapter twenty-one, verse 11. As the above-quoted text book said in this connection: "Millions die each year from heart trouble and cancer." In fact, the Society tends to count all types of diseases among the pestilences of Luke 21:11, infectious or not, deadly or not.

An article in the May 1, 1983, issue of *The Watchtower,* for example, carried the title, "Disease—A Sign of the Last Days?" A table of diseases on page 7 in the same issue starts with cancer and ends

---

7   The Greek word *thánatos,* "death," was also used for pestilence or plague, for example at Revelation 6:8. The name of the rider on the pale horse was *Thánatos* (commonly translated "Death"). He was followed by *Hádes,* the god of the nether world in Greek mythology, here evidently used as a symbol for death or the grave. To them were given "power over a quarter of the earth, with the right to kill by sword and by famine, by pestilence (Greek: *thánatos*) and wild beasts." (*The New English Bible*) These scourges allude to Ezekiel 14:21, where the Hebrew word for pestilence, *deber,* is translated as *thánatos* in the Greek *Septuagint* version.

with multiple sclerosis. Except for these and for influenza and malaria, many of the other diseases mentioned in the table have little or no mortality today.[8]

Deadly though they may be, cancer and heart trouble are *not* pestilences in the Biblical sense. They are not "raging, *epidemic* diseases" or *infectious* diseases, even if *The New York Times Encyclopedic Almanac 1970* happened to call coronary catastrophe a "pandemic." Although this obviously was said figuratively (as a pandemic actually refers to a widespread *infectious* disease), the *Watchtower* soon seized upon the statement and cited it in support of the claimed increase of pestilences.[9]

However, when Luke, who was himself a physician, chose the Greek word *loimós*, we may certainly believe he did so on purpose. He knew that Jesus was not speaking of diseases of ordinary kind (*nósos*), but of *infectious, epidemic* diseases or *pestilences*. The fact that the Watch Tower Society counts cancer, heart diseases, and other kinds of non-infectious maladies among the predicted pestilences not only conflicts with the definition given in its own Bible dictionary. It also indicates that its writers know that genuine pestilences—pestilences in the proper (and Biblical) sense of the word—have *not* increased since 1914.

In his book *Approaching Hoofbeats*, Billy Graham correctly defines "pestilence" as a word meaning "any infectious malady which is fatal." (Page 186) Later, when referring to Jesus' statement about pestilences at Luke chapter twenty-one, Dr. Graham uses the word "plague" as a synonym of pestilence and, strangely, now widens out

---

8 Although *river blindness* may cause blindness, it is not fatal. After a ten-year campaign, WHO (the World Health Organization) has now succeeded in bringing river blindness under control in West Africa, where this disease has been most widespread. (See the *World Health* magazine of October, 1985, pp. 6, 8, 19, 24.)

   Lupus and *snail fever*, when treated, seldom cause death. Not only is the mortality in snail fever today negligible when compared to what it was in earlier centuries, but the geographical extent has also been sharply reduced in many countries that earlier were severely hit by the disease, such as China, Japan, the Philippines, Brazil, Venezuela, Puerto Rico, Egypt, Morocco, the Sudan, Congo, Malawi, Zimbabwe and Mali. (See the *World Health* magazine of December, 1984.)

   Chagas disease can lead to eventual death but is evidently no more prevalent today than in the past. And although perhaps as many as 350 million people today suffer from *malaria*, this is actually a *sharp decline* of this disease since 1914. In earlier centuries over a third of mankind suffered from it and many millions died of it each year. At the outbreak of the First World War, 800 million people—45 percent of earth's population at that time—still were afflicted by it. (Schrader, p. 184) Today (1986), despite rapid increase in recent years, only about 7.5 percent suffer from it.

9 See for instance *The Watchtower* of October 15, 1975, page 634.

its application to include such things as plagues of insects, even referring to an occasion in Florida when "millions of toads overran whole counties." He includes "shifting climate patterns" among the "plagues" of current times. (Pages 192, 193) None of such things fit his earlier-stated definition of "pestilence." Nor do toads or changing weather patterns fit the meaning of the words used by Luke and by John in his Revelation account.

Historians and pestilences

The fact is that we live in a time when epidemic diseases play a relatively unimportant role compared with their ravages in earlier centuries. Because of this people today find it difficult to imagine the horrifying scope of the catastrophes that time and again infested mankind during past generations. As Professor William H. McNeill, one of America's most distinguished historians, points out, the mortality count in many of the great pestilences in the past has been so high that many modern historians, who judge only from their own experience of epidemic infection, tend to discount as exaggeration the ancient reports about massive die-off from many of the great plagues in the past. He states:

> Epidemic disease, when it did become decisive in peace or in war, ran counter to the effort to make the past intelligible. Historians consequently played such episodes down.[10]

But physicians and other researchers who, like McNeill, have studied the history of pestilences, do not agree with the attempt by some historians to downgrade the enormity of the effect of such plagues of earlier centuries. Professor Folke Henschen, for example, a pathologist of international reputation, notes in his historical review of infectious diseases:

> Infectious diseases . . . have probably been the most dangerous enemies of mankind, much more so than war and mass murder. When one studies the constant epidemics of the past and the deficiency diseases on land and at sea, one realizes that the whole of civilization could have succumbed, and one is constantly surprised that mankind has survived.[11]

10 William H. McNeill, *Plagues and Peoples* (Anchor Press/Doubleday, Garden City, New York, 1976), unabridged edition, p. 4. See also pages 120, 135.
11 Folke Henschen, *The History of Diseases* (London: Longman, Green and Co. Ltd, 1966), p 21.

Let us review, then, the various periods and ages of mankind that followed the time of Christ, so that we can then be in better position to assess today's situation and circumstances as they relate to our subject. What follows below are just a few examples gleaned from the history of pestilences. We recommend that those who want to go deeper into the subject might read the book by McNeill (*Plagues and Peoples*), which probably is the best-researched and best-documented survey of the pestilences that have visited mankind during the past 2,000 years.[12]

Pestilences during the Roman Period

A great number of widespread and very deadly pestilences visited the world during the Roman period. The following were some of the most severe:

1. *In A.D. 165* an epidemic (probably smallpox) was brought to the Mediterranean area from Mesopotamia by Roman soldiers. History shows that it spread through the whole Roman empire and raged for about fifteen years. The mortality was enormous. A quarter to a third of the population in affected places died. The plague **"inaugurated a process of continued decay of the population of the Mediterranean lands that lasted, despite some local recoveries, for more than half a millennium."**[13]

2. *From 251 to 266 A.D.* another great plague ravaged the Roman world. This time the mortality was even greater. At the height of the epidemic 5,000 a day died in the city of Rome alone. Other calamities also set in during this century: civil wars, barbarian invasions and repeated periods of famine. The overall devastation was so great that a population expert, J. C. Russell, estimates that the population of the Roman empire was reduced by 50 percent between Augustan times and A.D. 543.[14]

3. *In the years 310–312* China was hit by a pestilence that virtually wiped out the population in the northwestern provinces, killing 98–99 percent of the people there. It was followed ten years later, in 322, by

12 The work is also available in an abridged pocket edition in the Anchor Books series.
13 McNeill, p. 116. At about the same time, in A.D. 161–162, a similar pestilence broke out in China, killing 30–40 percent of the army serving on the northwestern frontier. (McNeill, p. 132) All quotations in the following are from the unabridged edition.
14 McNeill, pp. 116–118, 321. Contemporary authors say that the plague of A.D. 251 spread "over the whole known world."—Raymond Crawfurd, *Plague and Pestilence in Literature and Art* (Oxford, 1914), p. 74.

another epidemic that killed 20–30 percent of the population over a wider region of the country.[15]

4. *In the years 542–543,* during the reign of the Byzantine emperor Justinian (527–565), the so-called "plague of Justinian" reached Europe. It originated either in northeastern India or in central Africa. We have good information on this plague, because a contemporary eyewitness, the physician, historian and prefect Procopius, has left a careful and detailed description of the misery of his days. Thanks to his description it has been possible to identify the plague as the *pneumonic* and/or *bubonic,* the same plague that swept over the world in the 14th century and later was called the Black Death.[16] Before it reached Europe in 542, Constantinople, Procopius' home town, was severely hit:

> In Constantinople it killed 5,000–10,000 people a day. Through Greece it spread to Italy, and after fifteen years it reached the Rhine. There it turned and on its way back it passed through Constantinople again, having then in no way lost its virulence. It is estimated that the Eastern Empire lost half the number of its inhabitants. Many cities died out.[17]

In all, the "Justinian plague" is thought to have claimed 100 million lives.[18] McNeill and Henschen both stress that the plagues of the third and the sixth centuries played a substantial role in the decline of the Roman Empire.[19] The bubonic plague returned and raged periodically up to A.D. 750. McNeill compares it with the *Black Death* in scope and mortality:

> Historic evidence, indeed, suggests that the plagues of the sixth and seventh centuries had an importance for Mediterranean peoples fully analogous to that of the more famous Black Death of the fourteenth century. The disease certainly provoked an initial die-off of a large proportion of the urban dwellers in affected regions, and the over-all diminution of population took centuries to repair.[20]

---

15 McNeill, pp. 132, 135.

16 Procopius, *Persian Wars,* II, 22.6–39; McNeill, p. 322.

17 The Swedish medical historian Matts Bergmark in his book *Erån pest till polio* ("From Pestilence to Polio"), third edition (Stockholm, 1983), page 11.

18 See *The Watchtower* of June 15, 1977, page 359.

19 McNeill, p. 120; Henschen, p. 78. Professor Henry E. Sigerist, in his *Civilization and Disease* (Ithaca, New York, 1945), argues that the Justinian Plague put an end to the Roman Empire both in the east and the west and concludes: "Thus the 6th century marks a turning-point in the history of the Mediterranean world, and the great plague of Justinian appears as a demarcation line between the two periods. . . . The old world broke down, and on its ruins a new civilization began slowly to rise." (Pp. 113–115)

20 McNeill, p. 127

The bubonic plague also visited Asia in several deadly waves. The earliest Chinese description of it dates from A.D. 610. In 642 it ravaged the Kwantung province. In 762 it broke out in the coastal provinces, and "more than half the population of Shantung province died."[21] In 806 it killed off more than half the population in Chekiang province.[22]

During the same period, Japan underwent a number of very severe epidemics. As the result of a pestilence that broke out in A.D. 808 "over half of the population perished," and similar devastation is reported for another disease that struck in 994–995.[23]

Pestilence continued to ravage numerous countries at short intervals. Anglo-Saxon sources mention no less than forty-nine outbreaks of epidemics between A.D. 526 and 1087. Arabic sources list over fifty different visitations of pestilences in Egypt, Syria, and Iraq between 632 and 1301. Chinese records report as many as 288 pestilences from A.D. 37 to 1911! As McNeill points out, the sources are, of course, far from complete.[24]

The Late Middle Ages, Time of the Black Death

Toward the end of the year 1347 the frightful pneumonic/bubonic plague again visited Europe. Before its arrival there it had already swept over all Asia. As early as 1331 the epidemic broke out in the province of Hopei in China, where it is reported to have killed nine out of every ten persons. In 1353 and 1354 it raged in eight different and widely scattered parts of China. Contemporary chronicles report that "two thirds of the population" of those areas died.[25]

Rumors that had reached Europe in 1346 told of the terrible plague's spread from China "through Tartary (Central Asia) to India and Persia, Mesopotamia, Syria, Egypt, and all of Asia Minor." As historian Tuchman relates, they told of "a death toll so devastating that

---

21 Ibid., p. 134.
22 Ibid., pp. 134, 135.
23 Ibid., pp. 140, 141.
24 Ibid., pp. 128, 334, 293–302. Egypt underwent constant plagues from A.D. 541 on into the nineteenth century. In the famine period of 1053–1060, at one point 10,000 a day died in Cairo, and in 1201 two-thirds of the whole population of Egypt died within a few months! "Syria, too, appears to have lost half its population between the second and eighth centuries A.D."—T. H. Hollingsworth, *Historical Demography* (London and Southampton, 1969), pp. 308, 309.
25 McNeill, p. 162.

all India was said to be depopulated, whole territories covered by dead bodies, other areas with no one left alive."[26]

The pestilence was brought westwards via the caravan routes and reached the Crimea in 1346. From there it was spread by ship throughout the Mediterranean area. The fatalities (or "die-off") were devastating. "About a third of Egypt's population seems to have died in the first attack, 1347–1349."[27] Through Sicily, where half a million people died, the plague reached Italy, killing over half of its population.[28]

From Italy the catastrophic infection spread westward and northward over the European continent. In France, at least one third (according to some estimates, three quarters) of the population was annihilated. ("Hearth tax" records are available for this period and clearly support the swift and remarkable wiping out of thousands upon thousands of entire households by the plague. Monasteries and similar places where considerable numbers were in close contact suffered particular damage, at times the number of residents dropping from as many as a hundred to just two or three.) Nineteenth century scholar J. F. K. Hecker estimated that Poland lost three quarters of its inhabitants, and in Germany his findings indicated that "200,000 small country towns . . . were bereft of all their inhabitants."[29]

By August 1348 the plague had crossed the channel into England. Within nine months it had wiped out half the population. In the same autumn an English ship brought the pestilence to Iceland, and there, too, half the population perished. In Norway, where the plague broke out in the summer of 1349, two thirds of the population died. In the same year it swept over Denmark, in some areas completely depopulating up to 40 percent of the villages, and reached Sweden in the spring of 1350. Before the end of the year one third of the population in Sweden had died.[30]

---

26 Barbara W. Tuchman, *A Distant Mirror. The Calamitous 14th Century.* London: MacMillan London Limited, 1979, page 93. See also McNeill, page 190.

27 McNeill, p. 187. In Cairo, as many as 20,000 died in a day in 1348. (Hollingsworth, p. 309) It is estimated that the whole Islamic world (Middle East and North Africa) suffered similar proportional losses: "By 1349, the entire Islamic world had been engulfed by the Black Death. About a third of the general population and perhaps 40% to 50% of those living in towns had died." (Robert S. Gottfried, *The Black Death*, London, 1983, p. 41.)

28 This is the estimate of the nineteenth century scholar J. F. K. Hecker, whose figures are the most conservative of all. See George Deaux, *The Black Death 1347* (in the series *Turning Points in History,* edited by Sir Denis Brogan, London, 1969), p. 75.

29 George Deaux, pp. 111–114; Bergmark, p. 52; Tuchman (1978), pp. 92ff.

30 Bergmark, pp. 28–30; K. Lunden in *Bra Böckers Världshistoria* ("Good Books' World History"), Vol. 6 (Höganäs, Sweden, 1984), p. 26.

THE PROGRESS OF THE BLACK DEATH IN EUROPE
DECEMBER 1347—DECEMBER 1350

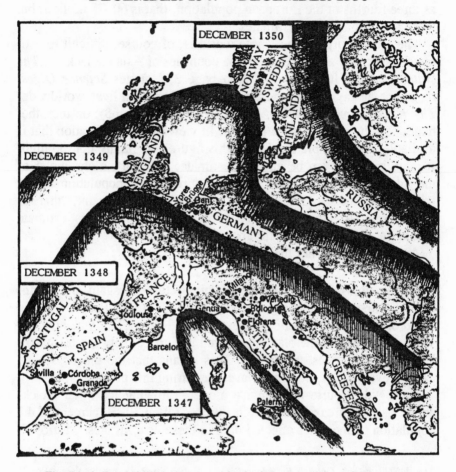

The Black Death killed about one-third of the population of Europe, and probably also of the whole world. In Europe alone, 25–40 million died between December 1347 and December 1350. No disaster since has equalled this terrifying devastation.

Europe was never to forget this incredibly massive visitation of death. Contemporaries called it *Magna mortalitas*—The Great Death.[31] Estimates of the total mortality in Europe vary from one fourth to as much as one half of the total population, which would

---

31 The "Black Death" is a later term given to subsequent visitations of the plague, although it is now generally used of the first attack in 1347–1350.

mean that between 25 and 40 million people were annihilated in the first attack of the plague in 1347–50.[32] A few estimates range as high as three fourths of the European population, that is 60–75 million, but these are probably overestimates.

The total figure for the whole world is, of course, difficult to estimate, especially as figures from the countries of Asia are lacking. *The Watchtower* of June 15, 1977, on page 359 quotes *Science Digest* magazine as saying that the plague took 62 million lives worldwide. *The 1983 Guinness Book of World Records* (page 465), on the other hand, sets the number at 75 million. In view of the information that *is* available, for example for China, this figure is certainly not too high. It may, in fact, even be an underestimate. Froissart, a chronicler of the 14th century, estimated that one-third of the population of the world died, and as pointed out by historian George Deaux, "there is widespread agreement with Froissart's estimate."[33] This estimate would put the death figure far above 100 million.

And yet this was not the end.

The pneumonic and bubonic plagues returned, again and again, after the first violent attack in the years 1347–1350. People lived in dread of it for nearly four centuries. From 1346 to 1720, when the last violent outbreak of the plague occurred in Europe, between 60 and 70 European epidemics are known. This means that the plague visited Europe every sixth year on the average during this period.[34]

During the fourteenth century alone, following its initial attack, another six outbreaks occurred in Europe. Often 30–50 percent of the population of the cities affected died in these new ravages.[35] Europe's

---

32 McNeill, p. 168. *Collier's Encyclopedia* (Vol. 4, 1974, p. 234) says that the total of 25 million deaths in Europe "are J. F. K. Hecker's statistics, which are the lowest of all authorities'." The most recent studies tend to show that Hecker's estimate was too low. (K. Lunden, pp. 17–22) In 1931, Professor A. M. Campbell concluded that "the figures would seem . . . to support the estimates that one-half more nearly than that of one-fourth as the population loss sustained by Europe in consequence of the Black Death." (*The Black Death and Men of Learning*, New York, 1931, p. 145)

33 George Deaux, pp. 111, 144. Earth's population is estimated to have been about 450 million before the Black Death struck. (E. Hofsten, *Befolkningslära*, Lund, Sweden, 1982, p. 16)

34 Bergmark, p. 37.

35 Swedish historian Michael Nordberg says that the result of the epidemics was "at least as terrifying as in 1348–50." He gives the following examples: "London lost through plagues the following parts of its population: 1563: 25–30 percent; 1593: c. 18 percent; 1603: 22–26 percent; 1625: c. 25 percent; 1636: almost 10 percent; 1665 (The Great Plague) c. 28 percent. Still worse were the losses for many North-Italian cities in the severe epidemic in

WHAT LEADING AUTHORITIES SAY ABOUT THE BLACK DEATH

"Almost certainly the most terrible visitation to which mankind has ever been exposed."—Professor Folke Henschen, *The History of Diseases* (London, 1966), page 79.

"The Black Death was an unprecedented catastrophe for which the only parallels are the Biblical story of the Flood and the 20th-century predictions of the effects of an all-out nuclear war."—George Deaux, *The Black Death 1347* (London, 1969), pages 143, 144.

"Undoubtedly the worst disaster that has ever befallen mankind."—Michael W. Dols, *The Black Death in the Middle East* (Princeton, New Jersey, 1977), page vii.

"The most lethal disaster of recorded history."—Barbara Tuchman, *A Distant Mirror. The Calamitous 14th Century* (London, 1979), page xiii.

"[The] greatest of all crises faced by the human species."—Isaac Asimov, *A Choice of Catastrophes* (London, 1980), page 242.

"The only possible comparison would be with the hypothetical results of a modern nuclear or bacteriological war."—The renowned French historian Emmanuel Le Roy Ladurie, *The Mind and Method of the Historian* (Brighton, Sussex, England, 1981), page 71.

"The impact of the Black Death, the greatest ecological upheaval, has been compared to that of the two world wars of the twentieth century. To a degree this is true. But the Black Death . . . wrought even more essential change. . . . The effects of this natural and human disaster changed Europe profoundly, perhaps more so than any other series of events. For this reason, alone, the Black Death should be ranked as the greatest biological-environmental event in history, and one of the major turning points of Western Civilization."—Robert S. Gottfried, *The Black Death* (London, 1983), page 163.

"The greatest disaster ever suffered by the world was the pandemic spread of bubonic plague, which killed as much as one-third of the world's population before running its course across fourteenth-century Europe and Asia."—James Cornell, *The Great International Disaster Book* (New York, 1979), page 70.

population continued to decline. As of the year 1380 it had been reduced by about 40 percent, and toward the end of the century by
nearly 50 percent.[36] The lowest level was reached between 1440 and
1480.[37]

The same trend may be noted for other parts of the world. About
A.D. 1200 China had a population of 123 million. In 1393 it had
decreased to a mere 65 million. Although historians usually ascribe
this decrease to the civil war that raged at the same time as the plague
(the war being caused by Chinese reaction against Mongol dominion
and ending in the expulsion of the Mongols), McNeill is certainly
more realistic when he lays the heaviest responsibility for the drastic
decrease upon the plague.[38] Again, in the sixteenth century China is
said to have been almost depopulated by the bubonic plague.

Although this scourge practically disappeared from Europe after
1720, it continued to rage in other parts of the world. As late as between 1906 and 1911, 7.5 million were killed by the plague in India.[39]

In view of all this, it is not difficult to understand why authorities
make statements such as those shown in the accompanying boxed list,
in reference to the first attack in the fourteenth century.

Yet this pneumonic/bubonic plague, which repeatedly visited mankind for hundreds of years after 1350, was not the only epidemic to
ravage the world during these centuries. It was to be accompanied by
a series of other devastating pestilences, as we now see.

A.D. 1500 to 1800: era of syphilis and smallpox

The transoceanic expeditions that began in the year 1492 ushered in a
new era of pandemics that had fatal consequences for the entire globe.

At the end of the fifteenth century, syphilis came to Europe, perhaps imported from America by the sailors of Columbus. **"In the
years that followed the disease spread all over Europe, Africa and
Asia, and everywhere it took a very malignant turn."**[40] In spite of

---

1630: Milan 35–40 percent; Venice 35 percent; Padova 44 percent; Parma 50 percent;
Verona 59 percent; Brescia 45 percent; Cremona c. 60 percent and Mantova 69 percent!"
(*Den dynamiska medeltiden*, Stockholm, 1984, p. 32)

36 Tuchman (1979), p. 119. Similar ravages occurred in Africa and Asia. In 1380, for instance, the plague killed another 13 million people in China. (*Collier's Encyclopedia*, Vol.
4, 1974, p. 234)

37 McNeill, p. 169.

38 Ibid., pp. 163, 190.

39 *Awake!*, July 22, 1956, pp. 22–24.

40 Bergmark, p. 59.

all the talk about syphilis today, it is the sixteenth century, not the twentieth, that may be called "the century of syphilis." The disease was everywhere, in all classes of society, in the homes, at the public baths, in public houses, among children and adults. The frequency of the disease was frightening and the organic lesions were very serious. Millions died of it. The disease was also inherited by the offspring, and blind, deaf, and otherwise malformed children were born.

Since the sixteenth century syphilis has grown weaker and less disastrous. Syphilis was considered incurable up to the beginning of our century, but from then on different antibiotics have been developed against it. Today the mortality has decreased to a fraction of what it was before the First World War. Though still with us, syphilis no longer kills the millions that it did in the sixteenth century.[41]

Even if syphilis was brought to the Old World from America by Columbus' sailors, as some researchers believe, this disease was by no means as disastrous to the Europeans as the pestilences the American aborigines got in exchange from the Europeans.

When the Europeans came to America, they brought with them epidemic diseases that had been raging in the Old World for centuries, and against which the Eurasian populations had developed a certain degree of immunity.

The Amerindian populations, on the other hand, were entirely defenseless against these new infectious diseases. The result was a complete catastrophe, the real magnitude of which only recently has become clear. The reason is, as McNeill explains, that historians before World War II systematically underestimated the pre-Columbian populations of America, putting the total between eight and fourteen million.

> Recent estimates, however, based upon sampling of tribute lists, missionary reports and elaborate statistical arguments, have multiplied such earlier estimates tenfold and more, putting Amerindian population on the eve of the conquest at about one hundred million, with twenty-five to thirty million of this total assignable to the Mexican and an approximately equal number to the Andean civilizations.[42]

41 Bergmark, pp. 83, 87, 91. See also René Dubos, *Mirage of Health* (New York, 1959), chapter six, and *Awake!*, September 8, 1984, page 3.

42 McNeill, pp. 203, 204. Compare also the discussion of the distinguished European historian Fernand Braudel in his *Civilization and Capitalism 15th–18th Century: The Structures of Everyday Life* (London, 1981), pp. 35–38. Also Emmanuel Le Roy Ladurie, *The Mind and Method of the Historian* (Brighton, Sussex, England, 1981), pp. 72, 76, 77.

It was not Cortez' soldiers but *smallpox* that conquered the king-dom of the Aztecs in Mexico in 1520. Cortez' soldiers brought with them the disease from Hispaniola (the island now occupied by the Dominican Republic and Haiti), where it had arrived from Europe two years earlier. The smallpox epidemic that broke out in Mexico quickly spread to Guatemala and then farther south. By 1525 or 1526 it reached the Inca domain in South America, where it paved the way for Pizarro's conquest in the same way that it had conquered Mexico for Cortez a few years earlier. The mortality was frightful. After the initial ravages, about one third of the total population had died![43]

Smallpox was followed by other pestilences. In 1530–1531 an epi-demic of measles spread through Mexico and Peru, killing large num-bers. It was followed fifteen years later by another epidemic, probably typhus. Then, in 1558–1559, a deadly influenza epidemic ravaged America. This epidemic seems to have been global. It had broken out in Europe in 1556 and lasted for four years, with disastrous conse-quences. It is estimated that England lost 20 percent of its entire pop-ulation, and similar losses occurred in other countries. Contemporary Japanese sources also mention this dreadful influenza, telling that "very many died" in it.[44]

The consequences for the Amerindian populations of these and other outbreaks of pestilence were devastating. In 1568, fifty years after Cortez' conquest, the epidemics had reduced the population of Mexico from 25–30 million to less than three million. By 1605 it had decreased to one million. Similar declines occurred in other parts of America.[45]

By the middle of the seventeenth century two other very lethal dis-eases had been brought to America from Africa: *malaria* and *yellow fever*. Both diseases were new to the Amerindians, and the results, therefore, were extremely serious. Malaria "appears to have com-pleted the destruction of Amerindians in the tropical lowlands, so as to empty formerly well-populated regions almost completely."[46] And yellow fever, which had reached the Caribbean from West Africa in 1648, had a similar devastating effect on Amerindian populations. Since no immunity had developed (as it had to some degree among

43 McNeill, p. 209.
44 McNeill, p. 209. Although death figures are lacking, it is quite possible that this influenza epidemic was comparable to the Spanish flu of 1918–1919 with respect to extent and mortality.
45 Braudel, p. 36; McNeill, pp. 204, 205.
46 McNeill, p. 213.

many in Africa), it almost unerringly killed every adult that contracted it.[47]

After all these ravages, what was the final result for the native populations of the Americas? McNeill summarizes:

> Overall, the disaster to Amerindian population assumed a scale that is hard for us to imagine, living as we do in an age when epidemic disease hardly matters. Ratios of 20:1 or even 25:1 between pre-Columbian populations and the bottoming out point in Amerindian population curves seem more or less correct, despite wide local variations. Behind such chill statistics lurks enormous and repeated human anguish, as whole societies fell apart, values crumbled, and old ways of life lost all shred of meaning.[48]

In plain language this means that the total decrease of the Amerindian populations in North, Central, and South America was 95 or 96 percent, that is, a decrease from about 100 million to as low as 5 or 4 million!

The pestilences that devasted America also visited Europe, although the consequences were not as severe. Smallpox appeared in Europe after the decline of the Roman Empire, but did not become widespread until the sixteenth century. In 1614 a pandemic spread from Asia over great parts of Europe and Africa. In the eighteenth century smallpox killed sixty million of the population in Europe alone. Mortality was especially high among children. 25–35 percent of those infected died—and practically all children caught the infection![49] Millions of homes throughout Europe were bereaved of younger members by the onslaught of smallpox.

Nineteenth century: time of cholera, measles and scarlet fever—and time of change

Cholera was the great plague of the nineteenth century. It is spread mainly through water or food contaminated by excrement of infected persons. No pestilence killed as quickly as cholera and, until recent times, the mortality rate was very high: from 50 to 80 percent.

Up to 1817 this plague was known only in India. In that year it began to move northwest, reaching the Russian town of Astrachan at

47 Ibid., p. 214.
48 Ibid., p. 215.
49 Bergmark, pp. 114, 115.

THIRD CHOLERA PANDEMIC, 1846–62

Woodcut created by artist Alfred Rethel depicting the tragic effect of the third cholera pandemic in 1846–62. (Republished by M. Bergmark, *Från pest till polio,* Stockholm 1983, p. 204.)

the Caspian Sea in 1823. Another thrust in 1826 brought it to Russia again in 1829, and from there it suddenly spread to Europe, America, and the rest of the world, spreading horror and death everywhere for seven years. Another four pandemics swept over the whole world during the next sixty years, the last in 1883–1896. The five outbreaks are estimated to have killed about 100 million people worldwide.[50]

Measles and *scarlet fever* also belonged to the nineteenth century more than to any other century. Up to 1840 measles was the most common cause of child mortality. From 1840 to 1880 that role was taken over by scarlet fever, which was responsible for four to six percent of all deaths during this period, not only among children but among all age groups. From 1880 to 1915 measles again held the

50 Bergmark, pp. 191, 207–209; Herbert L. Schrader, *Und dennoch siegte das Leben* (Stuttgart, 1954), pp. 64–67, 70, 71. Cholera still rages in some parts of the world, especially Asia, where it is pandemic. But effective measures of treatment (liquid supply) are applied, and the mortality rate is low today.

position as the greatest child killer.[51] Other great pestilences of the past century were *typhus* and *tuberculosis,* the last of which still kills some three million people annually.

Despite its calamitous plagues, the nineteenth century was to mark the turning-point for most of the great pestilences. As early as the beginning of the century large-scale inoculation and vaccination against smallpox were started in one country after another. After Louis Pasteur's discovery of microorganisms, the real causes of epidemic diseases began to be understood, and this in turn brought about a series of dramatic medical discoveries, especially from the 1880's and on.

Since then vaccines, antibiotics, and other prophylactics, controls and cures have been developed against most of the great pestilences, for example against the bubonic plague, cholera, yellow fever, syphilis, typhus, tuberculosis, and malaria. In our century smallpox has been virtually exterminated. The last known case was reported from Somalia in October 1977.

In fact, only one of the *great* plagues remains to be brought under control by modern medical science: *Influenza.* True, cholera still breaks out in some areas, particularly Asia, but improvement in sanitation and in sewage disposal systems has reduced its incidence; effective treatment (notably of liquid supply) is now applied and mortality today is low. Influenza, by contrast, still produces occasional pandemics that are worldwide.

Because this plague caused some twenty million deaths in the great pandemic of 1918–1919, the Watch Tower Society constantly refers to it as its best evidence in support of its claim that pestilences have been increasing since 1914. It seems proper, therefore, to conclude this survey of past centuries and their plagues with some observations on the Spanish flu of 1918–1919. Was this pandemic disease really unique in the history of pestilences? Was it even unique in the history of *influenza* epidemics?

Influenza—"the last great plague"

In almost every age most people seem to have thought that the problems and catastrophes of their own time were so great that they must

51 Dubos, chapter 6.

have been unparalleled in the history of mankind.[52] The reason for this is that most people, while well aware of the calamities of their own days, such as wars, famines, crimes, earthquakes and epidemics, usually know very little about the extent and frequency of such miseries in the past.

It is no surprise, therefore, that the problems of today may seem unique to many. Even experts, who may know a lot about hunger, diseases, and similar calamities in the world today, have seldom delved deeply into the extent of these problems in earlier centuries. Thus, they may sometimes make sensational statements about the "uniqueness" of this or that catastrophe of our century—statements that simply are not true, although these opinions may be widely publicized and accepted. Some statements about the *Spanish influenza* of 1918–1919 quoted in the Watch Tower literature clearly belong to this category. What, then, are the facts about the "Spanish flu"?

According to noted bacteriologist Dr. Edwin Oakes Jordan, the Spanish flu of 1918–1919 killed 21,642,283 persons.

More than half of these, or twelve and a half million, died in India.

Another two million died in Europe, and about seven million in other parts of the world.[53]

As pointed out at the beginning of this chapter, the Watch Tower Society, quoting an American magazine, maintains that this influenza was the greatest plague in world history, and that more people died of it **"than had died of any disease epidemic in the history of mankind."** From the discussion already presented about plagues of the past it should now be clear to every attentive reader that this claim is in direct conflict with the historical evidence. The claim is totally false.

A number of great pestilences in the past took more lives than the Spanish flu. As shown above, the "plague of Justinian" in the sixth century is estimated to have claimed 100 million lives. The Black Death of the fourteenth century probably killed as many as 75 million. The smallpox epidemic in the 1520's may have killed over 30 mil-

---

52   See the pertinent observations of Dr. N. W. Pirie in the "Introduction" to his book *Food Resources Conventional and Novel* (London, 1969).

53   Dr. Edwin Oakes Jordan, *Epidemic Influenza* (1927); *Encyclopaedia Britannica*, Vol. 12 (1969), p. 242; *Awake!*, March 8, 1971, p. 6. One expert, cited on page 29 of the *Awake!* of February 22, 1977, feels that a total death figure of 21 million "probably" is "a gross underestimation," as that number may have died in India alone. If this could be supported, the total death figure would be raised to about 30 million.

lion—a third of the total Amerindian population—in America alone. And in the nineteenth century cholera took about 100 million lives in five great pandemics. Some of these cholera pandemics killed far above twenty million each, and were, therefore, each fully comparable to the Spanish flu. Obviously, the Spanish flu was not the "greatest" or "most destructive" epidemic in the history of mankind.

Perhaps for this reason Watch Tower claims about the Spanish flu sometimes focus on its *mortality rate*, that is, the claim is made that it killed a higher *percentage* of those infected with it than any other known pestilence. Thus an article on the Spanish flu in the *Awake!* magazine of March 8, 1971, was given the title "The Deadliest Killer of All Time." On page three the article then quoted an unnamed authority as stating:

> **Had the epidemic continued its mathematical rate of acceleration, civilization would easily have disappeared from the earth within a matter of a few more weeks.[54]**

This statement is, however, totally absurd. It is generally estimated that about 525 million—over a quarter of mankind—fell ill with the influenza. Of these 15–25 million died and about 500 million recovered. The average mortality, then, was about *four percent*.[55] What does this mean? It means that even if every single person on earth had fallen sick with the influenza, the great majority of mankind—about 96 percent—would have survived. *Civilization obviously was never in danger!*

Influenza epidemics commonly develop quickly and spread swiftly to a high percentage of the population. Often 25–40 percent are affected. But mortality is commonly low.

These features were also shared by the 1918–1919 epidemic, although the approximately four percent mortality was higher than

---

54 The statement is repeated in the Watch Tower Society's new book on evolution, *Life— How Did It Get Here?* (1985), page 225, where the reference shows the source to have been Joseph E. Persico, *Science Digest*, March, 1977, page 79.

55 Bergmark, p. 260. According to Jordan and Henschen about 50 percent of mankind (one billion) fell sick, which would lower the average mortality to two percent. Henschen puts it as low as 0.25 percent, which is too low. (*Encyclopaedia Britannica*, Vol. 12, 1969, p. 242; Henschen, p. 52) In most places the mortality was much lower than the two percent global figure suggested by Jordan and Henschen, for instance in the U.S.A., where it was 0.5 percent. In a few places it ran considerably higher. In India four percent of the population died, and in Western Samoa 20–25 percent of the population, or 7,500 out of 38,000 perished. (W. I. Beveridge, *Influenza: The Last Great Plague*, London, 1977, p. 31; *The Watchtower*, August 1, 1978, p. 29)

usual.[56] The fact is, however, that most of the great pestilences throughout history had a *far higher* mortality than did the Spanish flu. *Typhoid fever* and *dysentery*, both of which used to be the constant followers of wars in the past, sometimes killed as many as 20 and 50 percent of the infected, respectively. *Yellow fever* had a mortality of 60 percent or more.[57] *Cholera* killed from 50 to 80 percent of those who fell ill with it. Mortality due to the *bubonic plague* varied between 30 and 90 percent, while *pneumonic plague*—the other type of infection during the Black Death pandemic of 1347–1350—had a mortality of 100 percent, with no known survivors![58]

Clearly, it would be far from correct to describe the Spanish flu, with an average mortality of 4 percent, as "the deadliest killer of all time," as the Watch Tower Society does. Compared with the other great plagues of history it was, instead, one of the *least* deadly of those killers!

The swiftest killer?

A third claim is that the Spanish flu took its death toll *more swiftly* than any earlier plagues. **"In all history there had been no stronger, swifter visitation of death,"** said *The Watchtower* of June 15, 1977, on page 359, citing *Science Digest* magazine. It was then pointed out that while the Black Death took 62 million lives worldwide *in three years*, the Spanish flu took 21 million lives *in just four months*.

What the article does not point out to the reader is that the Spanish flu did not last for only four months. It lasted for about *twelve* months, from the early spring of 1918 to the spring of 1919.[59] It reached a peak in the autumn months of 1918, when mortality was highest. But comparing *the peak period* of greatest mortality of the Spanish flu with *the total duration* of the Black Death and other earlier plagues, such as the plague of Justinian, will certainly give a warped picture of the mortality rates, because these earlier plagues had their peak periods too! To get a correct result we must 'compare apples with apples' and not apples with pears. We must either compare the mortality rate during the *peaks* of both the Spanish flu and the Black Death, or the

---

56 *Encyclopaedia Britannica*, Vol. 12 (1969), page 242. The mortality was not unique among the influenza epidemics, however. Some of the earlier influenza epidemics had a much higher mortality!

57 Bergmark, pp. 141, 154, 232.

58 McNeill, p. 168.

59 Beveridge, pp. 21, 42, 43.

average mortality rate of both during the *whole periods* of their duration. Thus, the Spanish flu killed 21 million persons in about one year, while the Black Death took at least 62 million lives in three years—which is likewise about 21 million a year![60]

This is a noteworthy matter, for two reasons. First, because the fastest means of transportation at the time of the Black Death was the sailing vessel or ship. By contrast, at the time of the Spanish flu automobiles, trains and steamboats provided for swifter modes of travel. Thus, viruses and bacteria that earlier took several weeks or months to spread from one continent to another could now cover the same distance in relatively few days.

Second, it is noteworthy because the world population at the time of the Black Death was only a fourth of what it was in 1918. In three years the Black Death killed at least *14 percent* (the most conservative estimate being 62 million out of 450 million) of the population of the earth, or about 5 percent per year, while the Spanish flu in one year killed slightly more than *one percent* of mankind (21 million out of 1,800 million).[61]

The Black Death, therefore, far more than the Spanish flu, deserves to be called the *sternest* and *swiftest* visitation of death in history.

The most widespread killer?

Finally, the Spanish flu is proclaimed "noteworthy because it raged world wide."[62] But many earlier pestilences also had spread all over the world, including some influenza epidemics. These included the influenza epidemics of 1556–1559, 1580, 1732–1733, 1781–1782, 1830–1833, 1857–1858, and 1889–1890. All of these spread rapidly over the whole world and affected a high percentage of the population.[63]

One of the most fatal influenza epidemics was the global pandemic of 1556–1559 which, as noted earlier, killed off about one out of every

---

60 If it is objected that the Spanish flu may have killed *more* than 21 million, perhaps 25 million or more, it should be remembered that the Black Death, too, probably killed more than 62 million world wide—perhaps 75 million or more.

61 Isaac Asimov, in pointing out that the Black Death "may have killed a third of all the human population of the planet," compares it with the Spanish flu and concludes: "However, the influenza epidemic killed less than 2 per cent of the world's population, so that the Black Death remains unrivalled." (*A Choice of Catastrophes*, London, 1980, pp. 241, 243.)

62 *The Watchtower*, August 1, 1978, p. 29.

63 Beveridge, pp. 26–30; McNeill, p. 209.

five persons of the entire population of England and of some other European countries. Again in 1580, an epidemic started in Asia and spread to Africa, Europe, and America. Contemporary records report that **"in the space of six weeks it afflicted almost all the nations of Europe, of whom hardly the twentieth person was free of the disease, and anyone who was so became an object of wonder to others in the place."**[64] In some areas the mortality was very high. In the city of Rome 9,000 died; some Spanish cities were said to be "nearly entirely depopulated by the disease."[65]

The influenza pandemic of 1781–1782, which "was reported from all European countries, China, India, and North America," attacked up to two-thirds and three-quarters of the population in some places.[66] Some of these pandemics reached a considerable mortality. In Britain, the "great influenza of 1847" was compared to the ravages of cholera, "as there were more influenza deaths than there had been cholera deaths during the great epidemic of that disease in 1832."[67]

To sum up, on all counts the Spanish influenza of 1918–1919 was far from being the "greatest" plague in the history of mankind. As regards total loss of life, several other plagues in the past killed more people than the 1918–1919 epidemic.

Nor was its *rate* of mortality the highest of all the great plagues of the past. Rather, the mortality rate was low compared with many earlier pestilences. In this regard, it would rank, not as the "deadliest," but among the least deadly of the great plagues of history.

The claim that the Spanish flu was the "swiftest" killer of all time has been shown to be false, also, as this claim is based upon a faulty use of statistics.

Finally, the worldwide extent of the 1918–1919 influenza was in no way "noteworthy," as many earlier epidemics, including a number of influenza epidemics, raged worldwide also.

In what way, then, was the Spanish flu exceptional? Was it unique in *any* respect? It *may* have been unique in *one* respect, although even this is impossible to prove. The Spanish flu may have killed more people than any earlier *influenza* epidemic. This seems to be the opinion of many experts. According to the *Encyclopaedia Britannica*,

64 Beveridge, p. 26.
65 Ibid., p. 26.
66 Ibid., p. 28.
67 Ibid., p. 29; McNeill, p. 209.

"The 1918 epidemic was the most destructive [influenza epidemic] in history."[68] Dr. Beveridge, in his review of influenza epidemics, tends to agree, describing it at first as "the greatest visitation [of influenza] ever experienced by the human race."[69] And yet he is far from convinced of this. Mankind has been periodically visited by influenza epidemics since ancient times, several of which were worldwide in scope and had a high mortality. The historical records, however, are far from complete and mortality figures are usually missing. Beveridge, who briefly describes sixteen major epidemics of influenza during the 200 years that immediately preceded the Spanish flu, concludes his discussion of this last-mentioned disease by saying:

> The 1918–19 pandemic was by far the most serious in recent times and we have come to think of it as quite exceptional. However, perhaps it is not unique. Judging from historical accounts, some epidemics in former times that may have been influenza were just as devastating."[70]

Even in this respect, then, the Spanish flu may not have been unique.

Have pestilences increased in this century?

For the modern picture to fit the claim that we now live in a unique and prophetically marked period, there should be evidence of an increase in pestilence in our time. While not specifically stating that this is happening, Dr. Graham, in his treatise on the four horsemen of the Apocalypse, nonetheless writes of "the lifeless forms of the 40,000 children who died from hunger and disease in the short time you were sleeping," and adds, "Count up the Third World victims of plague and pestilence that now sweep the famine and drought-ravaged towns and villages of the earth." (*Approaching Hoofbeats*, page 184) Later, stating that the Lord "warned us there would be plagues," he goes on to say, "We are being warned by scientists today about bacteria, viruses and insects that are highly resistant to radiation, antibiotics or insecticides. Some feel the tilt of nature has already been affected by modern chemicals." (Page 192)

What do we actually find if we 'count up the Third World victims of plague and pestilence'—or even those of the rest of the earth—in

---

68   *The Encyclopaedia Britannica*, Vol. 12 (1969), p. 242.
69   Beveridge, p. 32.
70   Beveridge, pp. 32, 33.

our time? Do we find the increase that many end-times expositors warn of? Are there even substantial indications of darkening prospects for the near future?

The answer that all qualified researchers—historians, physicians and other scholars who have studied the subject—give to this question is unanimous: Pestilences have *not* increased during this century. *They have decreased.* Consider these observations:

Professor Folke Henschen, pathologist:

> Infectious diseases, which only one or two generations ago formed the largest group in our statistics on morbidity and mortality, have been driven back by the advance of medicine.[71]

Matts Bergmark, medical historian:

> . . . it is precisely the infectious diseases that have decreased.[72]

Herbert L. Schrader, medical historian:

> . . . the subjugators of pestilences have won the greatest victory that ever has been gained during six thousand years of world history: the victory over a premature death.[73]

Professor William H. McNeill, historian:

> In most places epidemic diseases have become unimportant, and many kinds of infection have become rare where they were formerly common and serious. The net increment to human health and cheerfulness is hard to exaggerate; indeed, it now requires an act of imagination to understand what infectious disease formerly meant to humankind, or even to our own grandfathers.[74]

This enormous *decrease* in the ravages of pestilences, a decrease that has been steadily going on since the end of the last century, is a fact firmly established by medical history, a fact that no informed person would dream of denying. Though placing the start of the end-time generation in 1948, author Hal Lindsey acknowledges that **"In this day of modern medical science, plagues seem to be things of the past."** He therefore can only express anticipation of their possible

71 Henschen, p. 1.
72 Bergmark, p. 326.
73 Schrader, p. 278.
74 McNeill, p. 287.

revival in the near future, saying: **"But there are new factors which make plagues a real possibility for the future."**[75]

The Watch Tower Society, however, flatly refuses to accept the fact that epidemic diseases have decreased in this century. It is forced to deny this *because its widely publicized prophetical interpretations and claims imply that pestilences have not decreased but increased.* Thus it desperately clings to its list of the infectious diseases that still are prominent in different parts of the world and constantly refers to them in support of the idea that the "sign" has appeared on earth since 1914.

One example, often referred to, is *malaria. The Watchtower* of May 1, 1983, for instance, points out that this disease annually kills a million children under the age of five in Africa, and that **"more than 150 million people worldwide now suffer the chills, fever and other symptoms of malaria."** (Page 7)

The readers are not told, however, that the extent of this disease has been *sharply reduced* in our century. As was pointed out in a previous footnote, *over one-third of mankind* suffered from this disease in earlier centuries and *mortality from malaria in the past was much higher* than it is today, when it can be suppressed medically by the use of drugs.[76] In earlier centuries, malaria profoundly influenced human societies throughout the world:

> **In India many centuries before the present era, it was called the 'King of Diseases,' and was also known in ancient China. Whether, as some historians assert, it was decisive in the downfall of Greece and Rome and caused the mysterious depopulations that left massive ruins at Polonnaruwa, Sri Lanka, and at Ankor-Wat, Democratic Kampuchea, cannot be determined; but it is certain that malaria has been one of the great scourges of humanity."**[77]

At the outbreak of the First World War, 800 million persons still suffered from malaria. Since then modern medicines have greatly reduced the mortality of the disease, and, particularly since the end of

---

75 Hal Lindsey, *The 1980s Countdown to Armageddon* (New York, 1981), pp. 30, 32. The "new factors"—the number of starving or malnourished people tied in with overpopulation of the world's poorest regions, and resulting sanitation problems, shortages of medicines and doctors—are "turning these poor areas into breeding grounds for disease," says Lindsey. (Page 32) However, apart from overpopulation, none of the "new factors" are really new in these areas. They are age-old problems.

76 See earlier footnote 8.

77 J. H.-G. Hempel in *World Health*, the magazine of the World Health Organization, April, 1982, p. 6. "Not Vandals and Goths, but malaria was the final conqueror of Rome." (Bergmark, p. 223)

World War II, DDT and other insecticides have freed large geographical areas from it. As one authority writes:

> In geographical terms, malaria has been eliminated from the whole of Europe, almost all of USSR, from several countries of the Near-East, the USA and most of the Caribbean, large areas of the northern and southern parts of South America, Australia, and large parts of China.[78]

Thus the cases of malaria were reduced from 800 million to about 250 million in 1955, and to some 150 million in the 1970's. Unfortunately, the last ten years has seen an upswing in the number of cases, due to increased resistence of mosquitoes to insecticides in some areas. According to the last count by the World Health Organization, the number of cases presently (1985) is 365 million. (See *Awake!* of January 8, 1985, page 29.) This is still less than half the number affected at the time of World War I. Future prospects appear promising as new insecticides and anti-malarial medicines are being developed; recent research suggests that a malarial vaccine may be available within the next few years.[79]

Possibly even more notable has been the progress in reducing *tuberculosis,* which according to the same issue of *The Watchtower* referred to earlier (May 1, 1983, page 4) annually kills some 3 million people. Here again, the reader is not told that this disease had its greatest extension in the middle of the last century, when it implacably killed one-tenth of the population. During the nineteenth century tuberculosis was still "the deadliest of all diseases in Europe."[80] Since the discovery of the tubercle bacillus in 1882, different vaccines and medicines have been developed against this disease, resulting in a steady decrease in mortality, particularly after the First World War.[81] (See accompanying figure.)

As evidence that "The fourth horseman [of the Apocalypse] rides" in our time, Dr. Graham lists herpes simplex II and AIDS among "noxious plagues" and "destroyer diseases."[82]

---

78 Hempel, p. 9. In many places progress has been very dramatic: "In India the number of malaria cases had been estimated in 1935 at 100 million annually, with one million deaths. Once the use of DDT started, notifications of malaria dropped sharply, until by 1965 there were only 100,000 cases with no deaths reported." (Ibid.)

79 *World Health,* September, 1983, p. 30; *Science,* August 10, 1984, pp. 607, 608; *Nature,* August 16, 1984.

80 Schrader, p. 213.

81 Schrader, p. 241–246.

82 *Approaching Hoofbeats,* pp. 193, 194.

DECLINE IN TUBERCULOSIS MORTALITY, 1870–1950

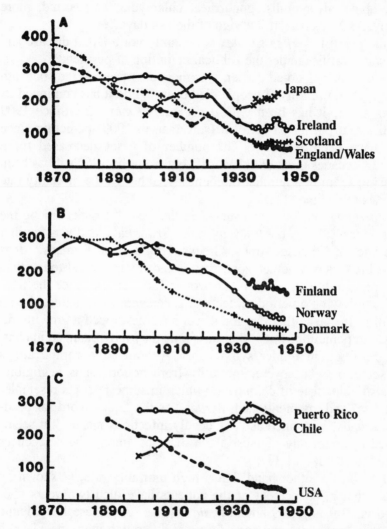

Mortality resulting from tuberculosis per 100,000 population in different countries 1870–1950. At the beginning of our century, about one million people died annually from tuberculosis *in Europe alone*. In many underdeveloped countries tuberculosis remains high, but worldwide there has been a remarkable decline since the start of this century. (Dr. Britt-Inger Puranen, *Tuberculosis*, Umeå, Sweden, 1984, pp. 115, 318, 348. (Republished from: R. & J. Dubos, 1953, Diagram C.)

The Watch Tower Society also regularly includes the *venereal diseases*, above all syphilis, gonorrhea, chlamydia, herpes and, more recently, AIDS as part of its "sign of the last days."[83]

While painful, *herpes simplex* is certainly not a lethal disease and in no way qualifies under the Biblical definition of pestilence.

Syphilis, as was noted earlier, was most disastrous in the sixteenth century, when millions of people died of it. While it has continued its ravages since, it has been with *a decreasing mortality*. Since 1909 remedies that partially control it (salvarsan in 1909, penicillin since 1943) have been available. The number of cases decreased for a couple of decades after World War II, but from the 1960's it has been increasing again in a number of countries, although the mortality rate continues to decline.[84]

Gonorrhea, too, was widespread in the past. "It ranks among the oldest diseases," says the *Encyclopaedia Britannica*, and was familiar to the ancient Chinese, Arabs, Greeks, Hindus, and Romans.[85] It is impossible to say whether gonorrhea is more widespread today than in the past, although it has had a worldwide increase since the mid-1950's, following a period of decline. Like syphilis, it is treated with penicillin. It is true that the gonococci have developed a growing resistance to penicillin, but at the same time they have changed in character, resulting in milder symptoms.[86] Although the complications may sometimes be severe, mortality from gonorrhea is negligible. This also holds true of *chlamydia* (which in some respects resembles gonorrhea) and, as mentioned, *herpes*. As the Greek word for pestilence, *loimós*, is defined as "any deadly infectious malady," it seems strained to count any of these three diseases among the pestilences referred to at Luke 21:11.

AIDS, on the other hand, has a high mortality rate, as shown by the fact that c. 80 percent of the patients have died two years after diagnosis. But is AIDS an *epidemic* disease? A disease is epidemic when it is "prevalent and spreading rapidly among many people in a

---

83 *Awake!*, September 8, 1984, pp. 3–10.
84 *The Encyclopaedia Britannica*, Vol. 22 (1969), p. 946; P. R. Cox, *Demography*, 5th edition (Cambridge, 1976), pp. 126, 127. In some countries the number of cases has continued to decrease. Sweden, for example, had only 176 cases of syphilis in 1984. (Statens Bakt. Lab., Sweden)
85 *Encyclopaedia Britannica*, Vol. 22 (1969), p. 949.
86 Bergmark, pp. 97, 98. In some countries it has continued to decline. Sweden had 34,624 cases in 1969, but only c. 7,000 in 1984. (Stat. Bakt. Lab.)

community, as a contagious disease."[87] Can this be said of AIDS today?

Certainly the number *infected* by the AIDS virus (HTLV-III) is high in some countries.[88] As far as is known, however, only a minority— between 5 and 20 percent of those within the high risk groups who become infected—will actually develop the disease.[89] Further, as the virus is not transmitted via the air, or by common contacts, but instead through sexual, especially homosexual, contacts, by transfusions of infected blood and blood products, and via intravenous injections of drugs, the risk of being infected is small outside the direct "risk groups" (active homosexuals, hemophiliacs and abusers of intra-venous drugs).

The proportion of AIDS cases in the United States outside the risk groups is not increasing, but has remained constant—about one per-cent—during the last few years, and it is estimated that in the United States the chances for people outside the the risk groups of contracting AIDS "are less than one in a million." (The *Discover* magazine of December 1985, pp. 31, 49) By June, 1986, about 30,000 cases of AIDS were known worldwide, of which more than 21,000 had oc-curred in the United States. About half of these had died. A few years ago the doubling period for the reported cases in the United States was six months, but since then it has been protracted, to about 12–14 months at present (1986). This indicates that the spreading rate is slowing down. All this also means that the disease does not spread rapidly, as does a general epidemic.

Undoubtedly, AIDS is a very dangerous infection that eventually could kill hundreds of thousands of people if it is not brought under control.[90] But it seems very unlikely that it will ever reach comparable proportions to the great pestilences of the past. Professor Sten Iwar-

---

87 *Webster's New World Dictionary,* Compact Desk Edition (1963), p. 160.

88 Estimates of the number infected in the United States range from a half million to one million. In Central Africa, where the disease is supposed to have originated, as much as 6–10 percent of the population in the big cities is thought to be infected.

89 The Swedish *Läkartidningen* ("The Medical Magazine") of May 15, 1985, pp. 1849, 1868. Because of the long incubation period—up to five years, perhaps longer—the exact figure is not known. Of the 0.5–1 million infected in the United States "more than 10 percent . . . are likely to develop the disease over the next five years." (*Nature,* April 25, 1985, p. 659)

90 In April, 1984, researchers announced that they had isolated the virus that causes AIDS, but a vaccine "is still several years away." (*Nature,* April 25, 1984, p. 659) Some estimate that about 300,000 will have contracted AIDS by 1991.

son, head of the infection clinic in Gothenburg, Sweden, and a leading authority on AIDS in that country, explains in an interview in the Swedish *Göteborgs-Posten* of June 2, 1985:

> AIDS is the most dangerous disease today, but as a pestilence it is limited to certain risk groups. AIDS cannot be compared to the Black Death or the Spanish Flu in which people died by the millions. The way of transmission is different, and the society is different. . . . AIDS is transmitted through intercourse and via blood transfusions and is limited to certain risk groups. Although a lesser number outside the risk groups may also be stricken, there is actually nothing to indicate that it will develop into a general pestilence.

Only the future, of course, can tell what will become of this new infection. At any rate, the mere possibility of a *future* epidemic cannot be used to prove that pestilences have increased since 1914, and a review of venereal diseases during the past seventy years since that date gives no support to that claim either.

In the light of these facts it is not at all surprising that end-times expositors, and notably the Watch Tower Society, attempt to improve the "pestilence sign" by going outside the limits of true pestilence and bringing in other, non-infectious diseases as added "evidence." Thus, in discussing the "sign of the last days," *The Watchtower* of May 1, 1983, said on page 5:

> Science is far from conquering sickness and disease. For example, *heart disease* remains the leading cause of premature death in industrialized countries.

While the statement of itself is accurate, it actually proves very distinctly that pestilences, in the true sense of the term, have *decreased* in our century. How so?

Because the principal cause of premature death in previous centuries was not heart disease, referred to by the Society, but was precisely *pestilences* or *infectious diseases*. Showing the change that has come, Professor Hofsten states:

> Everywhere in the world mortality is now considerably lower than in the past. A more marked development toward a reduced mortality started in northern and western Europe around 1800.

Of the situation in the developed countries, Hofsten goes on to say:

> If the causes of death are considered, one finds that the infectious diseases now have almost disappeared as a cause of death. Formerly, these

diseases affected people of all ages and were the most important reason why the mortality among children and youth in those days was quite high.[91]

Before the nineteenth century the *average* length of life was between 20 and 30 years.[92] Today, on a worldwide basis, it is more than double that figure. In the industrialized countries life expectancy is up to 75 years or more, while in the developing countries it has increased to between 30 and 60 years.[93]

Obviously, all people die sooner or later. The causes are different. If death comes late in life, the causes are usually *degenerative* or *aging* diseases. And cancer and heart diseases are—primarily—*aging diseases*.[94] Writing of cancer, Bergmark says that **"This dreaded disease is comparatively rare in ages under 50 years."**[95] And of both cancer and heart diseases, Schrader states:

> The two most common causes of death [in the developed countries] at the turn of the last century were still tuberculosis and cholera. Today it is heart and circulatory diseases and cancer, two sufferings that an old or a prematurely worn out body is exposed to.[96]

We thus need to distinguish between "deaths due to aging of the organism (essentially, diseases of the heart and of the circulatory system, and cancer), and deaths from infections or accidents."[97] Pestilences are infections. Heart ailments and cancer are not. If, as shown, the latter are the leading cause of death in the developed nations, this proves that deaths from pestilence have been markedly reduced in these countries.

Although heart diseases and cancer are presently the leading causes of death in the developed nations does this automatically mean that these ailments are on the rise in those countries? The Watch Tower Society maintains that they are, saying in the *Watchtower* of January 15, 1985, on page 11:

91 Erland Hofsten, *Världens befolkning,* 2nd edition (Uppsala, 1970) pp. 90, 91.
92 Poul Chr. Matiiessen, *Befolkningsutvecklingen—orsak och verkan,* (Lund, 1972), p. 34.
93 Mathiessen, pp. 36, 42. See also Roland Pressat, *Demographic Analysis* (Chicago, 1972), pp. 71–75.
94 This is, of course, with the exception of lung cancer caused by smoking. In Sweden, about 15 percent of all cases of cancer are caused by smoking; in England this percentage is twice as high.
95 Bergmark, p. 327.
96 Schrader, pp. 278, 279. See also T. H. Hollingsworth, *Historical Demography* (London and Southampton, 1969), p. 23.
97 Pressat, p. 84.

WHAT LEADING AUTHORITIES SAY ABOUT
PESTILENCES TODAY AND IN THE PAST

"The creation . . . of a 'common market' of microbes, passed through a particularly intense, rapid, dramatic, one might even say apocalyptic phase, during the period roughly 1300–1600. The sacrifice of human lives resulting from the global spread of pathogenic agents during these three centuries has had no parallel before or since."—French historian Emmanuel Le Roy Ladurie, *The Mind and Method of the Historian* (Brighton, Sussex, England, 1981), page 30.

"We who live in civilized countries where medicine has made such tremendous advances, and hygiene is preached and practised, know nothing of such plagues as swept across whole continents in the Middle Ages."—Leo Huberman, *Man's Worldly Goods. The Story of the Wealth of Nations* (New York and London, 1968), page 50.

"Infectious diseases, which only one or two generations ago formed the largest group in our statistics on morbidity and mortality, have been driven back by the advance of medicine."—Professor Folke Henschen, *The History of Diseases* (London, 1966), page 1.

"In many ways one can think of the middle of the twentieth century as the end of one of the most important social revolutions in history, the virtual elimination of infectious disease as a significant factor in social life."—Sir MacFarlane Burnet, *Natural History of Infectious Disease* (Cambridge, 1962), page 3.

"In most places epidemic diseases have become unimportant, and many kinds of infection have become rare where they were formerly common and serious. The net increment to human health and cheerfulness is hard to exaggerate; indeed, it now requires an act of imagination to understand what infectious disease formerly meant to mankind, or even to our own grandfathers."—Professor William H. McNeill, *Plagues and Peoples* (New York, 1976), page 287.

"The subjugators of pestilences have won the greatest victory that ever has been gained during six thousand years of world history: the victory over a premature death."—Herbert L. Schrader, *Und dennoch siegte das Leben* (Stuttgart, 1954), page 278.

"The most remarkable achievement of the twentieth century may be the eradication of the great pandemics that once swept over entire nations—and continents—crippling, maiming, scarring, and killing millions."—James Cornell, *The Great International Disaster Book* (New York, 1979), page 182.

In developed nations cancer, heart trouble, diabetes, cirrhosis, and emotional disorders are on the rise.

As regards cancer, this simply is not true. The world-famous cancer researcher Professor Richard Peto, in an interview for the Swedish newspaper *Göteborgs-Posten* (October 20, 1984), said that **"It is a common misconception among the general public that the number of cases of cancer is increasing. But this is wrong. When the frequency of the disease within the same age group is compared from year to year we rather find a decrease—with the exception of lung cancer."**

On the whole, the same is true of heart diseases. Although heart attacks are increasing in some countries, for example in Sweden, it is well known among researchers that they are now decreasing in most other industrialized nations, including the USA.[98]

What is happening, then, is that cancer and heart trouble tend to come later and later in life. The reason? Quite simply it is that in our time people as a whole are enjoying better health—and living longer lives.

Today, in this last quarter of the twentieth century, people still become ill and people still die. But only a small fraction die from pestilence, fewer than ever before in known history. Despite the dire forebodings and frightening scenes dramatically drawn by some authors and religious sources, the facts show that the health picture in our century is, not darker, but measurably brighter for mankind as a whole.

---

98 This was pointed out, for instance, by the Swedish heart researcher Dr. Lars Wilhelmsson, in the Swedish newspaper *Göteborgs-Tidningen*, February 10, 1985, p. 5. See also Dr. A. E. Harper, "Nutrition and Health in the Changing Environment," in *The Resourceful Earth*, edited by J. L. Simon and H. Kahn (Oxford and New York, 1984), pp. 490, 507–511)

CHAPTER 5

Some Remarkable Facts About Wars

NO SENSIBLE person would wish to belittle the threat created by modern warfare. War has increased in destructive power during the past five hundred years due to a series of technical advancements, which may be divided into three stages:

1) The introduction of *gunpowder* on the battlefield in the fourteenth century led to the replacement of bows and crossbows with gunpowder weapons in the fifteenth century.

2) The next stage arrived in the eighteenth century with the *Industrial Revolution*. With it came the invention of a number of new and more lethal weapons during the nineteenth century, such as revolvers, machine guns, hand grenades, field mines and underwater mines ("torpedoes"). All of these and many other kinds of new technological means of waging warfare were used, for example, in the American Civil War (1861–1865). This development has continued at an ever-increasing rate in our own century. The most important weaponry news before World War II concerned tanks, submarines, and airplanes, all used to some degree in World War I, though still in the experimental stage at that time.

3) The third and most dramatic step in the development took place in 1945, when the first *atomic bomb* was dropped over Hiroshima, and mankind suddenly entered the *Nuclear Age*. With this step the human race for the first time in history found itself confronted with the specter of global self-destruction.

However, does this situation imply, as some claim, that our twentieth century is the most warlike period of human history? Does it serve to clearly identify our day as one marked in Bible prophecy as the "time of the end"?

In *The Late Great Planet Earth,* the author cites the modern state of war as evidence that Jesus' words in Matthew chapter twenty-four find fulfillment in our time. **"War has greatly increased in frequency and intensity in this century,"** he states and refers to the **"continuous fighting on our globe"** since World War II.[1]

Adventist writer Robert Pierson, stressing that **"there have been wars during the last sixty-five years on a scale this world has never witnessed before,"** sees these as signs of the end, with prophecy being fulfilled in a way unique to our time.[2]

Dr. Billy Graham, while not fixing on specific dates, similarly expresses the belief that Jesus' expression about wars relates to some unique intensification and escalation of warfare. Speaking of the 'signs that seem currently to be coming into focus,' he says:

> **. . . one of the major signs that He indicated was the increasing intensity of warfare.**
>
> **Mankind has always had wars, but never on the scale that Jesus predicted in Matthew 24 and Revelation 6.**[3]

The most specific, detailed and remarkable claims, however, are those made by the Watch Tower Society, with tremendous importance placed upon the war which broke out in Europe in 1914. They present this as strong evidence that Christ returned and "the conclusion of the system of things" began in that year. The claim is made that Jesus, in Matthew chapter twenty-four, verse 7, foretold the *first world war* as the initial feature of the sign of an "invisible presence" since 1914. Was 1914 really the great "turning point" in history the Watch Tower Society claims it was?

What of other impressive claims in Watch Tower publications about the 1914–1918 conflict? Was it actually the first world war of history? Did it really break out wholly unexpectedly, suddenly terminating a long era of peace? Is the claim true that this one war was "seven times greater than all the 901 major wars of the previous 2,400 years?"[4] In other words, do the statistics of the Watch Tower Society tally with

---

1 Hal Lindsey, *The Late Great Planet Earth,* p. 147.

2 Robert H. Pierson, *Goody-bye, Planet Earth,* pp. 8, 11–15.

3 Billy Graham, *Approaching Hoofbeats, The Four Horsemen of the Apocalypse,* pp. 127, 128.

4 This statement, cited (evidently without first verifying its accuracy) from a brief news-item in the *Collier's* magazine of September 29, 1945, has often been repeated in Watch Tower publications. See for instance *The Watchtower* of October 15, 1975, page 633, also April 15, 1982, page 8, and *You Can Live Forever in Paradise on Earth* (1982), page 150.

the facts, or have the figures been "improved on" in an effort to make the year 1914 stand out as marked as possible?

Did Jesus predict the First World War?

When Jesus, in Matthew chapter twenty-four, verses 6, 7, foretold that there would be wars, did he then refer to *world wars?* Do his words contain *any* statement about wars that no generation before 1914 saw fulfilled in the wars of their own time?

The idea that Matthew chapter twenty-four, verse 7, points to the First World War and the wars that followed thereafter is based upon the expression "nation shall rise against nation, and kingdom against kingdom."[5] It is felt that the wording indicates that Jesus had a great war in mind, a war in which many nations and kingdoms would be involved: *The First World War!* It should be observed, however, that in the original Greek text the words for "nation" (*éthnos*) and "kingdom" (*basileía*) are in the *singular* number. Thus the *Anchor Bible* (W. F. Albright and C. S. Mann, *Matthew,* 1971) says: **"For one people will rise against another, one kingdom against another."** (See also J. B. Phillips translation, the 1972 revised edition.) This carries one's thoughts to wars in general, not especially to "world wars" or even necessarily major wars.

This is also confirmed by the fact that Jesus framed his statement in terms borrowed from similar expressions found in the Hebrew Scriptures or Old Testament, for instance at Isaiah chapter nineteen, verse 2 and Second Chronicles chapter fifteen, verse 6. None of these texts deals, of course, with world wars. The first of them even refers to a war *within one nation only, a civil war:*

---

5 Earlier the Watch Tower Society held that the "wars and reports of wars" mentioned in verse 6 referred to the wars that occurred previous to World War I, while verse 7 describes World War I and other major wars since 1914. (*From Paradise Lost to Paradise Regained,* 1958, pp. 178, 179.) But the two verses cannot be separated from each other in this way, because the word "for" (Greek *gar*) in verse 7 clearly shows that this verse simply is *an explanation of the preceding verse!* The thought is: "You will hear of wars and rumors of wars, but don't be frightened into believing that the end is coming. *For* there will be many wars and other troubles," etc. The Society finally realized that the two verses refer to the same kinds of wars. Thus *The Watchtower* of January 1, 1970, admits: "By going on to say that nation would rise against nation and kingdom against kingdom, Jesus is explaining why it is that they would hear of wars and reports of wars." (Pp. 43 and 44) This view is still retained in *The Watchtower* of April 1, 1983, where it is stated on page 4 that Jesus, in verse 7, "went on to explain" what he had just said in verse 6. This is quite correct— but the consequence for the Watch Tower Society is that it is forced to apply, unnaturally, both verses to the wars since 1914!

And I will stir up the Egyptians against the Egyptians: and they shall fight every one against his brother, and every one against his neighbor; city against city, and <u>kingdom against kingdom</u>.[6]

That Jesus did not use the expression "nation against nation and kingdom against kingdom" especially of world wars is also evident from the fact that his description *included* the wars and revolts within the Roman Empire that preceded and culminated in the destruction of Jerusalem and its temple in A.D. 70. Even the Watch Tower Society agrees about that, but holds that the wars and other difficulties that led up to the destruction of Jerusalem in A.D. 70 were a prophetic proto-type of the troubles on earth since 1914.[7] The Society, therefore, attempts to portray the period before A.D. 70 as a particularly violent and troublesome period, filled with wars, revolts, famines and earthquakes.

But the simple truth is that this period was no worse in these respects than many other periods in history. In fact, the first century of our era was comparatively one of the most peaceful and undisturbed eras in history! It was a part of the long and well-known peace period called *Pax Romana,* "the Roman peace," extending from the year 29 B.C. to about A.D. 162. **"This, the era of the *Pax Romana,* was perhaps the least eventful period of military history,"** according to the two military historians R. Ernest Dupuy and Trevor N. Dupuy.[8] The most important break in this peaceful period came from the above-mentioned revolts within the Roman Empire, which in Judea caused the destruction of Jerusalem and its temple in A.D. 70.[9]

Consequently, neither in the actual wording nor in the subsequent events that took place is there anything to indicate that Jesus' state-

---

6 Isaiah 19:2, ASV. Isaiah's prophecy was evidently fulfilled in the concluding decades of the eighth century and early decades of the seventh century B.C., when Egypt had fallen apart into several smaller "kingdoms" or provinces, governed by local kings repeatedly in war with each other, until Ethiopian kings of the 25th Dynasty finally took control of the country.

7 See the book *God's Kingdom of a Thousand Years Has Approached* (173), chapter 16. *The Watchtower* of May 1, 1975, admits that "Jesus' expression 'nation against nation and kingdom against kingdom' also had a first-century application, <u>so it is not limited to world wars</u>." (Page 274)

8 R. Ernest Dupuy and Trevor N. Dupuy, *The Encyclopedia of Military History* (New York, 1970), page 122.

9 The Jewish revolt against Rome was part of a more widespread rebellion that spread all over the Roman Empire and culminated in the year after Nero's death, A.D. 68–69, "when Servius Galba, consul for the second time with Titus Vinius as his colleague, began the year that brought death to both and almost meant the downfall of Rome." (Tacitus' *Historae,* I, 11)

ment about coming wars at Matthew chapter twenty-four, verses 6, 7 refers particularly to the world wars and other major wars that have occurred since 1914. His words fit any of the kinds of interstate and civil wars that have been fought throughout history and those words were obviously uttered as a warning, to teach his disciples not to look upon such calamities as a "sign" of his coming and the end of the age. What, then, of the impressive claims of a supposed unique and momentous change in 1914 as made by the Watch Tower Society?

Did the First World War mark the "turning point" of history?

When Jesus returns, "with power and great glory," his intervening in human history will mean a *conclusion* of the present age. He comes in order to conclude it. His disciples knew that, and therefore they asked for the sign that would indicate *both* his coming and the conclusion of the age.[10] Jesus' intervention to conclude this age will not be a drawn out affair. In possession of "all authority . . . in heaven and on earth," he will quickly overthrow this whole system of things, and therefore he compared his future intervention with the coming of the flood in the days of Noah which suddenly overtook the unsuspecting people of that time and quickly brought an end to the then exising age. **"So shall be the coming [Greek, *parousía*] of the Son of man."** (Matthew 24:37–39) Similarly, Jesus likened his coming to the sudden and swift destruction of the city of Sodom in the days of Lot, and added; **"After the same manner shall it be in the day that the Son of man is revealed."** (Luke 17:28–30) The verb "reveal" (*apokalúpto*) is here clearly used as a parallel to the "coming" (*parousía*) at Matthew chapter twenty-four, verse 39. Both words refer to the same event: Christ's coming for bringing the present age to a close.

The coming of Christ and the conclusion of the present age will indeed be a great *turning point* in the history of mankind. When the Watch Tower Society dates the coming of Christ and the beginning of the "conclusion of the age" as from 1914 onward, it is not only forced to stretch out this "conclusion" over a whole lifetime (from 1914 to Armageddon, which is supposed to occur shortly), thus making it a very lengthy event in contrast to Jesus' own statements. It is also forced to make the year 1914 *the great turning point* in history. As

---

10 Matthew 24:3. The Greek expression *synteleía tou aiōnos* in this verse literally means the "conclusion of the age." See the Society's *The Kingdom Interlinear*, page 141.

proof for this, the Society often quotes what some historians, newspaper editors, and politicians have said about World War I and 1914. **"Many historians correctly point to that year as <u>the pivotal one</u> for mankind,"** claimed *The Watchtower* of October 15, 1980, page 14. Is this true?

No, it is not. It is a gross misrepresentation of what these historians actually have said. None of them has stated that 1914 was *the* pivotal year for mankind. The historians quoted by the Watch Tower Society say that 1914 was <u>"one of"</u> the turning points in history, "the turning point <u>in our time</u>," and so on. None of them has claimed that 1914 was *the* turning point in history. The Society in its quotations consistently fails to include the fact that historians point to many different turning points in history, *of which 1914 is only one*. This method employed of quoting only those portions that appear to support their argument can be seriously misleading, as shown by the following examples.

The Watch Tower publication *"Let Your Kingdom Come"* (1981) quotes, among others, historian Barbara W. Tuchman as saying the following in her book *The Guns of August* (1962): **"The First World War was one of the great convulsions of history."**[11] On examining Tuchman's statement, however, we find that the Society chose not to include an important part of it. Her full statement is that, **"like the French Revolution, the First World War was one of the great convulsions of history."**[12] Why did the Watch Tower Society pass over the words, "like the French Revolution"? Evidently because the unique claims for 1914 would have been weakened by a quotation that placed the French Revolution on an equality with the 1914–1918 conflict. Historians, in fact, hold the French Revolution to have been an even *greater* turning point in history than World War I!

On the same page of *"Let Your Kingdom Come"* the Watch Tower Society also quotes *The Economist* magazine of August 4, 1979, in which the editor said that, **"In 1914 the world lost a coherence which it has not managed to recapture since. . . ."** But it is hidden from the reader that the editor in the very same article compares the period after 1914 with the period from 1789 to 1848, which was as unstable, filled with wars, disorder and violence, as our own time, and suggests that history follows a rhythmic pattern—**"Two genera-**

---

11 *"Let Your Kingdom Come"*, Watchtower Bible and Tract Society, 1981, p. 115.
12 Barbara W. Tuchman, *The Guns of August—August 1914*, the Four Square Edition, 1964 & 1965. The quotation is found under "Sources" at the end of the book.

tions of upheaval and violence, followed by two generations of consolidation and calm, followed by two more generations of upheaval, followed by . . . ?" (Page 10) So what did the editor *really* say about the period since 1914? Only that it seems to follow the general cyclical pattern of history in the past!

There have actually been many "turning points" and convulsions in history, and it would be easy to fill numerous pages with quotations from historians in proof of this. A few examples may suffice.

On the decline of the Roman Empire in the fifth century:

> This period witnesed one of the great turning points of world history.[13]

On the Industrial Revolution that began about the 1780's:

> By any reckoning this was probably the most important event in world history, at any rate since the invention of agriculture and cities.[14]

On the French Revolution 1789–1799:

> The French Revolution is the most important event in the life of modern Europe. It deserves to be ranked with the Reformation and the rise of Christianity because, like them, it destroyed the landmarks of the world in which generations of men had passed their lives.[15]
>
> Even today in the middle of the twentieth century, despite all that has happened in the lifetime of men not yet old, and even here in America or in any other part of a world in which the countries of Europe no longer enjoy their former commanding position, it is still possible to say that the French Revolution at the end of the eighteenth century was the great turning point of modern civilization.[16]

On the Russo-Japanese War 1904–1905:

> Psychologically and politically, Japan's victory in the war marked a turning point in world history.[17]

On the dropping of the first atomic bomb on Hiroshima in 1945:

> A new era in warfare and a new era in history dawned in the closing days of this period: the nuclear age, ushered in by the first atomic bomb drop, on Hiroshima, August 6, 1945.[18]

---

13 Dupuy & Dupuy (1970), p. 166.
14 E. J. Hobsbawm, *The Age of Revolution* (London, 1962), p. 29.
15 *Cambridge Modern History*, Cambridge University Press, 1904, Vol. 8.
16 The noted historian R. R. Palmer in the preface to George Lefebvre's *The Coming of the French Revolution* (New York: Vintage, 1947), p. v.
17 Dupuy & Dupuy, pp. 926, 1014.
18 *Ibid.*

That the world war of 1914–1918 marked *one* of the many turning points in world history no one would try to deny. But the question is: Was it the supreme turning point the Watch Tower Society wants to make out of it? Was it such a turning point that the disciples had in mind when they asked Jesus for the sign of his coming and the end of the age? Such a conclusion can neither be drawn from the answer Jesus gave to the question of his disciples, nor from the statements of historians.

Did the 1914–1918 war suddenly "take peace from the earth"?

Peace and security were suddenly and unexpectedly taken from the earth in 1914, claims the Watch Tower Society, quoting Revelation chapter six, verse 4 about the rider on the fiery-colored horse to whom "there was granted to take peace away from the earth so that they should slaughter one another." (NW) Since the Society holds that this rider started his death-dealing ride on earth in 1914, it attempts to show that peace prevailed on earth before that year, a peace that suddenly and unexpectedly was "taken away" through the outbreak of the war.

To prove this the Society quotes, not historians, but a couple of elderly statesmen and—two of Jehovah's Witnesses! The two statesmen, Konrad Adenauer and Harold Macmillan have often been referred to in Watch Tower publications, as they in their old age remembered their youth as a time of peace, security, and optimism, something which "suddenly, unexpectedly" disappeared in 1914.[19] The *Awake!* magazine also quotes Ewart Chitty, who was 16 years old when the war broke out, and George Hannan, who was 15 yeas old at that time. Mr. Hannan states that **"Nobody expected World War I. . . . People had been saying that the world had become too civilized for war. But world war came out of nowhere, like a bolt from the blue."[20]**

Does this picture of the pre-war period match up with the historical reality, or does it just reflect the habit of many elderly people to idealize the "good old days"? Where can we more likely learn the genuine facts about the pre-war era: from an elderly person's childhood mem-

19 *The Watchtower*, May 1, 1982, p. 14.
20 *Awake!*, May 8, 1981, p. 6. Chitty and Hannan are both Jehovah's Witnesses of long standing. See *The Watchtower*, February 15, 1963, pp. 118–120, and *The Watchtower*, January 15, 1970, pp. 56–61.

ories, or from an historian who has thoroughly studied the epoch? Chitty and Hannan are both lifelong Jehovah's Witnesses, something *Awake!* fails to mention. That their picture of the period before 1914 agrees with that of the Watch Tower Society is, therefore, of little note. Hannan's statement that "Nobody expected World War I" should be compared with what the first president of the Society, C. T. Russell, said about this 22 years before the war broke out. In 1892, referring to the fear and unrest then in the world, Russell explained:

> ... **the daily papers and the weeklies and monthlies, religious and secular, are continually discussing the prospects of war in Europe. They note the grievances and ambitions of the various nations and <u>predict that war is inevitable at no distant day, that it may begin at any moment between some of the great powers, and that the prospects are that it will eventually involve them all.</u>**[21]

The truth is, that the great war of 1914 did not come as any surprise at all. *It was expected by virtually everyone!* The world had been preparing for the war for decades, and the nations stood armed to the teeth. Everybody was waiting for the "igniting spark." In their book *A History of the Modern World Since 1815,* historians R. R. Palmer and J. Colton say:

> **Never had the European states maintained such huge armies in peacetime as at the beginning of the twentieth century. . . . Few people wanted war; all but a few sensational writers preferred peace in Europe, but <u>all took it for granted that war would come some day</u>. In the last years before 1914 the idea that war was bound to break out sooner or later probably made some statesmen, in some countries, more willing to unleash it.**[22]

For some years Pastor Russell and his followers to some extent shared these expectations. But they never expected the war to come as late as in 1914. In 1887, for instance, Russell, commenting on the widespread fear and the armaments race in Europe, wrote in the February issue of *Zion's Watch Tower:*

> **This all looks as though *next Summer* would see a war on foot which might engage every nation in Europe.** (Page 2)

When this did not happen, Russell expressed himself more cautiously about the war prospects. "We do not share them," he wrote in

21 *The Watch Tower,* January 15, 1892, pp. 19–21. *Reprints,* p. 1354.
22 R. R. Palmer and Joel Colton, *A History of the Modern World Since 1815,* fifth edition (New York, 1978), pp. 654, 655.

1892, "That is, we do not think that the prospects of a general European war are so marked as is commonly supposed." Such a war did not fit into the prophetic scheme of Pastor Russell, who instead envisioned worldwide anarchy as due to come. Should a general European war break out, it had to come long before 1914. Thus, Russell said:

> **Even should a war or revolution break out in Europe sooner than 1905, we could not consider it any portion of the severe trouble predicted. At most it could be a forerunner of it, a mere 'skirmish' as compared with what is to come.**[23]

Believing that worldwide anarchy and the destruction of all human government would be accomplished before 1914—by which time the climax of Armageddon would have arrived and the Kingdom of God would be established on earth—Pastor Russell and his associates thus held that the generally expected war in Europe had to come long before that date, probably "about 1905," Russell said.[24]

Was what is now known as World War I really preceded by a long era of peace and security? It is certainly true that the period from 1848 to 1914 was somewhat calmer as compared with the convulsions that both *preceded* and *succeeded* this period, a period that is sometimes termed a *belle epoque,* a "beautiful epoch." But this name is misleading. Barbara W. Tuchman, an historian of international fame, made a special study of the decades that preceded World War I. In the foreword to her study, which covers the period 1890–1914, she says:

> **It is not the book I intended to write when I began. Preconceptions dropped off one by one as I investigated. The period was not a Golden Age or *Belle Epoque* except to a thin crust of the privileged class. . . . We have been misled by the people of the time themselves who, in looking**

---

23 *The Watch Tower,* January 15, 1892, pp. 19–21. *Reprints,* p. 1354.
24 Pretending that Russell's predictions came true, the Watch Tower Society has often quoted *The World Magazine* of August 30, 1914. (Most recently quoted in *The Watchtower* of April 1, 1984, pp. 5,6.) In an article headed "End of all Kingdoms in 1914" in that magazine it was claimed that "The terrific war outbreak in Europe has fulfilled an extraordinary prophecy." Then Pastor Russell's publications are copiously quoted, and this in a way that gives a reader the impression that Russell had foreseen the war. The intimate knowledge of the many publications of Pastor Russell and the ability to select suitable statements from them indicates, however, that the author of the article either was a close collaborator of Russell or got his material from one. It would be practically impossible for an ordinary neutral journalist to be so versed in the publications of Pastor Russell. In reality, the predictions of Russell quoted in the article referred to the "great trouble," the "battle of Armageddon," the "end of all kingdoms" and the establishment of God's Kingdom on earth. *None of these events was fulfilled in 1914,* as Russell had predicted. On the other hand, what *did* come, the world war, could not be found among Russell's prophecies.

The World Magazine, August 30, 1914.

AWAKE! — OCTOBER 8, 1973

The Turning Point Foreseen— by Whom?

But did you know that, long before 1914—in fact, more than a quarter of a century before—persons were pointing ahead to that year as one to be of great significance for all mankind? History shows that sincere Bible students, known today as Jehovah's witnesses, did just that. Note this:

Back on August 30, 1914, the New York *World*, in its magazine section, said, "The terrific war outbreak in Europe has fulfilled an extraordinary prophecy." It went on to state:

"For a quarter of a century past, through preachers and through press, the "International Bible Students' [Jehovah's witnesses] ... have been proclaiming to the world that the Day of Wrath prophesied in the Bible would dawn in 1914."

As shown by the New York *World Magazine* of August 30, 1914, Watch Tower founder C. T. Russell expected that Christ's Kingdom would end all earthly Kingdoms in 1914. The prediction obviously failed. The nations not only survived, they have since tripled in number. However, because the *World Magazine*—at the outbreak of the war—inaccurately claimed that "The terrific war outbreak in Europe has fulfilled an extraordinary prophecy," Watch Tower publications have repeatedly referred to the article. Yet, when they finally printed a picture of the actual article in *Awake!*, the embarrassing title, "END OF ALL KINGDOMS IN 1914," was cut off. Not until eleven years later did the full picture, with the title restored, appear in *The Watchtower* of April 1, 1984. The organization had *not* foretold the coming of World War I, and what it *had* predicted, the end of all human government in 1914, had proved false. Yet the article was still presented as favorable to their claims about 1914, claims that today are almost totally different to what they were *before* 1914.

back across the gulf of the War, see that earlier half of their lives misted over by a lovely sunset haze of peace and security. It did not seem so golden when they were in the midst of it. Their memories and their nostalgia have conditioned our view of the pre-war era but I can offer the reader a rule based on adequate research: all statements of how lovely it was in that era made by persons contemporary with it will be found to have been made after 1914.[25]

It is true that *Europe* had experienced one of its longest peace periods before 1914. The Watch Tower Society quotes an unnamed European historian as saying of August 1914: **"During the first days of this fateful month one of the most peaceful periods our continent had ever experienced came to an end."**[26] *But this held true only of Europe,* and it should be noted that the same continent has experienced *a peace period of approximately the same length since 1945!*

The stark fact is that, for the rest of the world, frequent wars raged practically everywhere before 1914. Says the Austrian scholar Otto Koenig:

> If, however, someone would start to talk about the good old days, about the long peace period from c. 1871 to 1914, he should just open the closed pages of the history book: the Boer War in South Africa, the Boxer Rebellion in China, the Russo-Japanese War, the Illinder Rebellion in Macedonia, the Balkan Wars and the occupation of Bosnia, the war between Italy and Abyssinia, the Mahdi Rebellion, the Herero Rebellion in German South-west Africa, the wars between the Berbers and the French in Algeria, wars in Indo-China, revolutions in South America—and this is just a selection from among the war events during this long 'peace period.'[27]

Millions of people were killed in these wars. It was certainly not a peaceful epoch. Even the so-called "peace" in Europe was just a peace between the great powers. Other wars were being fought in Europe, for example the two Balkan Wars in 1912 and 1913, involving Bulgaria, Serbia, Greece, Montenegro, Turkey and Rumania. Besides, the "European peace" was absolutely not a peace *with security.* On the contrary, it was a peace *in fear*—fear of the war all knew would come.

---

25 Barbara W. Tuchman, *The Proud Tower.* A Portrait of the World Before the War, 1890–1914 (New York, 1966 [first printing 1962]), pp. xiii, xiv.
26 *The Watchtower,* April 15, 1984, p. 5.
27 Otto Koenig, *Das Paradies vor unserer Tür* (Wien, München, Zürich, 1971), p. 391. (Translated from German.)

Historians generally call this European peace period "the era of armed peace."[28]

The pre-war situation, then, was very much like the situation that has prevailed on earth since 1945: A generation of relative peace in Europe, with numerous limited wars in many other parts of the world. The claim that World War I ended a long era of world peace and security is, therefore, a false claim. The pre-1914 era was filled with fear, insecurity, violence and wars the same as most other epochs in history.

World War I—the first "world war"?

"No generation previous to that of 1914 ever experienced a world war, never mind two," claimed the *Watchtower* of July 15, 1983 (page 7). **"Historians widely agree that World War I was the first war on a global scale,"** stated the *Awake!* magazine of May 8, 1981 (page 8). Is this true?

No, it is not. Historians do not "widely agree" on this claim. That World War I is now called the First World War does not mean that it was, factually, the first world war in history. Though many today may not realize it, the people who lived through the 1914–1918 conflict simply called it "The Great War." It was when yet another world war broke out in 1939 that the terms "first" and "second" came into use to distinguish one conflict from the other. *But other wars before 1914 had also been "world wars" in exactly the same sense as World War I!*

The "era of world war" actually began early in the eighteenth century.[29] In a period of eighty years, *three* world wars occurred, and before the end of that century the *fourth* had begun! These facts are stressed by many historians. Consider:

1. *The War of the Spanish Succession* (1702–1713) in which France, Britain, Holland and Austria figured prominently, with the conflict extending into North America, was, according to historians Palmer and Colton, **"the first that can be called a 'world war,'** be-

---

28 Field-Marshal Viscount Montgomery of Alamein, in *A History of Warfare*, Collins (London 1968), page 443, states: "The years between 1870 and 1914 were years of armed peace in Europe and of frequent small wars throughout the rest of the world." Swedish historian Anton Nyström says that "a state of half-war" prevailed in Europe between 1870 and 1914. (*Före, under och efter 1914*, Stockholm, 1915, p. 141.)

29 Montgomery, p. 315.

cause it involved the overseas world together with the leading powers of Europe."[30]

2. *The Seven Years' War* (1756–1763) was the *second* world war of the eighteenth century: **"The Seven Years' War was to a greater degree than the War of the Austrian Succession [1740–1748] a world war."**[31] The global extension of this conflict is stressed by all: **"It came to embrace all the four continents of the world and all the great oceans."**[32] Prussia, Austria, Britain, France, Russia, Sweden, Spain and most of the German States of the Holy Roman Empire became embroiled in the struggle. Issues included control of North America and India. It was this war that brought Britain to its position as the leading imperial power of the world, thanks in great measure to its renowned statesman and leader William Pitt. Pitt, who acceded to power in 1756, the same year the war broke out, won through his brilliant strategy a series of victories all over the world. Montgomery, therefore, calls him "a strategist of world war."[33] Some historians consider him even greater than Churchill in this respect.

3. *The War of American Independence* (1775–1783) was the *third* war in the same century that is classifed as a "world war" by historians: **"The Revolutionary War was several wars in one. It was among other things a war for national independence, a civil war and in the end a world war."**[34] It was the British defeat at Saratoga in 1778 that turned the war into a world war. **"The defeat at Saratoga . . . marked the beginning of a general war waged throughout the**

---

30 R. R. Palmer & Joel Colton, *A History of the Modern World to 1815*, fifth edition (New York, 1978), p. 184. On discussing the War of the Spanish Succession, *The New Cambridge Modern History* (Vol. VI, Cambridge, 1970) also mentions the Great Northern War (1700–1721), fought at the same time, and concludes: "The two great conflicts which ushered in the eighteenth century added up to a real world war." (Page 410) See also *The Encyclopedia Americana*, 1984, Vol. 23, p. 86.

31 The highly esteemed Swedish *Världshistoria* (World History), edited by Sven Tunberg and S. E. Bring, Norstedt & Söner, Vol. 10 (Stockholm 1930), p. 182. If, as this work indicates, the War of the Austrian Succession (1740–1748), also is to be termed a "world war," the Seven Years' War was, in fact, the *third* world war! Another historian who terms the War of the Austrian Succession a "world war" is Eirik Hornborg, who points out that it was fought "in Europe, in America, on the West-African coast, in India and on the world seas." (*Världshistorien*, Stockholm, 1962, p. 224)

32 Stig Boberg, *1700-talets historia* (Copenhagen, Oslo, Stockholm: Scandinavian University Books), p. 31. The *Awake!* magazine of December 8, 1970, page 21, admits that the Seven Years' War "involved nearly every nation of Europe and was fought worldwide—in India, North America, Germany and on the seas."

33 Montgomery, pp. 317, 320.

34 *The United States. A Companion to American Studies;* Ed. by Dennis Welland (London, 1974), p. 158.

world," says historian Piers Mackesy.[35] Part two of his work on the war, therefore, bears the subtitle: *The World War 1778*.[36] Viscount Montgomery, too, emphasizes this change in 1778: **"The war was now another world war."**[37]

One historical biographer describes the war in this way:

> . . . what had started as an American revolution against England had exploded into a worldwide war. French and Spanish fleets fought the British in the English Channel, the West Indies and Gibraltar. The Spanish captured West Florida. Russia, Denmark, Sweden and Prussia joined to break England's blockade on France and Spain. Holland, too, ran naval stores to France, and supplied America so abundantly from the West Indies that England declared war on her. Their two navies fought to a standstill in the North Sea. England's line of ships and men was now stretched thin to circle the globe.[38]

4. *The Napoleonic Wars* (1792–1815), a multi-national conflict that followed upon the French Revolution, was the *fourth* world war beginning in the eighteenth century. Historians Palmer and Colton explain:

> It is convenient to think of the fighting from 1792 to 1814 as a 'world war,' as indeed it was, affecting not only all of Europe but places as remote as Spanish America, where the wars of independence began, or the interior of North America, where the United States purchased Louisiana in 1803 and attempted a conquest of Canada in 1812.[39]

Other historians concur in describing the Napoleonic Wars as a world war. The noted Norwegian historian and statesman Halvdan Koht calls this conflict **"a more than twenty-year-long world war, fought on all continents."**[40] And Cyril Falls, a professor of the history of war, mentions the major wars that followed the Napoleonic Wars and comments:

> None of these, however, was a world war of the type of those of the first fifteen years of the nineteenth century [the Napoleonic wars during 1801–

---

35 Piers Mackesy, *The War for America 1775–1783* (London, 1964), p. 147.
36 Mackesy, p. 121. Compare page xvi.
37 Montgomery, p. 321.
38 Irving Stone, *Those Who Love* (New York: Doubleday & Company, 1965), pp. 311, 312.
39 Palmer & Colton, *A History of the Modern World to 1815*, fifth edition (New York, 1978), pp. 382, 383. Winston Churchill, having termed both the Seven Year's War and the War of American Independence "world wars," calls the Napoleonic Wars "the longest of the world wars." (*A History of the English-speaking Peoples*, Vol. III, London, 1957, p. 312 [cf. Vol. II, London, 1956, pp. 123, 163]).
40 Halvdan Koht, *Folkets Tidsålder*, Stockholm 1982, p. 7.

1815] which had involved not only all Europe but in a lesser degree <u>every continent of the globe</u>.[41]

Consequently, the Watch Tower Society's claim that World War I was "the first war on a global scale" is demonstrably false, as is also the statement that "no generation previous to that of 1914 ever experienced a world war, never mind two." Historians *do not* "widely agree" on such erroneous claims, as they usually are better informed than that. On the contrary, they know that the "era of world war" began in the eighteenth century, which saw *three great world wars* within a period of eighty years (within one "generation" according to the Society's definition), with the fourth world war breaking out before the end of that same century!

But perhaps World War I was more extensive, more "global," than the world wars that preceded it? This is alleged in the *Watchtower* of May 1, 1984:

> The first world war was <u>by far the widest</u> and most destructive human conflict up to that time. (Page 4)

Unfortunately, this claim is not true either. In contrast to some of the earlier world conflicts, World War I was largely limited to Europe. General Montgomery, who fought in both World War I and World War II and played an important role in each, explains:

> However, all in all, it can be said that the war in theatres outside Europe was of minor strategical importance. The 1914/18 war was <u>essentially a European war</u>. It came later to be called a 'world war' because contingents from many parts of the British empire served in Europe, and because the United States joined the Entente Powers in 1917. But in reality, since the role of sea power was mostly passive, <u>this was less a 'world war'</u> than some previous conflicts such as the Seven Years' War.[42]

Comparing World War I with World War II, Montgomery further says:

> Whereas <u>the 1914/18 war could hardly</u> be called a world conflict, there can be no such thoughts about the war brought on by Hitler in 1939.[43]

Such balanced and discerning judgments by an experienced and well-informed historian and military general of world repute should

41 Cyril Falls, *A Hundred Years of War* (London, 1953), p. 161.
42 Montgomery, p. 470.
43 *Ibid.*, p. 497.

be weighed against the enormous and unique claims that the Watch Tower Society attaches to the 1914–1918 war.

The first "total war"?

But is it not true that World War I was the first *total* war? This is another claim often put forth in the Watch Tower publications. Thus the Society's new book *Reasoning from the Scriptures* (1985) says on page 235 that **"For the first time, all the major powers were at war."** And the *Awake!* magazine of May 8, 1981, can even quote *The World Book Encyclopedia* as saying:

> In World War I, for the first time in history, makind came to know total war. (Page 6)

What is not made known to the readers, however, is that most historians evidently do not agree with this statement.

What is a "total war"? Generally a "total war" is defined as a war in which not only the military but also the economy and the industry of a nation are mobilized for war.[44]

Total war as thus defined did not begin with World War I. Military historians R. Ernest Dupuy and Trevor N. Dupuy state that the American Civil War (1861–1865) was the first total war in this sense:

> With the national economies on both sides fully integrated into their respective war efforts, the American Civil War was truly the first modern war, and the first 'total' war in the modern sense.[45]

Despite this, it appears that historians commonly identify the earlier *Napoleonic Wars* as the first total war. Montgomery, who agrees that the American Civil War was indeed "an example of total war, ruthlessly conducted," says that total war was first introduced in 1793, when the French, by their Law of August 23, 1793, "announced the era of total war."[46] And E. J. Hobsbawm, in describing the crisis that followed the French Revolution, explains:

---

44 Dupuy & Dupuy, pp. 916, 1016. G. Graninger and S. Tägil point out that "No war in history has been total in the sense that every major nation, maybe all nations, have been involved in the conflict." (*Historia i centrum och periferi*, Part 3, Lund, 1973, p. 164)

45 Dupuy & Dupuy, p. 820.

46 Montgomery, pp. 332, 550.

In the course of its crisis the young French Republic discovered or invented total war; the total mobilization of a nation's resources through conscription, rationing and a rigidly controlled war economy, and virtual abolition, at home or abroad, of the distinction between soldiers and civilians.[47]

History professor Cyril Falls, too, traces the origin of total war back to the Napoleonic Wars. In *A Hundred Years of War,* when discussing World War II he says:

On the political side the war witnessed a further advance towards 'totality,' a process which may be said to have begun in the Napoleonic Wars.[48]

Thus, what is called the First World War cannot be characterized as markedly different from a number of earlier world conflicts. It was preceded by several other *world wars* and *total wars*. But, insists the Watch Tower Society, it was much greater than all previous wars, even **'seven times greater than all the major wars during the preceding 2,400 years combined.'** Is that correct?

How "great" actually was "The Great War"?

The need to emphasize the 1914 date has induced the Watch Tower Society to blow up World War I to completely absurd proportions in the minds of Jehovah's Witnesses. What about the claim, for instance, that this war was "seven times greater than all the 901 major wars of the previous 2,400 years" combined?

There is not the slightest truth in this statement, as will soon become apparent.

Statements about the size of the war, the number of persons involved, the number of casualties, and so forth, often vary considerably. It is not difficult to select the most horrifying figures given by certain writers, columnists and politicians in various books and newspaper columns, and thus create a picture of a war that has only a remote semblance to reality. This is exactly what the Society has done with World War I.

---

47 E. J. Hobsbawm, *The Age of Revolution. Europe 1789–1848*, (London, 1962), p. 67. Churchill agrees: "For the first time in history the entire man-power and resources of a state were being marshalled for total war." (Churchill, Vol. III, p. 229)
48 Cyril Falls, p. 350.

To gain as clear a perspective as possible regarding World War I and others wars that preceded it, we must turn to historians and other scholars who have made a genuinely profound, scientific study of wars throughout history. Such a scientific study of wars has been going on since the 1930s, and the two pioneers of such study are Lewis Richardson and Quincy Wright. In more recent years, their work has been taken up by others, such as J. David Singer, Melvin Small and Francis A. Beer. The information that follows is mainly taken from their works, with some from other trustworthy historical sources.

How many nations participated in the 1914–1918 conflict? The Watch Tower publication *Happiness How to Find It* (1980) quotes a newspaper columnist as saying that the countries involved in World War I comprised "more than 90 percent of the world's population." (Page 146) It is not explained, however, *how many* of these countries there were, or, more importantly, just *in what way* they were "involved" in the war. Similarly, the *Watchtower* of October 15, 1980, on page 15, claims that World War I "affected nearly every country on earth"—but no explanation is given as to *how* these countries were "affected."

As stressed by General Montgomery, World War I was "essentially a European war" and thus "less of a 'world war' than some previous conflicts." Although it is true that the total number of nations directly or indirectly involved in it at some stage were 33—about *half* of the then-existing nations—the fact is that most of these played a very insignificant role in the war.

Thus we find that the Allied Forces consisted of 10 nations, the Central Powers of 4, which makes 14 nations in all.[49] Francis Beer lists only 12 contending parties, explaining in a footnote that **"This list excludes non-European belligerents such as China, Japan, Thailand, Latin American countries, and also certain smaller European belligerents such as Greece, Luxembourg, and Portugal, who all played a relatively minor role in the war."**[50] Singer and Small, who give particularly accurate data, show the number of independent belligerent parties to have been fifteen.[51]

---

49 Quincy Wright, *A Study of War,* abridged edition (Chicago, 1969), p. 58; Dupuy & Dupuy, p. 990.

50 Beer, p. 37.

51 J. David Singer and Melvin Small, *The Wages of War 1816–1965.* A Statistical Handbok (New York, London, Sydney, Toronto, 1972), pp. 116, 117.

In its scope, then, World War I was certainly not greater—and assuredly not "seven times greater" than all previous major wars combined for over two thousand years. Its scope was not even greater than the quartet of "world wars" of the eighteenth century described earlier. Those earlier multi-national wars extended beyond a single continent, such as Europe, in a very real sense.

The most frightening aspect of World War I was the death toll. If, as claimed, it was worse than previous wars in any respect, it would seem that it must be in the number killed. How "great" was World War I in this regard, as compared with some of the major wars of the past?

Deaths from World War I compared with pre-1914 wars

By far the most serious aspect of war is, obviously, the killing. **"Casualties give the wars their importance. This is the aspect of war that makes it most like a disease."**[52]

How many were killed in World War I? 37,508,686 persons claims the *Awake!* magazine of February 22, 1961, pages 6, 7. It refers to the *World Almanac* of 1946 as the source of this information.

The *Awake!* magazine should have mentioned, however, that this figure does not refer to deaths due directly to the combat but includes the many millions of people that died from causes other than the war, such as famines and *the Spanish flu!*

Thus the *Awake!* magazine of October 8, 1983, page 12, nearly halves the above-mentioned figure, reducing it to about 21 million (9 million soldiers and 12 million civilians.) But this figure, likewise, is much too high. An earlier issue of *Awake!* (October 8, 1971, page 16), gave 14 million as the death toll (9 million soldiers and 5 million civilians). Even this figure is probably misleading.

The most accurate tables show that between 8 and 8.5 million soldiers were killed in the war.[53] The number of civilian dead varies greatly. Dupuy and Dupuy give the figures as 6,642,633, but they state explicitly that this number includes deaths from epidemic diseases and malnutrition, not deaths due directly to military action.[54]

52 Beer, p. 34.
53 Dupuy and Dupuy, p. 990.
54 *Ibid.*

The table of Francis A. Beer gives 1,374,000 civilian deaths, although he points out that figures are missing for some countries.[55]

The total number of those who were killed as a direct result of the war—soldiers and civilians—was, then, according to the most trust-worthy estimates, 10–12 million, perhaps a little more. Millions of others died from other causes during the war period, such as from malnutrition and epidemic diseases, especially the Spanish flu in 1918.

What then of the wars that took place before 1914? How do these compare with World War I in fatalities? If, as the Watch Tower publications claim, World War I was "seven times greater" than all the major wars during the preceding 2,400 years combined, then it would seem that it is from this aspect, the killing, that the comparison, first and foremost, must be made. This would mean that all of the 901 major wars previous to 1914 claimed only one-seventh of the 10–12 million that were killed in World War I, or about 1.5 million victims in all! Or, if we include other war-related causes such as famine and disease and take the far larger 1946 *World Almanac* figure of 37,508,686 persons dying from World War I, it would still limit the total number of those killed in 901 previous major wars to only about 5 million. Does the available evidence give any substance to such a view?

Losses of life in past wars are, for obvious reasons, not a simple matter to estimate. Gaston Bodart, who made a careful study of the losses in wars fought in the past three hundred years, observed:

> Conscientiously compiled records of the actual losses of armies are to be found in the archives of most of the military Powers only after the War of the Spanish Succession, i.e. after 1714. Even after that date, reliable data are limited to the greater battles, the more important engagements and sieges. The total losses for each war were not compiled until after 1848.[56]

When it comes to civilian fatalities, the situation is yet more difficult:

> Official records of this character have been kept by the different Governments only in more recent times, not at all until the second half of the

---

55 Francis A. Beer, *Peace Against War* (San Francisco, 1981), p. 37. Beer says: "More than 8 million soldiers and 1 million civilians were killed in World War I." (P. 36) This would make a total of over 9 million soldiers and civilians, which is probably an underestimate.

56 Gaston Bodart, L.L.D., *Losses of Life in Modern Wars* (London, New York, 1916), p. 12.

nineteenth century, and even in the records later than 1850 there are large gaps. Statistical reports or tables must, therefore, be practically limited to the losses of the armies.[57]

There is no reason to think, however, that the percentage of civilian deaths in proportion to the total losses was smaller in earlier wars than in World War I. On the contrary, it was often much higher, as for example in the Huguenot Wars, the Peasants' Wars (1524–1525), and in the Thirty Years' War.[58]

Is it really possible that just 5 million people were killed as a result of the 901 major wars during the 2,400 years that preceded 1914? To show how utterly absurd such an idea is, a few examples of wars from the centuries that immediately preceded 1914 are given below, *each of which claimed more than one million lives,* and in some cases several million.

1. *The Thirty Years' War* (1618–1648), an international conflict with about *10 nations* involved in it, is estimated to have killed *2–3 million soldiers.* The civilian fatalities, however, were much more frightening, not least because of the famines and diseases caused by the war.[59] Today most experts believe that 30–40 percent of the total German population, or *7–8 million* civilians, died due to the war![60] This is a stunning figure, surpassing by far the civilian mortality of World War I for that country. Historian R. R. Palmer observes that **"even the Second World War, in sheer depopulation, was not as devastating for Germany as was the Thirty Years' War. It is quite possible for human beings to die like flies without benefit of scientific destruction. The horrors of modern war are not wholly different from horrors that men and women have experienced in the past."**[61]

2. *The Manchu-Chinese War.* In 1644 China was invaded by the Manchus (from Manchuria), who started to conquer the country

---

57 Ibid., p. 12.

58 *The Watchtower* of April 1, 1983, quotes Professor Wright as saying that civilian deaths were exceptionally high in the Second World War. (Page 6) What they fail to mention is that Wright adds that, "until that war [World War II], civilian losses had tended to decrease since the seventeenth century." (Wright, p. 60) This decrease included World War I!

59 It was once estimated that as many as 25 million or three-quarters of the total German population died during the Thirty Years War, but this figure has been revised by modern historians. See *Awake!*, April 22, 1972, page 13; compare Beer, page 48.

60 Swedish historian Göran Rystad in *Då årat ditt namn . . . ,* Sveriges Radios förlag (Uddevalla, 1966), p. 63.

61 R. R. Palmer, *A History of the Modern World* (New York, 1952), p. 133.

in a lengthy war that is estimated to have claimed *25 million lives*—about twice as many as were killed militarily in World War I![62] The Manchus thereafter ruled China until 1912.

3. *The War of the Spanish Succession* (1701–1714), a war involving 10 European nations plus European colonies in other parts of the world, caused "well over a million" casualties (dead and wounded) in the armies, "of whom at least 400,000 sacrificed their lives."[63] But civilian losses must have been much heavier. **"In no other war have there been so many sieges as in the War of the Spanish Succession,"** says Bodart. **"The losses in sieges were much heavier on both sides than those in battles, ... The deaths among the inhabitants of besieged cities, those caused by diseases carried by armies, those of the Camisards, and finally from the famine which followed in the wake of this duel to the death, must have reached an enormous figure. Statistics on these points, however, are unfortunately totally wanting."[64]** Even a conservative estimate would place the total dead at over a million.

4. *The Seven Years' War* (1756–1763), fought all around the world, probably cost over one million lives in the armies alone. France lost about 350,000 soldiers and Austrian casualties were about 400,000 (dead and wounded). Prussian losses were "undoubtedly heavier."[65] Hundreds of thousands of others died in the armies of other nations and among the civilians.

5. *The Napoleonic Wars* (1792–1815) involved about the same number of nations as World War I. It is estimated that France lost about 2 million lives in these wars, half of which were lost in the period of the First Empire, 1805–1815.[66] During these last

---

62 E. L. Jones, *The European Miracle* (Cambridge, London, New York: Cambridge University Press, 1981), p. 36. Genghis Khan's conquests more than four hundred years earlier probably surpassed World War I also, measured by death figures. Historian Harold Lamb says of him that "when he had passed, wolves and ravens often were the sole living things in once populous lands. This destruction of human life bewilders the modern imagination—enriched though it be by the concepts of the last European war." (Harold Lamb, *Genghis Khan—The Emperor of All Men* (London, 1929), pp. 11, 12.) Genghis Khan's conquest of Northern China in 1211–1218, for instance, is said to have cost *18 million Chinese lives!* (The Swedish encyclopedia *Nordisk Familjebok*, Vol. 5, Malmö 1951, p. 795.)

63 Bodart, pp. 30, 96.

64 Ibid., pp. 96, 97.

65 Ibid., pp. 36, 100.

66 Ibid., p. 156.

eleven years it is estimated that 2 million soldiers died in the conflict.[67] The total death figure for the 23 years from 1792 to 1815 is set at 5 or 6 million![68]

6. *The Taiping Rebellion* (1850–1864), "perhaps the most destructive war of the entire 19th century."[69] This was a civil war in China that usually is stated to have claimed 20–30 million lives.[70] In connection with this war the *Awake!* magazine apparently overlooked its previous claim that World War I exceeded all previous wars in destructiveness. An article in its March 22, 1982 issue, trying to highlight religion's involvement in war, said that the number of victims was "possibly as many as 40 million," that is, *nearly four times as many as were killed directly by World War I!*[71] This one war alone demonstrates that World War I was *not* "the bloodiest war in history" up to that time, as has been sometimes stated. The reason why some historians make such an unfounded claim is, as E. J. Hosbawm explains, that the Taiping Rebellion "has been ignored by euro-centric historians."[72]

7. *The Lopez War* (1864–1870), in which Paraguay fought against Argentina, Uruguay, and Brazil, cost more than 2 million lives. The war "reduced the Paraguayan population from about 1,400,000 to some 221,000," that is, by 84 percent! The other three countries "lost an estimated 1,000,000 men."[73]

Compare the fatalities of just these seven wars, as seen in this chart, with those of World War I:

---

67 Ibid., p. 133.
68 Ibid., pp. 181, 182; *Awake!*, February 22, 1961, p. 7. The losses are, of course, difficult to estimate. Estimates of losses in just Napoleon's armies range between 400,000 and 2,500,000. See Beer, page 330, note 18.
69 Dupuy & Dupuy, page 864.
70 Palmer & Colton, *A History of the Modern World Since 1815* (1978), p. 632.
71 *Awake!*, March 22, 1982, page 7. *The New Encyclopedia Britannica* agrees with this: "A contemporary estimate of 20,000,000 to 30,000,000 victims is certainly far less than the real number." (Macropaedia, Vol. 4, 15th ed. 1980, p. 361) Swedish historian Gunnar Hägglöf (who spent a number of years as ambassador in China) says in his book *China as I Saw It* (*Kina som jag såg det*, Stockholm, 1978) that "the Taiping Rebellion, which in the middle of the nineteenth century shook the Chinese state to its foundations, cost over 40 million lives and actually marked the beginning of the end of the Chinese empire." (Page 62)
72 E. J. Hosbawm, *The Age of Capital 1848–1875* (London, 1975), p. 127.
73 Dupuy & Dupuy, p. 911.

Conflict	Estimated fatalities
The Thirty Years War	9–11 million
The Manchu-Chinese War	25 million
The War of the Spanish Succession	c. 1 million
The Seven Years' War	1–2 million
The Napoleonic Wars	5–6 million
The Taiping Rebellion	20–40 million
The Lopez War	2 million
Total estimated fatalities	63–87 million
Estimated fatalities in World War I	37.5 million

It can be seen that the mortality in just these seven wars is about double the figure of 37,500,000 war-related deaths cited earlier. And it would surpass many times over the number of 10–12 million deaths caused directly by World War I. It should be noted that these major wars from the three centuries immediately preceding 1914 are only *some* of the more important examples; the list of earlier wars causing a million deaths or more could be considerably extended.[74] These few examples, however, are enough to show how ludicrous the idea is that just 5 million (or, worse, 1.5 million) people died in the major wars of the 2,400 years preceding 1914. The simple truth is that *hundreds of millions of people died in wars during that period!*

To sum up, the 1914–1918 conflict (World War I) was primarily a European war, in which about fifteen, or about one quarter of the then-existing nations on earth, actively participated. It was not broader in scope than a number of earlier wars and in fact was actually narrower than several of these, such as the twenty-three-year-long Napoleonic Wars, in which *half* of the nations then existing on earth took active part.

About 90 percent of the 10–12 million direct victims of the 1914–

---

74 Many other wars fought during the same three centuries cost hundreds of thousands of lives each, for instance *The Spanish War* between France and Spain (1635–59), *The Great Turkish War* (1683–99), *The War of the League of Augsburg* (1688–97), *The War of the Austrian Succession* (1740–48), *The American War of Independence* (1775–83), *The Crimean War* (1854–56), *The American Civil War* (1861–1865), *The Franco-German War* (1870–71), *The Russo-Turkish War* (1877–78), and, at the start of our century, *The Russo-Japanese War* (1904–05), and *The Balkan Wars* (1912–13). As just two examples of fatalities, according to Hobsbawm, some 600,000 perished in The Crimean War and over 630,000 were killed in the American Civil War. (Hobsbawm, *The Age of Capital 1848–1875*, London, 1975, pp. 76, 78)

1918 war were Europeans. Other earlier conflicts, such as the Thirty Years War, had comparable death figures. The Manchu-Chinese War had *double* that number of fatalities and the Taiping Rebellion about *three times* that number.

The war was fought mostly with conventional weapons. Tanks, submarines, and airplanes (apparently used for the first time in the First Balkan War, 1912–1913) were still in the experimental stage and played an unimportant role in the war. The machine gun—a weapon developed in the previous century and used in several earlier wars (for example, the American Civil War)—was responsible for 80–90 percent of the casualties. The transportation on land was still done mainly by horses, as in earlier wars.

The 1914–1918 conflict was not the first *total* war in history, nor was it the first *world* war. In fact, according to Field-Marshal Montgomery, because it was essentially a European war, it is even questionable if it merits being termed a world conflict.

In whatever way, then, that the 1914–1918 war is measured—by its scope, duration, number of nations involved, combatants, or casualties—the claim that it was seven times greater than all the major wars of the previous 2,400 years combined stands out as pure fiction. It is so far from the truth that it is unbelievable that anyone—if he made a careful examination of the historical data—*seriously* or *honestly* could have made such a claim.

Is our century the most warlike in history?

World War II was, unquestionably, far greater than World War I in all respects and ended with the use of nuclear weapons. Yet, it has been followed by a forty-year period in which no repetition of the use of such weapons has occurred. Other wars have been fought but they have not been exceptional when compared with many of the major wars of past generations.

It is true that the *threat* of a war that could exterminate the greater part of mankind is obviously existent today. However, merely the *threat* or *possibility* of such a war does not in itself fulfill any supposed prophecy about wars in our twentieth century or specifically in the generation of 1914. What has actually happened?

From 1816 to 1965 the number of independent nations on earth quintupled, from 23 in 1816 to 124 in 1965.[75] This development multiplied, of course, the prospects of an increase in the number of international and civil wars, especially since the world population quadrupled during the same period. What do the facts reveal? Have we seen a notable increase in the *number* of wars in this century?

Those who proclaim that a "sign" clearly marks our twentieth century convey the idea that today's world is immensely more warlike than was that of the past. *The Late Great Planet Earth* asserts (page 147) that **"War has greatly increased in frequency and intensity in this century."** The author quotes the *US News and World Report* of December 25, 1967, as saying:

> **Since World War II there have been 12 limited wars in the world, 39 political assassinations, 48 personal revolts, 74 rebellions for independence, 162 social revolutions, either political, economic, racial or religious.**

Like Hal Lindsey, the Watch Tower Society feels there has been a tremendous increase in war frequency in our century. The *Watchtower* of April 1, 1983, page 3, quotes newspaper columnist James Reston as saying that our century has seen 59 interstate wars and 64 civil wars, or *123 wars in all*.

Further on in the same issue, however, it is claimed that "Over 130 international and civil wars have been fought since the end of World War II." (page 7)

Two years earlier, in the *Awake!* of May 8, 1981, it was stated that as many as *150* wars had been fought since the end of World War II. (Page 8)

But that record was almost doubled by the 1985 publication *Reasoning from the Scriptures* which cited retired Admiral Gene La Rocque to the effect that *270* wars have been fought since the end of World War II! (Page 235)

It is certainly not inappropriate to ask: What is the truth?

To find an answer to that question, it is necessary first to answer another: What *is* war? Is every armed conflict between two or more nations a war, however small the armed forces are, however few that are killed? Is every armed riot within a country a civil war? Obviously, the *number* of wars during a certain period is dependent on how war is defined.

75 Singer & Small, pp. 24–28.

To be able to make a meaningful comparison between wars today and those in the past, war researchers have had to give some kind of definition to war. Quincy Wright defined war as a conflict that involved at least 50,000 combatants.[76] He discovered that at least 284 wars of this kind occurred from 1480 to 1964, or about 60 wars per century on the average.[77] Very interestingly, however, only 30 wars of this kind had been fought in the twentieth century up to 1964. According to the definition cited, there is clearly no increase in the number of wars in our century compared with earlier centuries; the indication is for a decrease.[78]

Wright also points out that, although wars have become increasingly destructive in our century, they have not only decreased in number but also *in length*.[79]

Other war researchers confirm this trend. Singer and Small, who limit their discussion to international wars (that is, wars between nations in contrast to civil wars), define such a war as a conflict in which at least one of the participant nations has to be an *independent* nation, and which claims at least 1,000 battle deaths.[80] During the 150 years from 1816 to 1965, Singer and Small counted 93 such international wars. Of these, 35 occurred during the first 50-year period (1816–1864), 33 during the second (1864–1913), and 25 during the third 50-year period (1914–1965). Again, a clearly declining trend![81] This declining trend in war frequency is still discernible, even if the civil or domestic major wars during the period are included, as Beer observes.[82]

This declining trend in war frequency has been particularly manifest in Europe, which has experienced less than half as many wars in the nineteenth and twentieth centuries as in earlier centuries.[83] Since the end of World War II, Europe has had a whole generation of peace, which is one of the longest peace periods in its history!

---

76 Beer, p. 22.
77 Quincy Wright, p. 11.
78 Wright, p. 11.
79 Ibid., 55, 89.
80 Singer & Small, pp. 30–37.
81 Ibid., p. 38.
82 Beer, pp. 42, 43. Singer & Small (page 201) tend to feel that civil wars are on the increase. But if both kinds of wars—civil and international—are numbered together, as Beer does, the total number of wars is decreasing.
83 Beer, p. 43. As stressed by historian Michael Nordberg (*Den dynamiska medeltiden*, Stockholm, 1984, p. 12), "there were almost constant wars in Europe from the sixteenth century to 1815, most of them as devastating as the Hundred Years' War," 1337–1453.

Does war today play a greater and more destructive role in human life than in past generations?

Without doubt, most people today would unhesitatingly answer that question in the affirmative. But war researchers are not so sure. Some, such as war analyst Wright, state that "war has become increasingly destructive and disruptive" in our century, and columnist James Reston describes our century as "the bloodiest century in the history of the human race," although the figures he gives do not prove that.[84] A fact that must be taken into consideration, however, is that statements of this kind always have reference to war casualties *in absolute, not relative, numbers*. That is, they do not take into account the fact that both the number of people and the number of nations have doubled many times over in the past three centuries.

In view of this, the real question is: Have wars and victims of wars increased in our century *in proportion to the increasing number of nations and people on earth*? Does war play a greater part *in the life of mankind in general* today? Has the number of killed increased as a *percentage of the total population*?

The role played by wars in the past history of mankind has been much greater than most people imagine. **"As calculated by the Norwegian Academy of Sciences in 1969, the world has known only 292 years of peace since 3600 B.C.E., whereas 14,531 wars have been fought,"** declared *The Watchtower* of April 1, 1983 (page 3). For some reason the most frightening figure of the calculation was left out. According to this very same report, *over 3.6 billion (3,640,000,000) people were killed in those 14,531 wars!* The calculation referred to was not made by the Norwegian Academy of Sciences, however. It originated with Norman Cousins, chairman of the editorial board of *Saturday Review,* who published it in the *St. Louis Post-Dispatch* of December 13, 1953. Although he explicitly stated that his calculation was speculative, it has often been quoted as a scientific report.[85] But it may not be far from the truth.

Recently, Francis Beer has tried to verify Cousins' figures. On the

---

84 *The Watchtower,* April 1, 1983, page 3. Reston mentions 59 wars between nations with over 29 million combat dead, and 64 civil wars with almost 6 million casualties. But the Taiping Rebellion alone in the last century may have claimed almost *seven* times as many lives as all these 64 civil wars combined!

85 Brownlee Haydon, *The Great Statistics of Wars Hoax* (Santa Monica, 1962). (This is a paper of only 8 pages.) See also Singer & Small, pages 10, 11, and Beer, page 20.

whole, his study *confirms* Cousins' estimates. Beer concludes that **"there have been more than 14,000 major and minor wars and 3,500 major wars in the world since 3600 B.C."** As to casualties, he says: **"Our evidence thus suggests less than 1 billion *direct* battle deaths in world major wars since 3600 B.C."**[86] To this number must be added *civilian* deaths, including deaths *indirectly* due to wars, which would probably triple the figure to c. 3 billion.[87]

This testifies to the truth that the history of the human race as a whole, in all ages, is one marred by near constant warfare in one area or another and by a generally continuous flow of human blood shed in such conflicts.

Still, *The Watchtower* of April 1, 1983, page 7 claims that "historians have recorded years of peace prior to 1914" but "there have been none since." The object of the statement is, of course, to "prove" that peace was taken away from the earth in 1914, in fulfillment of Revelation chapter six, verse 4.[88]

The problem is that this statement has no support from war researchers.

Beer's research shows that there were only 52 years of peace from 1480 to 1965, or somewhat over 9 for each one hundred years. Eight of these 52 years of peace fell in the half-century period *after* 1914. As Beer points out, **"The general trend of peace diffusion and war concentration implies more peace and fewer wars today—less peace and more wars yesterday."**[89]

In a century that has seen two destructive "world wars," that has seen technical development explode in a series of new, more deadly weapons of extermination, and in a time that witnesses a frightening

---

86 Francis Beer, *How Much War in History: Definitions, Estimates, Extrapolations and Trends* (Beverly Hills, 1974), pp. 28, 30. Compare Beer, *Peace Against War* (San Francisco, 1981), pp. 37–40, 48, 49.

87 In *The Watchtower* of April 1, 1983, Quincy Wright is quoted as saying: "At least 10 per cent of deaths in modern civilization can be attributed directly or indirectly to war." (Page 6) But the reader is not told that Wright, in the very same passage, says that three quarters of these deaths may be attributed to *indirect* causes, such as famines and diseases, and that it is probable that "the proportion of such losses outside Europe and in Europe in earlier centuries has been greater." (Wright, p. 61)

88 The book *Reasoning from the Scriptures* (1985), for instance, says: "As foretold at Revelation 6:4, 'peace was taken away from the earth.' Thus the world has continued to be in a state of upheaval ever since 1914." (Page 235)

89 Beer, pp. 34, 48. Since Beer defines "peace years" as years "without *major* wars"—which he estimates at 600 since 3,600 B.C.—the real number of peace years in earlier times may have been even smaller, "perhaps even a number approaching zero."

armaments race, it may be difficult to believe that war and its actual effect on the human race remains essentially the same as in past centuries. The death toll of wars in our century is admittedly terrifying.[90] But that was also the case in the past. The real question is: Can it truly be said that a *higher percentage of the population* has died in wars in our century than in earlier centuries?

War researchers acknowledge that it is impossible to prove that either warfare or mortality due to warfare has actually increased in our century. Even scholars who tend to believe so are forced to admit that such a conclusion is an unproved hypothesis. Francis Beer, who, despite his previously quoted statements, feels there has been an upward trend in our century, writes:

> We must be careful to remember that this hypothesis has not really been confirmed, and that there may actually be no trend at all. Unlikely as it sounds, there may have been no significant change over time in the incidence of peace and war and in the casualties of violence. Peace and war may occur about as frequently and last as long as they ever did; casualties may also be very comparable to what they have always been.[91]

Probably the most accurate and minute examination of this question is that published by Singer and Small. They summarize their conclusion in the following way:

> Is war on the increase, as many scholars as well as laymen of our generation have been inclined to believe? The answer would seem to be a very unambiguous negative. Whether we look at the number of wars, their severity or magnitude, there is no significant trend upward or down over the past 150 years. Even if we examine their intensities, we find that later wars are by and large no different from those of earlier periods.[92]

Whatever claims or counterclaims may be made, one thing should certainly be very clear to us: Jesus' statement about wars has seen fulfillment—but not just in this twentieth century or just since 1914 or since 1948. It has come true *in every generation* since his day and up to the present.

He said nothing about "intensity," "escalation," or the "threat" of some holocaust of global proportions. His simple statement was that there would be wars and rumors of wars, with nation rising against

---

90 The number of deaths in World War II is difficult to determine. The best sources show that about 15 million soldiers were killed. The figures given for the civilian victims vary from 20 to 35 million. (Dupuy & Dupuy, p. 1198; Singer and Small, pp. 52, 48)

91 Beer, pp. 46, 47.

92 Singer & Small, p. 201.

WHAT HISTORIANS SAY ABOUT WARS TODAY
AND IN THE PAST

"The World War, 1914–1918, is thought by many to have touched a new high in bringing disaster and misery to the sections of Europe where the fighting raged. But the wars of this period [here speaking of the sixteenth and seventeenth centuries] were even more devastating—probably nothing quite so terrible as the Thirty Years' War in Germany (1618–1648) has ever been experienced."—Leo Huberman, *Man's Worldly Goods* (New York and London, 1968), p. 100.

"Even the Second World War, in sheer depopulation, was not so devastating for Germany as was the Thirty Years War."—Historian R. R. Palmer, *A History of the Modern World* (New York, 1952), p. 133.

"The 1914/18 war was essentially a European war. It came later to be called a 'world war' because contingents from many parts of the British empire served in Europe, and because the United States joined the Entente Powers in 1917. But in reality, since the role of seapower was mostly passive, this was less of a 'world war' than some previous conflicts such as the Seven Years' War."—Field-Marshal Viscount Montgomery of Alamein, *A History of Warfare* (London, 1968), p. 470.

On Genghis Khan: "When he marched with his horde, it was over degrees of latitude and longitude instead of miles: cities in his path were often obliterated, and rivers diverted from their courses; deserts were peopled with the fleeing and the dying, and when he had passed, wolves and ravens often were the sole living things in once populous lands. This destruction of human lives bewilders the modern imagination—enriched though it be by the concepts of the last European war."—Harold Lamb, *Genghis Khan, The Emperor of All Men* (London, 1929), pp. 11, 12.

"Unlikely as it sounds, there may have been no significant change over time in the incidence of peace and war and in the casualties of violence."—Francis Beer, *Peace Against War* (San Francisco, 1981), pp. 46, 47.

"Is war on the increase, as many scholars as well as laymen of our generation have been inclined to believe? The answer would seem to be a very unambiguous negative. Whether we look at the number of wars, their severity or magnitude, there is no significant trend upward or down over the past 150 years."—J. David Singer and Melvin Small, *The Wages of War 1816–1965*. A Statistical Handbook (New York, London, Sydney, Toronto, 1972), p. 201

"Even today in the middle of the twentieth century, despite all that has happened in the lifetime of men not yet old. . . . It is still possible to say that the French Revolution at the end of the eighteenth century was the great turning point of modern civilization."—Historian R. R. Palmer in the Preface to George Lefebvre's *The Coming of the French Revolution* (Princeton, 1947), p. v.

nation and kingdom against kingdom. This has happened repeatedly throughout human history. To add some other factor or inject some other meaning into his words is nothing more than human speculation or fabrication.

All attempts to limit Jesus' words regarding wars as though applying only to this twentieth century are, therefore, doomed to failure, for the claims made are contradicted by the established and overwhelming evidence of history, from his time till ours.

CHAPTER 6

Is Today's "Increasing of Lawlessness" Unprecedented?

NEVER BEFORE in history has there been so much news reporting. And news media—TV, radio, newspapers—seem to be preoccupied with the *bad* news. Every day people get their minds flooded with a concentrated dose of the latest miseries and evils in different parts of the world.

"After absorbing the news of today," noted historian Barbara Tuchman, **"one expects to face a world consisting entirely of strikes, crimes, power failures, broken water mains, stalled trains, school shutdowns, muggers, drug addicts, neo-Nazis, and rapists. . . . This has led me to formulate Tuchman's Law, as follows: 'The fact of being reported multiplies the apparent extent of any deplorable development by five- to tenfold.'"[1]**

No doubt this "Tuchman's Law" at least partially explains the feeling of so many that the world today is worse than ever before and that mankind today faces an unprecedented increase of lawlessness worldwide.

Increasing crime is yet another feature graphically portrayed as evidence of the last days by some expositors of prophecy. In *Good-bye, Planet Earth*, Adventist author Pierson says:

> **. . . we are witnessing the worst epidemic of lawlessness the human race has ever experienced. Our cities are beset with rape, murder, riots, looting, and arson.** (Page 3)

Later in the same publication (page 50) the author quotes from deceased Adventist leader Ellen G. White's *Testimonies,* in which she wrote:

---

1 Barbara W. Tuchman, *A Distant Mirror* (London, 1978), p. xviii.

The condition of things in the world shows that troublous times are right upon us. . . . Bold robberies are of frequent occurrence. Strikes are common. Thefts and murders are committed on every hand. Men possessed of demons are taking the lives of men, women, and little children. Men have become infatuated with vice, and every species of evil prevails. (Vol. 9, p. 11)

The interesting factor here is that Ellen White wrote these words over 75 years ago—and the picture she paints of crime then (about 1910) is certainly every bit as dark as that portrayed by current protagonists of end-times pronouncements.

Crime is frequently dealt with in the Watch Tower Society's publications, which attempt to give it the greatest proportions possible, since the Society explains Jesus' words about a future "increasing of lawlessness" (Matthew 24:12, NW) as describing one more feature of the supposed "composite sign," the fulfillment of which has been seen only since 1914.

Thus *The Watchtower* of June 1, 1983, pages 5 through 7, states that after World War I "the setting was ripe for an increasing of lawlessness on a magnitude never before beheld," and that mankind since 1914 has seen "the greatest increase of lawlessness in all history."

Evidently the Watch Tower Society trusts that the reader will have no difficulty in accepting these statements, because any discussion of the extent of lawlessness in the past is totally missing, and no historian, criminologist, or any other authority is quoted in support of the claim. The Society seems to take it for granted that lawlessness in the past was something rather trivial compared to that of our time.

The Watchtower of July 15, 1983, for instance, indicates that the newsmaking incidents of robbery combined with murder are features almost unique to our century:

There was a time when a burglar, or robber, took only valuables. Now they take lives as well. (Page 5)

Such a statement, of course, is nothing but an idealization of the past in order to put a special emphasis on today's lawlessness. Actually, robbery accompanied by murder may be found in every age, and it has been particularly rampant in times of famines and plagues. When syphilis scourged Europe in the sixteenth century, lawlessness and immorality saw an enormous increase everywhere. In Rome, for example, "murder and robbery were quite in the regular course of things."[2] Similarly, the generation that survived the Black Death in the fourteenth century witnessed a sharp increase of lawlessness and violence:

A striking feature about the last half of the fourteenth century is the greater amount of lawlessness then prevalent, and the number of outbreaks, both popular and intellectual, against authority.[3]

The simple truth is that violence, collective as well as individual, has always formed an integral part of man's history.

In the work *Violence in America* sociology professor Charles Tilly points out that **"Western civilization and various forms of collective violence have always been close partners."[4]** Of the period following upon the French Revolution, for example, he says:

Western history since 1800 is violent history, full enough of revolutions, coups, and civil wars, but absolutely stuffed with conflict on a smaller scale. The odd thing is how quickly we forget.[5]

What about today? Most experts seem to agree that for a number of years serious crimes have been increasing sharply in many countries. But is this circumstance really something new and unique to our time? Could it be that many have been given this impression only because of man's forgetfulness, or ignorance, of the past?

Industrialization, urbanization and crime

The Industrial Revolution that set in towards the end of the 18th century profoundly changed Western society. New machines and the use of mass-production techniques brought about a growing prosperity in many countries. One consequence of this was a rapid growth of city populations (urbanization). Many people in the 19th century, including sociologists, lawyers, judges, and so forth, feared that these changes would break down the traditional moral and social checks on man's behaviour, causing increasing lawlessness in society. A preva-

2 Matts Bergmark, *Från pest till polio*, 3rd ed. (Stockholm, 1983), p. 74.
3 A. M. Campbell, *The Black Death and Men of Learning* (New York, 1931), p. 129.
4 *Violence in America: Historical and Comparative Perspectives*. A staff report to the National Commission on the Causes and Prevention of Violence, edited by H. D. Graham & T. R. Gurr, Vol. I, Washington D.C., 1969, p. 5. This work will henceforth be referred to as *VIA*.
5 *VIA*, Vol I, p. 7

lent view in the 19th century, therefore, was that industrialization and urbanization were necessarily accompanied by rising crime.

To substantiate its thesis of an unparalleled increase of lawlessness, the Watch Tower Society draws extensively upon this supposed connection between industrialization, urbanization and rising crime. Evidently assuming that this idea is an established truth, *The Watchtower* of June 1, 1983, page 5, states that "the Industrial Revolution and the growing cities" paved "the way for our 20th-century increase of lawlessness," and even claims that **"These developments, unique to our modern age, have contributed to the greatest increase of lawlessness in all history."**

The facts, however, do not support this explanation. Though seemingly impressive and convincing, it has nevertheless been turned down by recent critical studies.

In the 19th century, the two major industrial countries were Britain and France. To test the theory that industrialization and urbanization breed an increase of lawlessness, the crime rates of these two countries in the last century have been carefully studied. In 1973 criminology historians A. Q. Lodhi and C. Tilly published their study of crime and violence in 19th-century France. Their investigation clearly demonstrated that rising crime *did not* accompany the growing industrialization and urbanization of this country. In fact, some types of crime even *declined* during the period! The authors concluded:

> **The linking of crime, violence, and disorder to urban growth must fall into the category of things people simply want to believe, for the belief rests on no substantial foundation of verified fact or systematic analysis.**[6]

The studies of crime rates in 19th-century Britain, the most advanced industrial society of that period, show similar results. **"The British data are quite clear as to decreases in official crime rates in the latter half of the nineteenth century,"** says Canadian sociologist Lynn McDonald in his summary of these studies.[7]

That crime does not experience a virtually automatic rise with the spread of urban industrial life was also demonstrated by history professor Roger Lane in his study of criminal violence in 19th-century Massachusetts. Rather than rising, crime tends to decrease with growing industrialization and urbanization. Lane explains:

---

6 A. Q. Lodhi and C. Tilly, "Urbanization, Crime, and Collective Violence in 19th-century France," *American Journal of Sociology*, Vol. 79, 1973, p. 296.

7 Lynn McDonald, "Theory and evidence of rising crime in the nineteenth century," *The British Journal of Sociology*, Vol. 33, 1982, p. 406.

All evidence points to the long-term drop in criminal activity as normative, and associated with urbanization. But the process was not complete without the accompaniment of rapid industrial development also. It was this which provided the means of absorbing raw immigrants, of fitting them into a 'system' which socialized and accommodated them into more cooperative habits of life.[8]

Thus the claim that the growing industrialization and urbanization of the last century paved the way for an unprecedented rise of lawlessness in our century is confuted by the actual facts. The claim is based upon a theory that, on closer examination, turns out to be scarcely more than a 19th-century myth.

The present "crime wave"

History demonstrates the fluctuating nature of crime waves, their surging and ebbing, and surging again. The pattern is seldom constant or uniform in every country. In a number of nations, crime has unquestionably been on the increase for a couple of decades.[9] In Italy, serious crimes have increased steadily since 1965, and in France since 1970. West Germany has experienced smaller increases from about 1965, while in England and Wales crime has been growing ever since World War II. Other industrialized countries, such as Japan, Switzerland and Norway, still have relatively low crime rates.[10]

How new, then, is the present growth in crime? Is it as novel or unique as some of the end-times expositors infer?

Attempting to prove the distinctiveness of today's crime increase, *The Watchtower* of June 1, 1983, on page 7, quotes the British criminologists Sir Leon Radzinowics and Joan King as saying, in their book *The Growth of Crime*, that **"the one thing that hits you in the eye when you look at crime on the world scale is a pervasive and persistent increase everywhere. Such exceptions as there are stand**

---

8 Roger Lane, "Urbanization and Criminal Violence in the 19th century: Massachusetts as a test case," *VIA*, Vol 2, p. 366. Thus, as Lane points out, "over a long term urbanization has had a settling, literally a civilizing, effect on the population involved." (Ibid., p. 359.)

9 Gwynn Nettler, professor of sociology at the University of Alberta, Canada, gives the following overall pictures: "Serious crimes have increased over the past decade or two in rich countries and in poor, 'developing' lands. . . . During this time, crime has probably declined or remained stable among two different categories of countries: (1) those under fresh totalitarian rule and (2) those that have been able to channel 'Western influence' in such a way that primary group control is maintained."—*Explaining Crime*, 2nd ed., (New York, 1978), p. 20.

10 Nettler, pp. 20, 21.

out in splendid isolation, and may soon be swamped in the rising tide."

True, these authors, writing in 1977, argue that crime has indeed been increasing in many countries for a couple of decades. They do *not* say, however, that this increase is unprecedented in history. Commenting upon the theory proposed by certain modern criminologists that 'there is not more violence about, but that we are much more sensitive to violence than were our less civilized ancestors,' the authors also admit:

> That is all very well if the comparison goes a fair way back. . . . A longer view, peering into the middle ages, or even the eighteenth century, might well give more substance to the theory. <u>With all our crime, our society as a whole is more secure, less savage, than theirs.</u> . . . The mere fact that towns had to be walled, that castles had to provide refuge for the surrounding villagers and their belongings, that travelers had to take their own protection with them, bears witness to the constant threat of brigands as well as the needs of warfare. Indeed the two would often be hard to distinguish.[11]

The end-times expositors we have cited in this book reside in the United States. Doubtless their view of the world is colored by the situation there. The United States, however, is hardly typical of the world as a whole. Perhaps these proclaimers of the end-times realize it, perhaps not, but few countries today compare in violent crime with the United States:

> In numbers of political assassinations, riots, politically relevant armed group attacks, and demonstrations, the United States since 1948 has been among the half-dozen most tumultuous nations in the world.[12]

---

11 Sir Leon Radzinowics and Joan King, *The Growth of Crime* (London, 1977), pp. 10, 11. The American criminologist J. S. Cockburn, writing in the same year, comments on the present "crime wave" in similar vein: "Crime for our generation has become a commonplace. Conditioned by a bombardment of criminal 'statistics,' we tend to regard a soaring crime rate and the attendant debates on law enforcement, capital punishment and gun control as the peculiar monopoly of, and to some extent the natural price for, our modern industrialized society. Viewed in a broader historical perspective, however, our preoccupation with crime appears less novel. Most nineteenth-century Englishmen were convinced that crime was increasing as never before; eighteenth century commentators were thoroughly alarmed by what they saw as a rising tide of violent criminality; and complaints of the imminent breakdown of law and order punctuated the Middle Ages." Of the increase in crime and lawlessness reported from many countries in the late sixteenth century, Cockburn remarks that "The trends were apparently universal." (*Crime in England 1500–1800*, Princeton, New Jersey, 1977, p. 49.)

12 *VIA*, Vol. II, p. 628.

In an article on homicide, the December 1984 issue of *Science* magazine observed that American murder statistics are higher than those for most other countries. American gun homicide, for example, is "50 times that of" England, Germany, Denmark and Japan![13] No wonder, then, that those currently stirring up religious expectations about the nearness of "the end" focus predominantly on crime in the U.S.A.

Back in 1970 Hal Lindsey, for instance, saw the increase in American crime as an important sign of the times. In his book, *The Late Great Planet Earth*, pages 100, 101, he wrote:

> A short time ago we saw a graph in a newsmagazine which indicated the climb in serious crime in the United States from 1960 to 1968. If you had been an ant on that page you would have had a very steep stairway to climb each one of those eight years. While the number of crimes in America was increasing 122 per cent, the population rose only 11 per cent.
>
> Many people have stopped talking about the 'crime rate.' They now refer to the 'crime epidemic.'

Similarly, in the Watch Tower Society's publications, crime in the U.S.A. has a central place. It is, in fact, the only country for which the Society has published crime statistics and crime curves covering a decade or more.[14]

Few expositors, however, honestly tell their readers that when it comes to crime—as well as to many other things—the United States is not representative of the world at large. But even taken by itself, how true is the claimed enormity of crime increase in that land? How reliable is the evidence upon which such claim is made?

The FBI Uniform Crime Reports

Most of the figures and curves published by the Watch Tower Society are said to be based upon the *Uniform Crime Reports* published by the

---

13 *Science*, December 1984, pp. 43, 46. Two-thirds of all homicides (murder and manslaughter) in the United States are committed with guns, which is explained by the fact that "Americans own more guns per capita than any other people in the world." (*Ibid*. p. 46)

14 Although these show terrifying increases, they are also a bit confusing. For the decade 1960–69 the *Awake!* of January 22, 1970, states on page 9 that *serious crimes* in the United States increased *88 percent*. The *Watchtower* of October 15, 1972, however, raised the figure for the period to *148 percent* (page 614). Still more impressive are the tables shown in the June 1, 1983 issue of *The Watchtower*, telling that "serious crimes in the United States increased over 1,000 percent from 1935 to 1980" (page 6). Most of this claimed increase must have occurred since 1960, as the figures given by the Watch Tower Society indicate an increase of only 77 percent up to that year!

FBI, the Federal Bureau of Investigation. The magazine which *The Late Great Planet Earth* quoted from regarding crime (*U.S. News and World Report*), also based its figures on this same source. (See footnote 3, for Chapter 9, of the book mentioned.) These FBI reports have been published annually since 1933 and include statistics on "serious crimes," namely, murder, forcible rape, robbery, aggravated assault, burglary, larceny and auto theft, with arson added in 1979.

This might seem to be an ideal, unimpeachable source of evidence on which to base discussions of American crime statistics. It may come as a surprise to many, therefore, to learn in what embarrassingly low esteem the trustworthiness of the FBI reports has been held by many authorities.

Actually, for at least the first three decades after 1933 the FBI's statistics are far from reliable. Until recently, and especially before 1967, sociologists and criminologists frequently debunked them, pointing out numerous flaws in the methods used for collecting the data.

Thus Thornstein Sellin, "the dean of American statisticians," has been quoted as describing the quality of the United States's crime statistics as 'the worst of any major country in the Western world,' while Harvard crime expert Lloyd E. Ohlin described the statistical data as "almost worthless—but it is the only thing there is."[15] Were the statistics really that bad? What effect does their trustworthiness—or lack of it—have on charts and comparisons with crime in earlier periods?

"The largest source of error," observes the well-known sociologist Charles E. Silberman, **"comes from the fact that the *Uniform Crime Reports* include only those crimes that are reported to the police and that the police, in turn, record and pass on to the FBI."**[16] The problem here is that the majority of crimes are never reported to the police. Additionally, the police often have not passed on to the FBI all crimes that are known to them. How this allows for manipulation of evidence, and the misleading effect this can create, is explained by Ramsey Clark, former Attorney General of the United States:

> **Most crime is never reported to police. And much crime is inaccurately reported. Erroneous crime statistics are often used to create the impression that the new chief is doing a good job, or to support a movement to**

---

15 *VIA*, Vol. II, p. 372. Sophia M. Robinson of the Columbia School of Social Work even stated that "the FBI's figures are not worth the paper they are printed on." (*Ibid.*, p. 372.)

16 Charles E. Silberman, *Criminal Violence, Criminal Justice* (New York, 1978), p. 448.

**add more police. Frequently an apparent increase in crime really reflects
an improved effectiveness in law enforcement, or in the reporting of crime
itself.**[17]

Changes in crime reporting, then, may create a statistical rise in
crime that does not correspond to the actual fact. As one example, in
Portland, Oregon, in 1973 and 1974 twice as many burglaries were
reported to the police as in 1971 and 1972. This would mean a *sharp
increase* in burglary during the period. An investigation, however,
revealed that burglaries had actually *decreased* during those years![18]
Many other similar cases could be cited.[19]

Due to constant criticism of its statistics, the FBI has periodically
revised and tightened its data-gathering system.[20] This has resulted in
an increased willingness among police officials to keep better records
of crimes and tell all about them to the FBI—thus causing additional
"paper increases" in the statistics.[21] Nevertheless, at the same time the
FBI's statistics have gradually become more reliable. Especially since
1967, when the U.S. government began to sponsor a number of national crime surveys as independent tests of the FBI's statistics, the

17 Ramsey Clark, *Crime in America* (Cassell & London, 1971), p. 45.
18 Nettler, pp. 70, 71. Increasing *willingness* to report crime at least partly explains the
    statistical increase in *rapes* in recent years. The women's liberation movement is supposed
    to have played an important part in this. (Nettler, p. 56; Silberman, p. 452.) Although a
    high number of rapes still go unreported, there is also evidence to show that many rape
    reports are *unfounded*. Of all rapes reported in 1968, for instance, 18 percent were, on
    investigation, found to be groundless! (Clark, p. 46)
19 The example of the New York police reports has nearly become classic: "Crime figures,
    the FBI thought, seemed remarkably low. On checking it found that in 1950, for example,
    the number of property crimes reported by the police were about half those reported pri-
    vately by insurance companies. . . . Following a survey by police expert Bruce Smith, a
    new system of central recording was installed. . . . In the one year following the change,
    assaults rose 200 per cent, robberies rose 400 per cent, and burglaries 1,300 per cent over
    1948 figures. As Smith concluded, 'such startling rises . . . do not in themselves represent
    an increase in crime, but rather a vast improvement in crime reporting.'" (Daniel Bell,
    The End of Ideology, Glencoe, Illinois, 1960, pp. 138, 139.) Similar improvements in the
    reporting system have created other "paper increases," for instance in Philadelphia be-
    tween 1951 and 1953 and in Chicago in 1960. (Bell, p. 138; Silberman, p. 449.) A dif-
    ferent type of artificial crime increase concerned *larceny*, defined as stealing of property
    valued at more than fifty dollars. The increase of this crime was for many years partly
    caused by *inflation*. Many items, that originally were worth less than fifty dollars, sooner
    or later passed the fifty dollar limit and so crept into the statistics when stolen. (Clark,
    p. 53.) Larceny-theft was not re-defined until 1973.
20 In 1958, for example, the whole statistical system was overhauled, after which the Bureau
    "doesn't consider the pre- and post-1958 figures to be entirely fungible [interchangeable]."
    (*VIA*, Vol. II, p. 376.)
21 *VIA*, Vol. II, pp. 380, 381; Silberman, p. 449.

attitude towards the *Uniform Crime Reports* has changed. Criminologists now usually agree that despite all inaccuracies, the *overall trends* depicted in the *Uniform Crime Reports* during the last 25–30 years are essentially correct, and that the increase in serious crimes since the 1960's is real.[22] If that is so, what significance does their earlier, and serious, unreliability have? And what is amiss in the use of U. S. crime statistics by some proclaimers of the last days?

The problem lies in the comparison of crime statistics from post-1960 years with those of pre-1960 years. To fail to recognize, or to acknowledge to readers, how unequal the reliability of the statistics for those two periods actually is, results in deception, unintentional or otherwise, for the readers.

In the Watch Tower publications the FBI *National Crime Reports* have been repeatedly referred to or quoted without any such acknowledgement, without a single word of caution. The statistics were even improved upon or "adjusted"—in *The Watchtower* of June 1, 1983—to show that "serious crimes in the United States increased over 1,000 percent from 1935 to 1980" (page 6). This statement, and the table presented on the same page to prove it, conceal another fact of the utmost importance: *that prior to the increase which set in in the 1960's, crime rates in the United States had been stable or even been decreasing during a whole quarter of a century!* That period may, in fact, have been unique in the history of American crime. As crime authority Silberman states:

> For a quarter of a century, the United States, perhaps for the first time in its history, enjoyed a period in which crime rates were either stable or declining and in which fear of crime was relatively low. The death rate from homicide dropped by 50 percent between 1933 and the early '40s; despite the FBI's highly publicized gun battles with John Dillinger and other criminals, the rate of other serious crimes (rape, robbery, assault and burglary) declined by one-third.[23]

As one clear evidence of this decline, we may take a closer look at homicide, the most serious of the "serious crimes." Homicide is, in fact, the only crime for which national long-term statistics exist that are *independent* of the FBI figures. Carefully kept by the Department

---

22 *VIA*, Vol. II, pp. 381–385; Silberman, p. 449. Yet there are still great discrepancies between the FBI's reports and the national crime surveys, that are difficult to explain. (See L. E. Cohen & K. C. Land, "Discrepancies Between Crime Reports and Crime Surveys," *Criminology*, Vol. 22, No. 4, November 1984, pp. 499–529.)

23 Silberman, p. 30.

of Health, Education, and Welfare, these statistics are considered "reasonably accurate," at least from the early 1930's onwards.[24]

In 1933, as shown by these figures, the murder rate in the United States was as high as 9.7 per 100,000 population. Then it began to decrease, until it reached a level of only 4.5 per 100,000 towards the end of the 1950's.[25] The increase since then has raised the number of homicides to over 20,000 annually, or to 9.8 per 100,000 population in the early 1980's. A large, certainly newsworthy, increase, true— *but this is nearly exactly the same rate as in 1933!* Although very high, the present American murder rate is not unique then, but represents a return to an earlier level.[26]

The weakness of much of the statistical evidence used by proclaimers of the nearness of the end is clear. Yet crime is admittedly high in a considerable number of countries. Does this make our twentieth century distinctive? Is it possible that such high crime rates in the post-1914 period (or the post-1948 period pointed to by Hal Lindsey) have no parallels in earlier centuries?

Crime in the historical perspective

While crime today is given much space in the Watch Tower publications, any discussion of the extent of crime in the past is wholly missing. The same is true of most expositors whose writings tend to whip up a feeling that these are, far and away, the worst of all times. The fact that crime reached high levels in a number of countries in the 1920's and 1930's, and then again in the 1960's and 1970's, does not prove that our century has seen more lawlessness than have earlier centuries. The evidence, in fact, is that crime was very often more prevalent in the past than it is today.

As observed by popular writer Colin Wilson, **"the history of mankind since about 2500 B.C. is little more than a non-stop record of murder, bloodshed and violence."** Thus he concludes that **"human history has been fundamentally a history of crime."**[27]

24 Silberman, p. 28; *VIA*, Vol. II, p. 375.
25 Ibid.
26 Criminal homicide in the U.S.A. passed 20,000 as early as in 1974. As this was twice the number murdered in 1965, the *Awake!* of November 22, 1975, expected that "there will be over 40,000 killings a year by the early 1980's." (Page 3.) Nothing of the kind took place. The murder rate in the early 1980's was still roughly the same as in 1974. Since then it has decreased!
27 Colin Wilson, *A Criminal History of Mankind* (London, 1985), pp. 4, 6. True, Wilson

Not only is this conclusion corroborated by a study of past crime, historians who have delved into the subject also conclude that there is probably less crime today than in the past. Professor John Bellamy at the Carleton University in Ottowa, Canada, even says:

> In most modern western countries the level of crime has been so reduced that the misdeeds of the few serve rather to provide the ordinary citizen with escapist entertainment than to instill a sense of fear.[28]

For those who have been victims of crime or who now live in high-crime areas, crime does indeed instill fear. But the fact remains that the actual percentage of the population affected is still not as great as it has been in earlier times of man's history. What a social evil crime often could be in the past is exemplified by Bellamy's own study of crime in England in the period 1290–1485:

> In the England of the later middle ages the preservation of public order was very often the biggest problem the king had to face. . . . Neither before that time nor since has the issue of public order bulked so large in English history.[29]

In the past, crime and disorder periodically seem to have been more or less out of control in many countries. It was with the growth of industrialization in the last century that the situation began to improve gradually in the western countries:

> During the first half of the nineteenth century, all cities were dangerous—those of Europe as well as the United States. In the second half, London, Paris, and other European cities were bringing crime and disorder under control, while American cities were not—or so it appeared to contemporary observers.[30]

In the middle of the twentieth century the situation in American cities gave evidence of having changed also. In 1960, crime researcher Daniel Bell, for example, judged that **"a sober look at the problem shows that there is probably less crime today in the United States**

---

also says, with reference to the outbreak of World War II, that the world at that time "exploded into an unparalleled epoch of murder, cruelty and violence" (page 5). This statement does not refer to ordinary social crime, however, but primarily to the bloodshed during the war. As was shown in the chapter on wars, the death figure during World War II was probably unparalleled if measured in *absolute* numbers, but not if measured *in proportion to the entire population*.

28 John Bellamy, *Crime and Public Order in England in the Later Middle Ages* (London and Toronto, 1973), p. 1.
29 Ibid., p. 1.
30 Silberman, p. 23.

than existed a hundred, or fifty, or even twenty-five years ago, and that today the United States is a more lawful and safe country than popular opinion imagines."[31] True, that was written before the most recent crime wave began in the early 1960's. But still in 1978 Silberman, commenting upon the fact that **"crime, violence, and lawlessness have been recurrent themes throughout American history,"** concluded that **"the country was more dangerous in the past than it is now."**[32] Recently performed long-term studies on crime trends give support to this conclusion, as will be demonstrated in the following section.

The evidence of long-term studies: The United States

While criminologists often point out that there is probably less crime today than for example in the last century, relatively few thorough long-term studies seem to have been done that show the trends during longer periods.[33] Those existing, though, give a most interesting picture of the overall trends of criminal activity.

For the United States, there seems to be no *national* long-term study reaching back to the period before the FBI's Uniform Crime Reports. But a number of reliable *local* studies have been done that cover individual cities and states. None of these indicate that crime today has increased above that of the nineteenth century.

> No comprehensive crime figures were collected prior to 1933, but studies of individual cities have been made, and they show that crime characteristically has its ups and downs, rather than a steady growth along with the population. James Q. Wilson, a crime expert at Harvard, has said that the early studies 'agree that during the period immediately after the Civil War the rate of violent crime in the big cities was higher than at any other time in our history.'[34]

The most recent studies even indicate a sharp decline in some places:

31 Bell, pp. 137, 155.
32 Silberman, pp. 21, 22.
33 Historical criminology is a new discipline. The first conference on the subject was held as recently as in February 1972. (*Nordisk Tidskrift for Kriminalvidenskab*, Vol. 61, Hefte 3.–4., 1973, p. 285.)
34 Attorney Fred P. Graham in *VIA*, Vol. II, pp. 374, 375.

None point to any clear proportional increase in serious crime within particular cities. And the most recent suggest, on the contrary, a sometimes striking proportional decrease.[35]

Crime statistics from the last century are, quite naturally, often very defective, but there are important exceptions. One example is Massachusetts, whose criminal records from the 19th century "are probably better than any kept elsewhere."[36] The conclusions drawn from these are, therefore, of major significance:

While all criminal statistics are subject to some doubt, the central conclusion about figures from Massachusetts may be stated with confidence: serious crime in metropolitan Boston has declined sharply between the middle of the 19th century and the middle of the 20th.[37]

Space does not permit a detailed discussion of the extent of crime in 19th-century U.S.A., but the following quotations from some cities may give a general idea of the situation:

Washington, D.C., just before the Civil War:

Riot and bloodshed are of daily occurrence, innocent and unoffending persons are shot, stabbed, and otherwise shamefully maltreated and not infrequently the offender is not even arrested.[38]

New York, in the 1850's:

A 'stone's throw' from Broadway, in the 1850's in New York was the Five Points, the most notorious place in the city. 'Policemen entered the Five Points only in pairs, and never unarmed. Respectable New Yorkers avoided the district in daylight. . . . It was the haunt of murderers, thieves, prostitutes and receivers of stolen goods.'[39]

Chicago, 1860's to 1890's:

In the twenty years after the Civil War, the murder rate quadrupled, far outstripping the growth in population, and muggings were commonplace; in 1893, one Chicago resident in eleven was arrested for one crime or another.[40]

---

35 History professor Roger Lane in *VIA*, Vol. II, pp. 359, 360.

36 Ibid., p. 360.

37 Ibid., p. 360. The most comprehensive study; "covering the years from 1849 to 1951, shows a drop of nearly two-thirds in those crimes which the FBI classifies as 'major.'" (P. 360.)

38 Silberman, p. 22. The quotation is taken from a report by a U.S. Senate committee investigating crime in the city.

39 Bell, p. 155.

40 Silberman, p. 23.

Los Angeles in the 1850's:

In a single fifteen-month period in the 1850's, a total of forty-four murders were recorded in Los Angeles, then a a town of only 8,000 inhabitants—about forty or fifty times as high as the city's current murder rate.[41]

San Francisco and the Barbary Coast, 1860–1880:

The *Annals* of San Francisco, a compilation of contemporary records of the 1860's, reports that in the downtown wharf sections 'no decent man was in safety to walk the street after dark; while at all hours, both night and day, his property was jeopardized by incendiarism and burglary.' From 1860 to 1880, there was not one night along the Barbary Coast without at least one murder and innumerable robberies.[42]

The long-term studies as well as the examples quoted above clearly show that the present crime rate in the United States is not unique in the history of American crime. As Silberman explains, many Americans may have come to feel that way because the present rate was preceded by an abnormally low, perhaps *uniquely* low, crime rate in the 1930's, 1940's, and 1950's:

Because domestic tranquility appeared to be the norm, Americans who came of age during the 1940's and '50s were unaware of how violent and crime-ridden the United States had always been. Although they continued to romanticize violence in detective stories and Westerns, an entire generation became accustomed to peace in their daily lives. To most Americans, therefore, the upsurge in criminal violence that began around 1960 appeared to be an aberration from the norm rather than a return to it.[43]

To be sure, most countries have not had the dramatic rise of crime seen in recent decades in the United States. If even such high-crime

---

41 Silberman, p. 23. This means a murder rate of 440 per 100,000 population annually! Today, when the average murder rate in the U.S. is about 7.9, Detroit has the highest, with a rate of 39 per 100,000. As this ranks among the highest in the world, Detroit has been given the title "murder capital of the world." (Nettler, p. 24.) Yet this is very much below the rate of many cities and places in the past. In the period 1680–1720, for instance, Corsica had 900 homicides annually in a population of 120,000, which means an annual rate of 750 per 100,000 inhabitants! (P. Arrighi, *Histoire de la Corse,* Toulouse, 1971, p. 275.) Some *states* in 19th-century America had a murder rate that surpassed that of Detroit today. In his study of murders in Texas from mid-1865 to mid-1868, Barry A. Crouch shows the annual murder rate in this state to have been at least 40 per 100,000 population during this period. (*Journal of Social History,* Pittsburgh, Pennsylvania, Winter 1984, pp. 218, 219, 229.)

42 Bell, p. 156.

43 Silberman, p. 31. Compare also page 19.

activity in the United States is not unprecedented, likely even being surpassed in the nineteenth century, we might therefore expect to find that current crime rates in many other countries are even more clearly below their 19th-century levels. Do long-term studies exist to corroborate this?

The evidence of long-term studies: The case of France

Probably no other country in the world can present more reliable crime statistics for the 19th century than France:

> The data available concerning urbanization, crime, and collective violence in France during that period are exceptionally rich and exceptionally uniform, compared with the data available for any part of the world today or yesterday.[44]

When, therefore, Abdul Qaiyum Lodhi of the University of Waterloo and Charles Tilly of the University of Michigan in 1973 presented their careful study of long-run trends in crime in France, covering the period from 1826 to 1962, their results cannot be easily dismissed. And their conclusions about that 136-year period are indeed surprising:

> Over the long run, crimes against property [burglary, larceny, theft] appear to have declined significantly in frequency, crimes against persons [murder, assault, rape] fluctuated mildly without trend, and collective violence varied sharply from year to year.[45]

While the rate of violent crimes remained essentially stable during the 136-year period, property crimes showed a very marked *decrease*. As shown by the curve on page 173, persons accused of crimes against property decreased dramatically from 174 per 100,000 population in 1836 to less than 10 per 100,000 in 1962![46]

Although long-term studies covering both the 19th and the 20th centuries are missing for most countries, the trend in France can hardly be unique. The evidence is, however, that the trends have varied, not only from one country to another, but also from one type of crime to another. In some countries certain types of crime have been

44 Lodhi and Tilly, "Urbanization, Crime, and Collective Violence in 19th-century France," *American Journal of Sociology*, Vol. 79, 1973, p. 297.
45 Lodhi and Tilly, p. 296.
46 Lodhi and Tilly, p. 301. Since 1970 serious crimes have been increasing. (Nettler, p. 20.)

CRIME IN FRANCE, 1826–1962

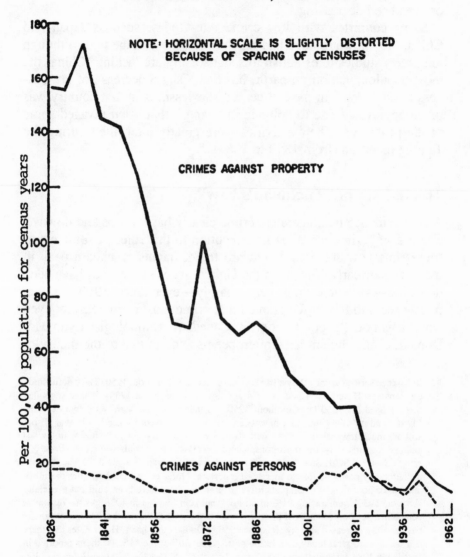

Persons accused of crimes against persons and property: France 1826–1962. (A. Q. Lodhi and C. Tilly, "Urbanization, Crime, and Collective Violence," *American Journal of Sociology,* Vol. 79, 1973, p. 301. Graph used courtesy of The University of Chicago Press.)

increasing over the long run, while others have remained rather stable or even been decreasing.[47]

Some countries with low crime rates today, such as Japan and China, are known to have had much lawlessness in the past, although long-term studies to establish this statistically are lacking. China, the most populous nation on earth, has had a sharp decrease of lawlessness since 1949.[48] In the last century lawlessness in that country was much aggravated due to "plundering gangs" that often ravaged some of the provinces. Their activities were greatly intensified during the Taiping rebellion (from 1850 to 1864).[49]

The impact of "Tuchman's Law"

As the evidence demonstrates, crime clearly has its "ups and downs." The recent "crime wave" is no exception to this rule. In some countries crime now shows a downward trend, having reached a peak in the 1970's or early 1980's. In the United States crime rates have been declining—violent crimes very sharply—ever since 1980.[50] Often people seem to take it for granted that crime must be increasing, even when it is not. As pointed out by Canadian criminologist Lynn McDonald, even scholars have often been so committed to the theory of

47 In Sweden serious crimes showed a very sharp increase after about 1950. The careful study by Hans von Hofer, published in 1984 and covering the period 1750–1980, reveals that thefts passed the 1850 level in about 1950 and then increased sharply for two decades. Murder and manslaughter, too, have been increasing in Sweden since World War II, but still are much lower than in some periods in the 19th century. As compared with the last century, assaults show the most conspicuous decrease. (See Hanns von Hofer, *Brott och straff i Sverige*, SCB, Stockholm, 1984, pp. 5:6 and Diagram 3:3 and 5:5.) The increase in thefts may partly be due to increased reporting. Hofer points out that, after the introduction of householder's comprehensive insurances, these have been built out especially since the 1950's, embracing 91% of all households in Sweden in 1978. As the insurance companies pay only in cases of thefts reported to the police, the number of *reported* thefts has certainly increased sharply since the 1950's. On the other hand, Hofer notes that there is a lot more to steal today than in the past. About *half* of the 515,000 thefts reported in Sweden in 1981 referred to motor vehicles, bicycles, and shoplifting. (von Hofer, pp. 3:2, 9f) Recent studies indicate that violent crime usually decreases with higher economic development, while property crimes tend to increase. (The *Development and Change* magazine, Vol. 13, No. 3, July 1982, pp. 447–462; *Sociology and Social Research*, Vol. 70, No. 1, 1985, pp. 96, 97.

48 The increase that began in the end of the 1970's has since been stopped by the application of more severe measures. See the *Awake!* July 8, 1974, pp. 5–9, and March 8, 1984, pp. 29, 30.

49 *Encyclopaedia Britannica, Macropaedia,* 15th ed., 1980, Vol. 4, p. 360.

50 *Time* magazine, April 8, 1985, pp. 35, 37. In Sweden the curve of serious crimes began to show a downward trend in about 1970. (von Hofer, page 5:6 and Diagram 5:5.)

rising crime that they have been blind to the factual data. Speaking of his own research on the crime rates in Canada, McDonald says:

> I know, personally, how long it took me to conclude that post-war crime rates in Canada were not rising (except for minor offences); I kept re-drawing the graphs and re-computing the slopes, thinking I had made a mistake![51]

Why, then, do people seem to take it for granted that the crime rate is rising, even when it is not? Without doubt, sensational, and some-times distorted, newspaper coverage is to a great extent responsible for this. Commenting on the newspaper headlines about street vio-lence, terrorism, rapes, and so on in Sweden, Johannes Knutsson of the Swedish Crime Prevention Council described **"the explosion of violence last summer [in 1983] as 'the journalists' brainchild' . . . The newspapers twist reality, and the politicians, deliberately or otherwise, abet them in doing so."** Emphasizing that a number of types of crimes have actually been *decreasing* lately, Knutsson said that society formerly **"used to incorporate a lot more everyday vio-lence. . . . Criminal violence too used to be more widespread, for example in Sweden at the turn of the century, when there was a lot more heavy drinking."[52]**

Escalating reporting on crime in the newspapers, then, may be a highly misleading indication of the true state of crime rates today. The validity of "Tuchman's Law"—quoted at the beginning of this chap-ter—was recently brought out in a study by sociologists Jason Ditton and James Duffy. They found that there is an "over-emphasis upon crimes of violence" in the newspapers, and particularly an "over-reporting of crimes involving sex."[53] Further, "an increasing body of evidence indicates that people's growing anxiety about crime is not commensurate with increases in crime itself," and that "the fear of crime is currently out of all proportions to its incidence."[54] As one example of this they refer to another study that revealed that **"In a period when the incidence of violent crime declined by 2.4 per cent, newspaper coverage of violent crime increased by 11.1 per cent"![55]** Lawlessness, then, often increases only in the newspapers,

---

51 Lynn McDonald, p. 417. An increase set in in 1966. (Nettler, p. 26.)
52 *News & Views* (an information paper for immigrants in Sweden), No. 28, Sept. 14, 1984, p. 1.
53 Ditton and Duffy, "Bias in the newspapers reporting on crime news," *The British Journal of Criminology,* Vol. 23, No. 2, April 1983, p. 162.
54 Ibid., p. 164.
55 Ibid., p. 164.

and, one may add, in some religious journals and literature seeking to create an excited state of mind regarding claimed fulfillment of a prophetical "sign."

The evidence to support the claim that our century is experiencing increasing lawlessness worldwide "on a magnitude never before beheld" simply does not exist. To the contrary, historical studies, including long-term studies of crime rates in specific cities, states and countries, indicate that there was often greater lawlessness in the past than today in many places. This may well have been true on an earthwide scale, in view of the fact that crime usually increases in times of famine, pestilence and war.

More than this, there is sound reason for understanding Jesus' words about increasing lawlessness (in Matthew chapter twenty-four) as applying, not to the world in general where criminality has always been widespread, but to conditions among professed servants of God, including those within the Christian congregation he would establish. His preceding words indicate this, for he describes what will befall his followers due to persecution and goes on to say that **"many will turn away from the faith and will betray and hate each other, and many false prophets will appear and deceive many people."** It is in such religious context that he then says, **"Because of the increase of wickedness [lawlessness], the love of most will grow cold, but he who stands firm to the end will be saved."** (Matthew 24:9–13, *New International Version*) Jesus, in fact, used the term "lawlessness" elsewhere in describing, not obvious criminals, but the hypocritical, dishonest conduct of religious persons. (Matthew 7:23; 23:28) In his parable of the wheat and the weeds he likened such doers of lawlessness to the spreading weeds and said that in the day of judgment his angels would **"collect out from his kingdom all things that are causing stumbling and persons who are doing lawlessness."**—Matthew 13:38–41, *New World Translation*.

The writings of Jesus' apostles amply testify to the growth of wickedness and lawlessness that developed among professed Christians in later years of the apostolic period. (First Timothy 4:1; Second Timothy 3:13; Second Peter 2:1–3, 10–14, 17–21) When Paul spoke of a coming revelation of "the man of lawlessness" he was not speaking of a source perpetrating common criminal activity such as robbery of physical property, or acts of physical violence such as murder, but of the greatest lawlessness of all, the usurpation of the place and authority that rightly belong only to the supreme Sovereign, God, combined with the religious deception of fellow humans. Paul also warned

Senationalist newspaper reporting creates a fear of crime that often is "out of all proportion to its incidence." Pictures like the above on the front page of *Awake!* of October 22, 1979, foster the idea that the whole world is as crime-infested as certain streets in New York City or other big-city areas of the United States.

WHAT AUTHORITIES SAY ABOUT LAWLESSNESS
TODAY AND IN THE PAST

THE UNITED STATES:
"Crime, violence, and lawlessness have been recurrent themes throughout American history. . . . the country was more dangerous in the past than it is today."—Charles E. Silberman, *Criminal Violence, Criminal Justice*, New York, 1978, pp. 21, 22.

"All evidence points to the long-term drop in criminal activity as normative, and associated with urbanization."—Roger Lane in *Violence in America* (ed. by H. D. Graham & T. R. Gurr), Washington, D. C., 1969, p. 366.

FRANCE:
"Over the long run [for the period from 1826 to 1962], crimes against property appear to have declined significantly in frequency, crimes against persons fluctuated mildly without trends, and collective violence varied sharply from year to year."—A. Q. Lodhi & C. Tilly, *American Journal of Sociology*, Vol. 79, 1973, p. 296.

FINLAND:
"Do we just now experience a boom period of crime? Well, the answer to that question lies in the future. But it must be pointed out that in Finland the population had lived through considerably worse periods."—Vaino Rantio, Commissioner at the Criminal Investigation Department in Helsingfors; in *Nordisk Kriminalkrönika 1982* (Scandinavian Crime Chronicle 1982), Göteborg, 1982, p. 21.

SWEDEN:
"Something we very often forget is that society used to incorporate a lot more everyday violence. . . . Criminal violence too used to be more widespread, for example in Sweden at the turn of the century, when there was a lot more heavy drinking."—Criminologist Johannes Knutsson in *News & Views* (an information paper for immigrants in Sweden), No. 28, Sept. 14, 1984, p. 1.

THE WESTERN WORLD:
"In most modern western countries the level of crime has been so reduced that the misdeeds of the few serve rather to provide the ordinary citizen with escapist entertainment than to instill a sense of fear."—John Bellamy, *Crime and Public Order in England in the Later Middle Ages*, London and Toronto, 1973, p. 1.

THE WORLD:
Comparing our modern society with those of the Middle Ages and the eighteenth century, the British criminologists Sir Leon Radzinowics and Joan King state: "With all our crime, our society as a whole is more secure, less savage than theirs."—*The Growth of Crime*, London, 1977, p. 11.

his contemporaries that "the secret power of [such] lawlessness is already at work."(Second Thessalonians 2:3–11, NIV) The writings of the apostle John in particular show that such increase of lawlessness within the first-century congregation did indeed cause the love of many to grow cold, making necessary John's strenuous urging on behalf of love of one's brother.—First John 2:9–11; 3:4, 10–18.

The preceding understanding of Jesus' words at least is in harmony with the known facts, confirmed by the Scriptural accounts themselves. The same cannot be said for the claims made by those who assert that our day is seeing a Biblically foretold increase of crime of unsurpassed proportions. The known facts are to the contrary.

CHAPTER 7

The Myth of the "Composite Sign"

THUS FAR we have considered on an individual basis those features of human life and circumstance which end-times proclaimers regularly emphasize: wars, famines, pestilences and earthquakes. Taken singly, it is obvious that none of them genuinely distinguishes our century from past centuries, whether we view these features since 1914, 1948 or any other date in this century.

Earthquakes are no more frequent nor greater in size than in previous centuries. Even war, despite its greatly heightened potential for destruction, evidently does not affect a greater percentage of the population than it did in the past. Despite all claims to the contrary, the number of wars—real wars—has actually decreased in our century. And famine and pestilence have not only decreased but have decreased sharply since the second decade of this century. The decrease is even more dramatic when compared with past centuries.

We cannot fail to note that the legitimate key to judging increase—particularly in the last three features—is that of the **percentage of population** affected. In a village of 1000 inhabitants, if 600 of them were in a state of starvation we would describe the village as famine-stricken, gravely so. That would mean that six out of every ten persons were starving. But in a city of 100,000 inhabitants even if 10,000 persons were in a state of starvation, that figure, while so much greater than the 600 previously mentioned, would mean that only *one* out of every ten persons was thus dying of starvation. The large city would, on the average, have a much lower incidence of starvation than the village. It would be, from that standpoint, the better place to live.

This is what we find in considering the world scene. The world's population has grown immensely right during this century and thus, whatever disastrous circumstance may be considered, it is only reasonable that a larger number of persons would be involved than several centuries, or even just one century, ago. In a time when commercial airplane flights were rare, limited to a few per day, five crashes in a year could rightly indicate a low degree of safety, could justify the conclusion that flying was a fairly hazardous way to travel. Today, when thousands of flights take place each day in just a single country, such as the U.S.A., even triple that number of crashes in a year would still not change the fact that airplane travel has become one of the safer modes of transportation in our modern times. The same principle properly applies in estimating the worldwide effect of the earlier-mentioned features of war, famine and pestilence, as well as the number of persons affected by earthquakes. To ignore that factor, deliberately or simply due to superficial thinking, is to distort reality and misrepresent the truth.

Those who would have us believe that we have visible evidence before us identifying our generation as strikingly marked by prophecy—because of supposedly being afflicted by such woes in some way special—may say that their claim is not based on these features taken singly. They may say that it is based on the *combination* of them, all occurring together during a single period.

Thus, religious author Hal Lindsey likened these disastrous features to **multiple pieces of a jigsaw puzzle** which are now said to be 'falling rapidly into place' since 1948. Evangelist Billy Graham hears in today's events the ominous pounding of the **combined hoofbeats** of the four horsemen of the Apocalypse. The Watch Tower Society presents these features as the individual elements of a **"composite sign."** The "sign," they say, is not any one of the features by itself but the combination of them occurring worldwide in one generation, a composite sign supposedly unique to the generation living from and after 1914.

So, while obliged by the facts to admit that none of these features individually has seen unprecedented incidence in this century, the claim might be made, "True, perhaps some century in the past saw more famine than ours, another century may have seen more or greater earthquakes, yet another century more disastrous pestilence, still another was equally or more wracked by war than our own. But it is not any one of these things individually but rather the *sum total* of all of them together happening in this one century, our twentieth century, that distinguishes this time as being, beyond question, the last days before world judgment occurs."

Is there any validity to that reasoning?

The syndrome of scourges

Most end-times proclaimers simply leave the record of the past out of their discussion and the majority of their readers are unlikely to know what that record shows in order to make a true comparison of conditions. The Watch Tower Society, however, at times seeks to counteract the evidence of the past and to deny its significance. This indicates that they recognize that there are problems with at least *some* of the features of their "composite sign," and that none of the afflictions are new to mankind. "None of these things are unique to our century," said the *Watchtower* of April 15, 1984 on page 5. How, then, could such things be used to identify the time of the end as beginning in 1914? The same issue of the *Watchtower* states that "they would, in some way, have to differ from like conditions in previous times," explaining:

> First, *every feature* of the sign would have to be *observed by one generation.* . . .
> Second, the effects of the sign would have to be *felt worldwide.* . . .
> Third, the combined conditions or symptoms would have to *grow progressively worse* during this period. . . .
> Fourth, the occurrence of all these things would be accompanied by a *change in people's attitudes and actions.* Jesus warned: 'The love of the greater number will cool off.'[1]

Thus they impose standards for judging the fulfillment of Jesus' words that are at least in part standards of their own making. Yet this fourfold attempt to save the "composite sign" from collapsing is indeed remarkably feeble. Have famines and pestilences, for instance, grown "progressively worse" since 1914? Are they more "worldwide" today than ever before? The truth is that the scope and mortality of both of these scourges have been progressively *reduced* in our century! Neither have earthquakes become "progressively worse" since 1914 or been felt more "worldwide" than before that date. As to wars, it is true that they have grown progressively in potential danger in our century. Yet the remarkable fact is that wars actually claimed more victims during the first three decades after 1914 than during the four decades that have passed since 1945! And though it is sometimes pointed out that wars during these four post-1945 decades have

---

1   The same reasoning is repeated in the book *Life—How Did It Get Here?* published by the Watch Tower Society in 1985, on page 226.

claimed some 30 million lives, this is less than the number killed in wars in the corresponding period of the past century (1845–1885).

A unique generation?

What of the argument that "every feature of the sign would have to be observed by one generation"? Does that single out the generation of 1914—or any generation of this century—as unique in this respect? By no means. Anyone who undertakes an honest and careful investigation of the matter will soon discover that it is practically impossible to find *one* generation during the past 2,000 years that *has not* observed the combined different features of the supposed "composite sign"! And this should not surprise us, really, as most of the scourges mentioned by Jesus are interrelated and, therefore, usually go together. This especially holds true of wars, famines, and pestilences. In *Hunger and History,* E. P. Prentice notes:

> Famine, War and Pestilence—the world knows them well, these three, and knows that they come not singly, one by one. Where there is Want, Pestilence makes her home and War is not far distant.[2]

Further emphasizing this commonality and simultaneousness of occurrence Ralph A. Graves explains:

> A survey of the past shows that war, pestilence, and famine always have been related, sometimes one and sometimes another being the cause, and the other two the effect. Where one of the trio has occurred the others, sometimes singly, but usually together, have followed.
>
> A veritable trinity of evil, the three are as one scourge, equal in their devastating power and in their sinister universality.[3]

This "trinity of evil" was even more closely tied together in the past than today, when improved communications and modern medical measures have greatly reduced the role of famine and epidemics in times of war.

In periods of war, famine and pestilence it is also quite normal to see crime and violence increase. History is full of examples of the

---

2 E. Parmalee Prentice, *Hunger and History* (Caldwell, Idaho, 1951), p. 137.
3 Ralph A. Graves, "Fearful Famines of the Past," *The National Geographic Magazine,* July 1917, p. 69. Walford expresses himself in similar terms: "Hence the sword, pestilence, and famine are now, as they have been in all time, the three associated deadly enemies of the human race." C. Walford, "The Famines of the World: Past and Present," *Journal of the Statistical Society,* Vol. XLII, (London, 1879) pp. 79, 80.

demoralizing effects of these scourges on the human mind and behaviour. In his discussion of famines, Professor Sergius Morgulis says:

> Famine is not merely destructive of health and physique, it is in a still greater degree a disrupter of morals and character. In the sharp struggle to maintain life all scruples are overcome, neighbor is against neighbor, and the strong are ruthless towards the weak.[4]

The history of famines, then, is also a history of demoralization, violence, brigandry, murder and cannibalism, a history of periods when lawlessness grows and love cools off. And exactly the same kind of degeneration occurs during pestilences. **"Times of plague are always those in which the bestial and diabolical side of human nature gains the upper hand,"** noted B. G. Niebuhr.[5] This interrelation between periods of wars, famines, plagues, or other disasters and an increase in crime has also been confirmed by findings of modern criminology. Swedish criminologist Hanns von Hofer, for example, in his thorough study of crime in Sweden from 1750 to 1982, notes that the historical development of violence and thefts **"is characterized by a series of very sharp increases and decreases that coincide with particular historical events, such as years of famine, alcoholic restrictions, and wars."**[6]

The saying that "misfortunes never come singly" clearly holds true of most of the miseries referred to by Jesus in his prophetic survey of the future course of world history. Wars, famines, plagues and crime are all interrelated and usually go together. Their "composite" appearance, therefore, is quite natural and understandable and is nothing new to our century. On the contrary, this *syndrome of scourges* has been a part of man's history throughout all centuries, and has been experienced by all generations since the time of Christ.

The fourteenth century—a "distant mirror"

The history of mankind is to a remarkable degree a history of crises and catastrophes. Although the Watch Tower Society admits this, unlike other end-times proclaimers it tries to belittle these past calamities, claiming that our century has seen them on a much larger scale.

---

4 Quoted by Prentice, p. 139. Some horrid examples are given by Graves, pp. 75–79.
5 Quoted by Philip Ziegler in *The Black Death* (London, 1969), p. 259. See also pages 83, 108, 109, 160, 192, 271, and 272 of the same work.
6 Hanns von Hofer, *Brott och straff i Sverige. Historisk kriminalstatistik 1750–1982*, Statistiska centralbyrån (Stockholm, 1984), p. 3:4 and Diagram 1:3.

Thus, in the *Watchtower* magazine of July 15, 1983 (page 7), this statement appears:

> **Certainly it is true that previous generations have experienced calamity. The 14th century was the time of the Black Plague when people across Europe lived in dread of pestilence, famines and wars. But just compare the scale of things in our century.**[7]

According to this the Watch Tower Society feels that the crises of the fourteenth century can by no means be measured against those of our own century.

Is that true? Is your life or that of people in general more plagued than was the case in the fourteenth century? Given a choice, would we choose conditions then—as regards wars, famines, pestilences and earthquakes—as preferable to those in this century? It was historian Barbara Tuchman who likened the fourteenth century to a "distant mirror" of our own. A closer look at the different features of that period will reveal how much—or how little—truth there is in the claim of the Watch Tower Society.

Time of war

History reveals the medieval world as a "world of constant war."[8] During the fourteenth century a number of long and bloody wars were fought in different parts of the world. In 1337 Western Europe saw the beginning of *the longest war in history,* the so-called *Hundred Years' War* between England and France, a war that actually lasted for 116 years and which, according to historian Tuchman, wrecked medieval unity.[9]

Other wars and endless civil wars raged in Europe, for example, the wars between the principalities of Germany and the wars between the commercial cities and principalities of Italy.

Not only Western Europe was embroiled in war. Eastern Europe and practically the whole Asian continent were dominated by the fierce Mongols, who had conquered those areas during the preceding cen-

---

7 *The Watchtower,* July 15, 1983, p. 7. *The Watchtower* of February 1, 1985, stated even more emphatically: "True, there had been wars, food shortages, earthquakes and pestilences down through the centuries of our Common Era until 1914. (Luke 21:11) Nevertheless, there had been nothing to compare with what has taken place since the Gentile Times ended in that momentous year." (P. 15)

8 *Collier's Encyclopedia,* Vol. 4, 1974, p. 234.

9 See the "Epilogue" of B. W. Tuchman's *A Distant Mirror.*

tury.[10] Of the period from 1200 to 1400 A.D., historians R. Ernest Dupuy and Trevor N. Dupuy say:

> During most of these two centuries [the 13th and 14th] the military and political history of mankind was dominated by one power. The Mongols— or their Tartar vassals—conquered or ravaged every major region of the known world save Western Europe.[11]

During the fourteenth century this vast empire gradually fell apart. Bloody civil wars raged for decades both in the western and the eastern parts of the huge Mongol empire. In China the alien rulers were finally overthrown in the 1360's after a long drawn-out civil war that evidently cost millions of lives.[12] In the same century the Turkish empire appeared on the scene, having first conquered Asia Minor and then the major part of the Balkan Peninsula.

Then, about 1370, one of the most ruthless world conquerors history has known appeared on the scene. He was *Tamerlane* (or, Timur Lenk), the awesome "Führer" of the fourteenth century. Having made Samarkand in Western Turkestan the center of his empire in 1370, he set out from there to conquer the rest of Asia. The countries of Khwarazm, Afghanistan, Beluchistan, Mongolestan, Russia, Western Siberia, Persia, Iraq, India, Syria and Anatolia were all conquered during the next three decades in a wave of incredibly cruel and bloody triumphs that cost millions of lives.

Like Genghis Khan of the previous century, Tamerlane mercilessly slaughtered whole populations—men, women and children—in any cities or areas that resisted him. The whole country of Khwarazm with its capital Urgentsj in Central Asia was thus completely obliterated

10 On the Mongolian conquests under Genghis Khan and his followers, see for instance E. D. Phillips, *The Mongols* (1969), R. Grousset, *Conqueror of the World* (1967), and J. A. Boyle, *The Mongol World Empire 1206–1370* (1977). The wars of Genghis Khan and his followers cost millions of lives, many more than the Napoleonic Wars and the First World War, because of the extensive massacres of the civilian populations of cities and countries. Thus, as noted previously in chapter five, footnote 62, the conquest of Northern China in 1211–1218 is estimated to have cost 18 million Chinese lives. And during the campaign in the west, 1218–1224, many cities in Persia were completely destroyed and the population often totally slaughtered. Whole countries were ravaged and depopulated. Afghanistan, for example, was turned into a desert.

11 R. Ernest Dupuy and Trevor N. Dupuy, *The Encyclopedia of Military History* (New York and Evanston, 1970), p. 330.

12 As pointed out earlier, historians generally ascribe the decrease of the Chinese population from 123 million in about 1200 A.D. to 65 million in 1393 to the wars with the Mongols. However, as suggested by McNeill (*Plagues and Peoples*, New York, 1976, p. 163), the Black Death "assuredly played a big part in cutting Chinese numbers in half."

from the map. Numerous populous cities, among them Tiflis, the capital of Georgia, Isfahan in Persia, Bagdad in Iraq, and Damascus in Syria, were devastated and plundered and their populations annihilated. During the conquests in India in 1398, it is estimated that one million people lost their lives within the space of a few weeks. Tamerlane finally died on his campaign against China in 1405, having then conquered almost all of Asia from Europe in the west to the Chinese border in the east.[13]

The feature of *war*—in all parts of the known world—was certainly not missing in the fourteenth century.

Time of famine

The fourteenth century opened with a change in climate, causing cold weather for a number of years, with storms, rains, floods, and then droughts—and crop failures. The result was a number of very severe famines. Apparently the worst of these was the universal famine of 1315–1317 (in some areas it lasted until 1319), a famine **"which smote all lands from the Pyrenees to the plains of Russia and from Scotland to Italy."**[14] The consequences were very severe. The poor ate almost anything, "dogs, cats, the dung of doves, and even their own children."[15] Reports from Livonia and Esthonia emphasize that "starving mothers ate their children," and that "famishing men often died on the graves while digging up bodies for food."[16] Chroniclers show similar conditions prevailing in other countries. In Ireland "the agony dragged on into 1318 and proved especially severe, for the people dug up the bodies in the churchyards and used them for food, and parents even ate their children."[17] In the Slavic countries, such as Poland and Silesia, the famine was still common in 1319, and reports tell that parents "killed their children and children killed their parents, and the bodies of executed criminals were eagerly snatched from the

---

13 One excellent work on Tamerlane and his conquests is *Timur, Verhängnis eines Erdteils*, by Herbert Melzig (Zurich & New York, 1940). In order to frighten the conquered areas into submission, Tamerlane used to build huge pyramids and minarets—using heads of the slaughtered populations as building material, together with mortar. Numerous such pyramids and minarets were built all over Asia.

14 Henry S. Lucas, "The Great European Famine of 1315, 1316, and 1317," *Speculum*, October 1930, p. 343. (Published by the Mediaeval Academy of America)

15 Lucas, p. 355.

16 Ibid., p. 364.

17 Ibid., p. 376.

gallows."[18] Along with the famine came a pestilence that swept away large numbers.[19]

Other great famines followed in the 1330's and 1340's. The Black Death was preceded by a very severe famine that is estimated to have affected one fifth of mankind. In Italy, for example, it "swept away by absolute starvation vast numbers of the inhabitants."[20] Throughout the rest of the century repeated famines visited the countries of Europe and other parts of the world, and in between, "universal want" prevailed, as shown earlier in chapter two. There is every evidence that the fourteenth century was plagued by famines and malnutrition far more than our twentieth century.

Time of pestilence

There is no need to repeat a description of the Black Death of the fourteenth century. We saw in chapter four that this plague in every sense far surpassed the Spanish flu of our century. Besides, it revisited Europe—and reportedly many other parts of the world—several times before the end of the century. Other pestilences that scourged mankind in the same period were dysentery and anthrax; several great epidemics of the disease known as St. Vitus dance broke out towards the end of the century.[21] (Though not notably contagious or necessarily deadly, leprosy reached its greatest scope in Europe during the decades previous to the Black Death.)

The plagues of the fourteenth century had an impact on the human race manifoldly more disastrous than the epidemics of our time, and many historians point to 1348, the initial year of the Black Death, as one of the most important turning-points of history. A. L. Maycock even maintains that "the year 1348 marks the nearest approach to a definite break in the continuity of history that has ever occurred."[22]

---

18 Ibid., p. 376.

19 Contemporary chroniclers often report that a third of the population died in some areas. Even conservative estimates show that the famine took an enormous toll. Thus, Dr. Henry Lucas estimates that one out of every ten persons in Europe north of the Alps and the Pyrenees perished. (Lucas, pp. 369, 377)

20 Walford, p. 439. Compare Ziegler, p. 44. Swedish historian Michael Nordberg, having mentioned the great famine of 1315–18 and other years of famine in the 1320's, says that the "years 1335–52 meant an almost continuous period of crop failures in nearly all of Europe due to the unfortunate combination of dry summers and very rainy autumns." (*Den dynamiska medeltiden*, Stockholm, 1984, p. 35)

21 Janken Myrdal, *Digerdöden* (Stockholm, 1975), pp. 19, 22. St. Vitus's dance attacked the nervous system, causing either death or disability.

22 A. L. Maycock, "A Note on the Black Death," in the *Nineteenth Century*, Vol. XCVII, London, January–June 1925, pp. 456–464. (Quoted by Campbell, p. 5.)

Time of earthquakes

It was commonly believed in ancient times that earthquakes, as well as heavenly phenomena such as eclipses, meteors, and especially comets, were omens of great calamities, particularly of wars, famines and pestilences.[23] Such sinister portents, therefore, usually caused great fear. This is probably the reason why, in discussing the things he said might mislead his disciples into believing the end was at hand, Jesus added earthquakes and, according to Luke chapter twenty-one, verse 11 (*The Jerusalem Bible*), "fearful sights and great signs from heaven." Thucydides, Diodorus Siculus, Livy and many other ancient writers claimed that earthquakes were omens of pestilence, and the Roman philosopher Seneca, a contemporary of the apostles, explicitly stated that "after great earthquakes it is usual for a pestilence to occur."[24] No wonder, then, that the great earthquakes preceding and accompanying the Black Death of the fourteenth century were interpreted as portents of the plague by contemporary chroniclers.

In China the years preceding the outbreak of the plague were marked by an imposing series of disasters: droughts, floods, swarms of locusts, famines and earthquakes. Even before the outbreak of the plague in 1337 the death toll must have been enormous:

> In 1334 there was drought in Houdouang and Honan followed by swarms of locusts, famine and pestilence. An earthquake in the mountains of Ki-Ming-Chan formed a lake more than a hundred leagues in circumference. In Tche the dead were believed to number more than five million. Earthquakes and floods continued from 1337 to 1345; locusts had never been so destructive; there was 'subterraneous thunder' in Canton.[25]

Europe also seems to have been hit by an unusual series of calamities, including disastrous earthquakes, in the years before and during the plague, accompanied by frightening portents in the sky and on earth:

> For year after year there were signs in the sky, on the earth, in the air, all indicative, as men thought, of some terrible coming event. In 1337 a

23 Fritz Curschmann, *Hungersnöte im Mittelalter* (*Leipziger Studien aus dem Gebiet der Geschichte*) (Leipzig, 1900), pp. 12–17.
24 Raymond Crawfurd, *Plague and Pestilence in Literature and Art* (Oxford, 1914), p. 65.
25 Ziegler, p. 13. Graves (p. 89) adds that "according to Chinese records 4,000,000 people perished from starvation in the neighborhood of Kiang alone," and climatologist H. H. Lamb says that the Chinese famine caused by the extraordinarily great rains and river floods in 1332 is "alleged to have cost 7 million lives." (*Climate, Present, Past and Future*, Vol. 2, London and New York, 1977, p. 456)

great comet appeared in the heavens, its far-extending tail sowing deep dread in the minds of the ignorant masses. . . . In 1348 came an earthquake of such frightful violence that many men deemed the end of the world to be presaged. Its devastations were widely spread. Cyprus, Greece, and Italy were terribly visited, and [the seismic tremor] extended through the Alpine valleys.[26]

"Europe was shaken from southern Italy to Bosnia and from Hungary to Alsace," geologist Haroun Tazieff states. The earthquake destroyed many cities and villages, including the city of Villach in Carinthia in Austria. Citing the eighteenth-century author Elie Bertrand, Tazieff says that:

The earthquake threw down thirty-six towns or castles in Hungary, Styria, Carinthia, Bavaria and Swabia. The ground opened in various places. It was thought that the stinking exhalations that this earthquake produced were the cause of that plague which spread over the whole world, which lasted for three years, and which according to calculations, killed a third of the human race.[27]

Tazieff, stating that "the fourteenth century was particularly hard hit" by destructive earthquakes, gives as another example the great earthquake that devastated the Swiss city of Basel in 1356:

On 18 October 1356 at ten o'clock at night the city of Bâle [Basel] and the towns and villages for seventeen miles round it were destroyed by a terrible earthquake whose after-shocks continued for over a year. . . .
Eighty castles, together with the towns and villages that depended on them, were ruined.[28]

As Tazieff notes, the fourteenth century seems to have been visited by an unusually great number of destructive earthquakes. Milne's catalogue, while very incomplete for this period and "practically confined to occurrences in Southern Europe, China and Japan," nonetheless lists 143 destructive earthquakes for the fourteenth century.[29] Death figures are, of course, generally missing, but there is no reason

---

26 Charles Morris, *Historical Tales: The Romance of Reality,* Lippincott 1893, p. 162 f. The famous 14th-century writer Petrarch, dwelling in Verona, Italy, at the time of the shock, wrote of it as follows: "Our Alps, scarcely accustomed to moving, as Virgil says, began to tremble on the evening of 25 January. At this same moment a great part of Italy and of Germany was so violently shaken that people who were not forewarned and for whom the thing was entirely new and unheard-of thought that the end of the world had come." (Haroun Tazieff, *When the Earth Trembles,* London, 1964, p. 155)

27 Tazieff, pp. 154, 155.

28 Ibid., pp. 155, 156.

29 See the information presented in chapter three of this work.

to believe that major earthquakes were less common or less destructive of human life in the fourteenth century than today. If anything, the available evidence points in the opposite direction.

Time of crime and time of fear

As demonstrated earlier, great calamities like war, famine and pestilence usually cause a sharp increase in crime and immorality. In *The Black Death and Men of Learning*, A. M. Campbell noted that rampant crime was "a striking feature about the last half of the fourteenth century."[30] Historian Tuchman in her famous study (*A Distant Mirror*, page 119) even states that brigandage reached such proportions that it contributed to the continuing decline of world population at the end of the 14th century! Crime and murder also spread during the great famine of 1315–1317:

> **Because of these conditions there was a great increase in crime. Persons who ordinarily led a decent and respectable life were forced into irregularities of conduct which made them criminals. Robbers and vagabonds appear to have infested the countryside of England, and they were guilty of all manner of violence. Murder became very frequent in Ireland. Robbery with assault was common; in fact all manner of articles that could be used for food were stolen, . . . in fact all things of value were readily taken.[31]**

Piracy, or robbery on the high seas, which plagued earlier centuries and was often organized and accompanied by much manslaughter, likewise increased during the fourteenth century.[32] Clearly, that time had its share of growing crime—and the fear created—as have other periods, our own included.

Materialism, pessimism, anguish and fear of the end of the world characterized the fourteenth century as much as they do our century, if not more. The problems of today are, to a much greater extent than people generally think, essentially a repetition of the past. Ziegler

---

30 A. M. Campbell, *The Black Death and Men of Learning* (New York, 1931), p. 129.
31 Lucas, pp. 359, 360.
32 The scope of this form of crime in the past is little known today, when it has practically disappeared. The Saracen pirates, for example, for long periods more or less dominated the whole Mediterranean area, fought a sea war that lasted for over a thousand years (8th to 19th centuries), plundered and devastated not only the coastal cities but ravaged cities far up into Middle Europe. Countless numbers of people were killed during these ravaging expeditions. (Erik-Dahlberg, *Sjörövare*, Stockholm 1980, pp. 49–63.)

quotes historian James Westfall Thompson, who compared the aftermath of the Black Death and of World War I and found that in both cases complaints of contemporaries were the same: **"economic chaos, social unrest, high prices, profiteering, depravation of morals, lack of production, industrial indolence, frenetic gaiety, wild expenditure, luxury, debauchery, social and religious hysteria, greed, avarice, maladministration, decay of manners."**[33]

Can it possibly be said that the calamities experienced by modern man are worse than those experienced by those of the medieval man? Ziegler, commenting upon the comparison of Thompson, concludes:

> **The two experiences are properly comparable but comparison can only show how much more devastating the Black Death was for its victims than the Great War [of 1914–1918] for their descendants.**[34]

Barbara Tuchman, who also refers to Thompson's comparison, agrees. She describes the fourteenth century as "a violent, tormented, bewildered, suffering and disintegrating age, a time, as many thought, of Satan triumphant," and adds:

> **If our last decade or two of collapsing assumptions has been a period of unusual discomfort, it is reassuring to know that the human species has lived through worse before.**[35]

Consequently, any claim that our century has seen the calamities of wars, famines, pestilences, earthquakes, and so forth, on a much larger scale than the fourteenth century is not supported by the historical evidence. It shows the opposite to be true. Taken as a whole, the supposed "composite sign" was certainly more palpable in the fourteenth century than it is today. The hoofbeats of the horsemen of the Apocalypse rang out equally as loud as in our present time.[36]

The testimony of the "population bomb"

Perhaps no other single factor testifies to the fictitiousness of calamitous claims about our century as does that of the world's population

33 Ziegler, p. 277.
34 Ziegler, p. 278.
35 Tuchman, page xiii.
36 Similar comparisons could be made with other periods in the past, the sixth century, for instance, when the "plague of Justinian" ravaged the world. As pointed out in chapter four, historians hold that the plagues of the third and sixth centuries contributed to the decline of the Roman empire, both the western and eastern parts thereof. Famine played a similar role.

growth. While the end-times proclaimers often employ it in an effort to support such claims it actually disproves them in a remarkable way.

It is therefore not surprising that the Watch Tower publications have been reluctant in telling the whole truth about this factor.

The *Awake!* magazine of August 8,1983, explained the present population growth in the following way:

> **The root of the problem lies in the way the population expands. It does not increase by simple consecutive addition (1, 2, 3, 4, 5, 6, etc.) but by exponential growth or multiplication (1, 2, 4, 8, 16, 32, etc.). (Page 5)[37]**

Does this rule explain the population growth from the distant past to the present time? Does it explain why it took milleniums for mankind to grow to one billion in about 1850, then double to two billion in the 1930's, and then double again to four billion in 1975? Let us see.

At present the population doubles in 35 years, which corresponds to an annual growth of 2 percent.[38] If the population had actually grown exponentially at constant doubling intervals of 35 years, it would have taken less than 1,100 years for it to grow from two individuals to the present 4.8 billion![39] Even if we were to allow for an annual growth rate of only 1 percent, corresponding to a doubling in 69.7 years, an exponential growth would lead to astronomical figures within just a couple of thousand years. As Professor Alfred Sauvy, Europe's great demographer, explains:

> **If for example the population of China, the size of which is estimated to have been 70,000,000 at the time of Christ, since then had increased by 1 percent per year, it would today have reached, not the recently estimated 680,000,000 [over one billion in 1984], but 21 million billions! Spread out all over the globe this population would give about 120 Chinese per square meter.[40]**

---

37 Exponential growth, also described in terms of *geometric* growth, means a doubling of the number at certain intervals. But it is essential that these intervals be constant, otherwise the growth is not exponential. See the discussion by Professor Erland Hofsten in *Demography and Development* (Stockholm, 1977), pp. 15–19.

38 This is the average annual growth for the past 35 years. But the rate of growth is *declining*. In later years it has been 1.8 percent, and according to the latest report it has now shrunk to 1.7 percent. The United Nations estimates that if this trend continues, population will stabilize at around 10 billion late next century.—*New Scientist*, August 9, 1984, p. 12.

39 H. Hyrenius, *Så mycket folk* ["So many People"] (Stockholm, 1970), pp. 9–11.

40 Jan Lenica and Alfred Sauvy, *Population Explosion, Abundance of Famine* (New York, 1962). Quoted from the Swedish edition, *Befolkningsproblem* (Stockholm, 1965), p. 17.

Clearly, exponential growth is not the correct explanation of the population development on earth. For some reason, the doubling intervals in the past were much longer. How much longer was pointed out on page 4 in the *Awake!* of September 8, 1967:

> It took from the first century to the seventeenth century before the population of the world doubled from 250 million to 500 million. Then, in a little over two hundred more years, in the nineteenth century, the population doubled again, reaching about one thousand million (1,000,000,000). But in only a hundred more years, in the twentieth century it once more doubled. And now? At today's rate of growth the population would double in just thirty-five years!

This pattern of tremendously shrinking doubling intervals, from as much as 1,600 years in the past to only 35 years at present, shows that there must have been something in the past that *prevented* an exponential growth, something that has been gradually removed during the past two hundred years. As the English economist Thomas Malthus, who often (but wrongly) is said to have been the originator of the theory of exponential (or geometric) growth, wrote in 1798, **"Population, when unchecked, increases in a geometrical ratio."**[41]

We could well ask, then: Why has the world population *not* grown exponentially during the past centuries? What factor, or which factors, *checked* the population growth in the past? The answer is completely devastating to the theory of the "composite sign" since 1914 or 1948 or to any claims that our century is 'the world's worst' as far as calamitous conditions are concerned.

The reason for the very slow population increase in past ages is precisely because *mankind then suffered much more than today from wars, famines and pestilences*. All population experts (demographers) today agree. These factors caused such high mortality that the population growth was effectively checked.

Often the high mortality even resulted in a *population decline*, for example through pestilence, as was shown earlier. "Until modern times epidemics and famines regularly reduced any population increase," says historian Fernand Braudel.[42] Demographer Alfred Sauvy, talking of the high "mortality factor" in the past, expounds the causes as follows:

41 Thomas Malthus, *Essay on the Principle of Population*, first published anonymously in 1798. Quoted by Hofsten (1977), p. 114.
42 Fernand Braudel, *Civilization & Capitalism 15th–18th Century: The Structures of Everyday Life* (London, 1981), p. 35.

This mortality factor was active in the past through three extraordinarily deadly fatal sisters: Famine, Disease and War. Due to its immediate effects Famine certainly occupied the first place in this terrifying trinity, closely followed by its near relative Disease.[43]

This mortality factor has been substantially reduced in recent times:

Of the three demographic fatal sisters only war has continued working unabatedly. We refer here to war in the strict sense of the word, because other forms of violence resulting from it have been considerably reduced. . . . Diseases still exist, but epidemics of the kind that earlier would decimate whole nations do not rage any longer. Famine and malnutrition still exist but acute and hopeless starvation has been eliminated, mainly owing to better means of transport.[44]

These are facts firmly established today, known not only among experts but found even within school textbooks. As an example, the following statement concludes a discussion of the population explosion in a civics textbook widely used in Swedish senior high schools:

In conclusion it can be said that we have arrived at a development that is unique to mankind. For thousands of years famine, disease and war have effectively put a check on all tendencies towards an accelerated population growth. But after the breakthrough of technics and medicine the earlier balance between the constructive and destructive forces of life has been upset, resulting in the population explosion.[45]

Consequently wars, and especially famines and devastating pestilences played *a decisive role* in checking earth's population in the past. Medical and technical advancements have combined to stem the ravagings of pestilences, to increase the food supply and improve the means of transporting it. The result has been a sharp decline of mortality, and this is particularly true of child mortality. This is the real cause of the population explosion.[46]

---

43 Lenica & Sauvy (1965), p. 12.
44 Lenica & Sauvy, pp. 20, 26.
45 Björkblom, Altersten, Hanselid & Liljequist, *Världen, Sverige och vi* (Uppsala, 1975), p. 31.
46 The Watch Tower Society is not totally unaware of these connections. The *Awake!* of August 8, 1983, for instance, began an article on the subject by stating that the present population explosion "is due in part to a worldwide decline in the death rate as a result of improved medical care and economic and social conditions," but then it quickly proceeded to an elaboration on the exponential growth as the cause. A much earlier article published in the *Awake!* of September 8, 1967, was more straight to the point by stating that "advances in disease control have drastically lowered the death rate in most countries," and that "mass control of infectious disease has produced a spectacular reduction in the death

WORLD POPULATION 3000 B.C.—A.D. 1985

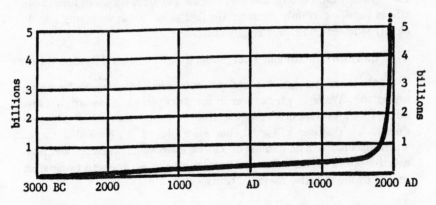

The common population curve

Let us take a closer look at the population curve, as it is commonly represented in various publications (see illustration above).

As we shall see presently, this idealized curve does not present the whole picture. To arrive at a more accurate picture, we must first take into account the real causes of the population explosion in our century. The long, almost horizontal line in the chart bears witness to the long ages when devastating famines, pestilences and wars caused the population to grow very slowly. The sharply rising curve to the right points to an enormous reduction of the effect of the first two of these scourges in recent times.[47] The curve in the chart is simply rather schematized and does not convey the whole truth about this phenomenal growth.

As Professor Erland Hofsten points out:

> . . . the usual picture of the population development is wrong. According to it earth's population has increased at a regular pace, slowly at first and then at an ever-increasing rate, until we have got what is now popularly called 'the population explosion.' But things have not come about

---

rate among infants and children." (Pages 4 and 5) The disastrous consequences of this "mass control of infectious disease" for the "composite sign" idea was, of course, not pointed out by the Watch Tower Society.

47 E. P. Prentice, concentrating on the impact of hunger on the human race, says that "the flat horizon represents the long level of want which man has known so well during many ages." Then, "about 1850, abundance came, and it is abundance which makes the steeple rise so sharply from a horizon which up to that time had suggested no possibility of such a change."—*Progress: An Episode in the History of Hunger?* (New York, 1950), pp. xx, xxi.

quite that simply. To all appearances there have been many periods when population has been stationary or even been declining, alternating with periods of rapid growth.[48]

Thus the population of China was nearly the same in A.D. 1500 as back at the time of Christ. The population of the Indian peninsula had *decreased* from 46 million at the time of Christ to 40 million in A.D. 1000. And the population of Southwest Asia had decreased from 47 million at the time of Christ to 38 million in A.D. 1900.[49]

According to French demographer Jean-Noel Biraben the total population on earth was about the same in A.D. 1000 as at the time of Christ, having gone up and down during those centuries due to devastating famines, pestilences and wars.[50] This non-increase testifies to the death of literally *thousands of millions* of people, including children and infants, in these calamities during those centuries. From the fifteenth to the nineteenth century famines, civil wars, epidemics and infanticide kept the Japanese population practically static for four centuries.[51] Many other examples could be given. The British demographer T. H. Hollingsworth states that "population must have gone down as often (or very nearly as often), and as much, as it went up."[52]

Modern demographers, therefore, present population curves that reflect these fluctuations. The example presented in the illustration is based upon a curve drawn up by Biraben, showing the changes in world population from around 400 B.C. to 1985.[53] It shows the population to have been the same in 1000 A.D. as at the time of Christ,

---

48 Erland Hofsten, *Befolkningslära* (Lund, 1982), p. 14.
49 These are figures of the French demographer Jean-Noel Biraben as quoted by Hofsten. (*Befolkningslära*, p. 17.)
50 Hofsten, *Befolkningslära*, p. 15.
51 Josué de Castro, *Geography of Hunger* (London, 1952), pp. 162, 163. *Infanticide*, "the wilful destruction of newborn babes through exposure, starvation, strangulation, smothering, poisoning, or through the use of some lethal weapon," was the principal means of birth control before the use of contraceptives and legalized abortions became widespread. Before the twentieth century infanticide was practiced on a large scale, not only in Japan and China, but all over the world, including Europe, claiming many millions of lives annually. Today the method has been replaced by abortions, which, although found unacceptable by many, including the authors, from a Christian point of view, yet clearly represent a development in a more humane direction. See William L. Langer, "Infanticide: A Historical Survey," *History of Childhood Quarterly,* Winter 1974, Vol. 1, No. 3, pp. 353–365; also Ping-ti Ho, *Studies on the Population of China, 1368–1953* (Cambridge, Massachusetts, 1959), pp. 58–61. (Infanticide still occurs in some areas in Africa and South America. See Barbara Burke, "Infanticide," *Science* magazine, May 1984, pp. 26–31.)
52 T. H. Hollingsworth, *Historical Demography* (London and Southampton, 1969), p. 331.
53 Hofsten, *Befolkningslära*, p. 15.

WORLD POPULATION 3000 B.C.—A.D. 1985

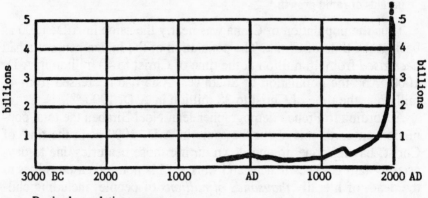

Revised population curve

as well as the impact of the Black Death upon world population from 1348 A.D. to about 1550.

When we turn our attention to curves drawn up for individual countries, the impression is even more telling. The curve shown in the next illustration, for example, relates to Egypt, and is based upon the figures and curve drawn up by Hollingsworth.[54] The dramatic changes between increases and decreases are in no way unique. Curves for many other countries show similar oscillations. The curve for Egypt shows very sharp population decreases due to wars and pestilences, but it should be remembered that wars and pestilences usually were accompanied by severe famines that contributed greatly to these decreases.

The modern "population explosion," then, through contrast reveals a terrible story about man's past, a story of famines, plagues and other calamities on a scale that—if seen as a whole—has nothing corresponding to it in modern times. Its testimony is there for all to see, and it is impossible to refute. And, very significantly, it deals a deathblow to the idea that we have seen a "composite sign" that could serve as an infallible indicator of Christ's *parousia* since 1914, or the start of some special 40-year time period since 1948, or any other similar claims.

54 Hollingsworth, p. 311. The curve has been redrawn and updated by a scholarly friend of ours, Fred Sørensen, who has also contributed much to other parts of this work.

POPULATION IN EGYPT, 664 B.C.—A.D. 1985

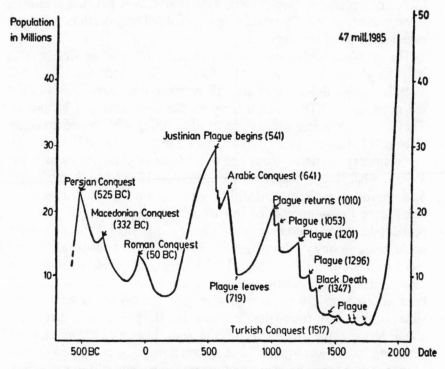

Population curve for Egypt, 664 B.C. to 1985 A.D. (Based on the information and curve drawn up by T. H. Hollingsworth in *Historical Demography*, London and Southampton, 1969, page 331.)

Possibilities versus realities

It goes without saying that the world picture is always subject to change, sometimes very sudden change. One can easily draw up an imaginary scenario of what *could* happen during the remaining years of this waning twentieth century. It is not difficult to find the factors upon which to build such a suppositional situation. The growing world population *could* lead to famines of unprecedented size and mortality. Since seismologists have for some time predicted that both Japan and California are due for some major earthquakes, one *could* envision such occurring and, if hitting very densely populated areas such as Tokyo, San Francisco and Los Angeles, bringing death to tens of thousands. In times of famine and other great catastrophes, epidemics can spread far more rapidly. So one *could* add such in uncontrollable proportions to the foreboding vision.[55] And, last but by no means least, the specter of nuclear war could be drawn into the scenario, since, were it to occur it *could* unquestionably bring death to millions, even hundreds of millions.

The problem with using such a scenario of horrible disasters as basis for claims about our century and specific periods since 1914 and 1948 is that all these things are still no more than possibilities. They are not realities. They *could* happen, but they have *not* happened. They cannot therefore serve as proof of anything with respect to either 1914 or 1948 or any other period thus far in our century. Even if such an imaginary scenario were actually to develop in, let us say, the 1990's, what would that prove about 1914 or 1948? The Watch Tower Society, for example, would still have to explain why the first seventy years since 1914—the period in which the "composite sign" was supposed to have appeared as proof of Christ's "invisible presence"—saw *no increase* in any of the respective features of that supposed "sign." Hal Lindsey's predictions regarding a forty-year period beginning in 1948 with the establishment of the Jewish state in Israel, would still be a jigsaw puzzle without any other pieces previous to such a possible, conjectured, future development. Dr. Billy Graham's statements about hearing the hoofbeats of the four horsemen "approaching, sounding louder and louder," would then have to be taken as evidence of prophetic hearing, a hearing of magnified sounds still in the future, since to the present day the facts show that none of the symbolic "four horsemen" are in greater evidence in our time than they were in past centuries.

The mere fact that something *could* happen does not necessarily mean that it will happen. Even before the development of the atomic bomb, nations had developed poison gases and bacteriological warfare with frightening potential. Nevertheless, while poison gas was used with horrible consequences in World War I, since then, even during the fiercely fought World War II, the nations have refrained from any known use of poison gas and have never resorted to the deployment of their fearsome weapons of deadly bacteriological warfare. Worth remembering also is that the last time an atomic weapon was used against humans was in 1945, now four decades ago. Predictions about

---

55 In an attempt to emphasize pestilence or disease as a noteworthy feature today, *The Watchtower* of April 15, 1984, quoted Dr. William Foege of Atlanta's Centers for Disease Control as saying: "I fully anticipate that possibly in our lifetime we will see another flu strain that is as deadly as 1918." (P. 6)

the future based on human reasoning and assumption remain a guessing game, unrelated to the actual outworking of divine prophecy.

Simply put, and setting aside conjecture and imagined circumstances, the reality is that our generation is no more plagued by famine, pestilence, earthquakes, war, crime or fear than other generations in the past, and in certain respects it is less so.

CHAPTER 8

"What Will Be the Sign of Your Coming?"

WHEN SPEAKING of a "sign of the last days," people commonly understand "the last days" to mean a period of time which immediately precedes the coming of Jesus Christ to carry out divine judgment. The belief is that such a distinctive period is an indicator signaling the nearness of that coming and the execution of judgment it brings. The Scriptures do, of course, speak of the "last days." But do they support the concept described? Is there to be such an indicator, a means whereby people can know beforehand that that day is about to break upon them?

Down through the ages, people in one generation after another have found reason to identify their time as "the last days." Their predictions and expectations have, in every case, ultimately led to failure with accompanying disillusionment. Quite evidently there has been a crucial mistake underlying all these failed expectations and erroneous claims.

The evidence is that they have understood and applied Jesus' words concerning wars, famines, pestilence, earthquakes and similar features, in a way exactly opposite to that in which they were directed.

In the first chapter of the present work it was pointed out that discerning Bible commentators do not understand the "woes" enumerated by Jesus in the beginning of his discourse to mean the *sign* asked for by the disciples. Quite to the contrary, Jesus warned his followers against being *misled* by such disasters. The subsequent chapters have presented evidence that fully confirms this conclusion. Because *every* century has had its share of wars, famines, pestilences, earthquakes, and so on—often to a greater extent than our own century—it would be very confusing to point to such things as the sign of Christ's *parousía*. As Roman Catholic scholar M. Brunec pertinently remarks:

"To set up signs of this type plainly amounts to little else than to create a psychological state of perpetual eschatological delirium."[1]

Jesus, before he answered the questions put to him, actually started with an enumeration of things that he knew might *mislead* his followers. The very first words of his reply indicate this. He began with this warning:

> Take heed that no one leads you astray.—Matthew 24:4, RSV.

By what means might they be led astray as to claims regarding his coming? He listed a number of things, beginning with false leaders, false Messiahs:

> For many will come in my name, saying, 'I am the Christ,' and they will lead many astray.—Matthew 24:5, RSV.

Christ's *parousía* or coming, "with power and great glory" and accompanied by "all the angels," will not be like that of a human being who appears with the claim of being God's anointed one, perhaps winning some followers. While there is no record of persons *specifically* taking to themselves the title of Christ or Messiah (both terms meaning Anointed One) between the time of Jesus' death and the destruction of Jerusalem, there were doubtless those who, as Theudas and Judas the Galilean had done, presented themselves as leaders and, at least by implication, as anointed by God for the task. (Acts 5:35–37; compare Acts 21:38.) Subsequent history knows more than 50 false Messiahs among the Jews alone, from Bar Kochba in the second century to Sabbatai Zebhi in the seventeenth, and numerous false Christs have likewise appeared among Christians.[2]

In addition to false Christs, according to the parallel text in Luke chapter twenty-one, verse 8, Jesus warned of many who would come and proclaim that "The time is at hand." This again indicates that Jesus viewed his coming as something *distant* in time, being preceded by *many false proclamations of its nearness.*

---

1 Quoted from a translation of Brunec's article on Matthew 24, Mark 13, Luke 17 and Luke 21, published in Latin in successive fascicles of Volumes 30 (1952) and 31 (1953) of the periodical *Verbum Domini,* published in Rome.

2 Professor J. A. Alexander, *The Gospel According to Mark,* 1858, page 348. (Reprinted in 1980 by Baker Book House, Grand Rapids, Michigan.) A number of false prophets, false teachers and fanatical imposters are known from the period up to A.D. 70, such as Simon Magus, Elymas, Theudas, Judas the Gaudonite, Dositheus, Menander and Cerinthus. The Jewish historian Josephus (*Ant.* XX,viii,5,6) also says that Judea, during the reign of emperor Nero, "was filled with robbers and imposters, who deluded the multitude."

This does not mean, of course, that it would be wrong for a Christian to live in expectation of Christ's coming, hoping it to be near, and conducting him/herself accordingly. On the contrary, true Christians are to be eagerly waiting for Christ's return from heaven even "waiting for and hastening [footnote: earnestly desiring] the coming of the day of God." (Philippians 3:20; 2 Peter 3:12, RSV) But this is not the same as relying on chronological calculations or date-settings, or on interpretations of the signs of the time, and hence pretending to *know* and announcing to others that "the time is at hand." Later on during his discourse, Jesus repeatedly and emphatically ruled out the possibility of such advance knowledge by stating that the "hour," the "day," and the "time" of his coming would be completely unknown, *even to his own followers:*

> So you also must be ready, because the Son of Man will come at an hour when you do not expect him.—Matthew 24:44, NIV.
> Therefore keep watch, because you do not know on what day your Lord will come.—Matthew 24:42, NIV.
> Be on guard! Be alert! You do not know when that time will come.—Mark 13:33, NIV.
> So you also must keep watch because you do not know when the owner of the house will come back—whether in the evening, or at midnight, or when the rooster crows, or at dawn.—Mark 13:35, NIV.

In fact, the central theme of the whole section from Matthew chapter twenty-four, verse 35, to chapter twenty-five, verse 13, is *the necessity of preparedness because of the suddenness and unexpectedness of Christ's coming and the impossibility of knowing anything about the time of it in advance!*[3]

---

3 In an effort to soften this plain teaching of Jesus, the Watch Tower Society has appealed to the statement in Amos 3:7: "The Sovereign Lord Jehovah will not do a thing unless he has revealed his confidential matter to his servants the prophets." (NW) See the comments on this text in *The Watchtower*, April 1, 1984, page 7, and especially March 15, 1974, page 163. However, Amos 3:7 does not imply that Jehovah will reveal "the times or seasons" of the kingdom and the *parousía* to his servants. Acts 1:7 rules that such knowledge "does not belong" to them. But he has revealed his "confidential matter," that is, his "plan" (Amos 3:7, NIV, NAB) or "purpose" (AT) to them. He tells them *what* he is going to do, not necessarily *when* he is going to do it.

   Another text that has caused some to conclude that Jesus wanted to give some indication about the time of his *parousía* is Matthew 24:34: "Truly I say to you, this generation (Greek, *geneá*) will not pass away until all these things take place." However, it seems strange first to state that the coming would take place within a certain generation, and immediately afterwards add that the time of the coming is *totally unknown, even to the Son of man himself*. (Compare Mark 13:32) As *geneá* does not only mean "generation,"

Farther along in his reply to his disciples Jesus did, in fact, refer to a "sign" of his coming. Was it, however, a sign that would tell watchful Christians that "the time is at hand," offering some period of opportunity to prepare themselves for that coming? No, obviously not. In his one and only specific reference to a "sign," Jesus described certain heavenly phenomena and then said:

> **At that time the sign of the Son of Man will appear in the sky, and all the nations [literally, "tribes"] of the earth will mourn. They will see the Son of Man coming on the clouds of the sky, with power and great glory.—** Matthew 24:30, NIV.

By these words he indicates that this sign will be so closely followed by the coming itself that it will then be too late for starting any further preparations. This is also the lesson of the parable of the ten virgins. (Matthew 25:1–13) A watchful Christian, therefore, is one who always is prepared, whenever his Lord may come. In none of the words of Jesus or his apostles are we encouraged to be watchful by means of chronological speculation or by trying to place special interpretations on world events. Rather, it is by living life in such a way that we will be found approved by our Master on his arrival. For that day arrives suddenly, unexpectedly, like the springing shut of a trap. —Luke 21:34–36; Romans 13:12, 13; 1 Thessalonians 3:12, 13.

It should be noted, too, that the true sign described by Jesus himself immediately makes it plain to all that the coming is right upon them. There will be no need for any "experts" on the "signs of the time" to explain to others what that sign means. As Jesus said when comparing that sign with the leaves on the fig-tree and on other trees: **"As soon as they put forth leaves, you see it and <u>know for yourselves</u> that summer is now near."** (Luke 21:30, NASB) Nobody needs some ex-

---

but also "race," and even "age" (see "geneá" in TDNT, Vol I), the problem would dissolve if it is supposed that Jesus referred to the *Jewish race,* or perhaps the *present age:* "This Jewish race (or, this age) will not pass away until all these things take place." On the other hand, many scholars point to the similarity of the statement to Matthew 23:36, where the contemporary Jewish *generation* that would see the destruction of the temple is clearly in view. They have therefore taken Jesus' statement at Matthew 24:34 as a reference back to Matthew 24:3, to answer the disciples' question, "When will <u>these things</u> (the destruction of the temple just spoken of) be?" See the excellent discussion along these lines by Dr. F. F. Bruce in *The Hard Sayings of Jesus,* Downers Grove, Illinois, 1983, pp. 225–230. Another point to be noted is that the word "this" (*haútē*) in "this generation" shows that Jesus spoke of the *geneá contemporary with himself,* as *haútē* always refers to something *close* or *present.* He cannot have meant a generation that would appear on the scene about 1900 years later, as the Society holds. He spoke of the *contemporary geneá,* so he was referring either to the "generation" (or, possibly, the "race" or the "age") *then existent.*

pert to tell him or her that the budding leaves indicate that the season of warmth is at hand.[4] Similarly, the meaning of the sign that actually and genuinely precedes Christ's coming will be obvious to all, with no need of further explanations.

This helps us understand why Jesus warned of people who would come, pretending to *know*—perhaps on the basis of some chronological formula or because they think themselves able to interpret current "signs of the time"—and assuredly making the exciting announcement that "The time is at hand!" (Luke 21:8) In spite of Jesus' warnings, and in fulfillment of his prediction, there has hardly been a single period in Christian history that has not seen the appearance of groups or individuals who claimed to *know,* from their chronological calculations or their interpretations of the "signs of the time," that "the time is at hand," often even predicting the exact year of Christ's coming, the expiration of the "Gentile times," the start of the millenium or other end-time events. The complete failure of the predictions of *all* these countless "prophets" and prophetic movements throughout the centuries proves that the advice Jesus added to his warning was a most appropriate one: "DO NOT GO AFTER THEM!" (Luke 21:8) They have all proved to be misleading guides, and following after them has always ended up in disappointment.[5]

The ultimate effect of their repetitious, unfounded predictions, is harmful. All too often it causes people to begin to doubt the reliability of God's Word. Or the claim of being "in the know" can cause a false sense of security, even of smug confidence, as of one who feels he or she is well informed as to just what to expect. This can contribute toward an exclusivistic attitude toward others, those who are "in the dark"; it can serve as a breeding ground for fanaticism. Persons putting trust in such baseless predictions may make unwise decisions in life, decisions affecting health, marriage, childbearing, home, education, employment and security. They may recover in time so that the scar of those unwise decisions heals; or they may not—and thus find themselves living the rest of their life unnecessarily burdened by the

---

4 One might think that Jesus should have referred to the "spring" rather than to the "summer" in this text. However, the Jews in Palestine spoke only of two seasons, summer and winter, essentially a warm, and mainly dry, season and a cold, rainy season. References to "the spring rains" and the "the autumn rains" in such texts as Deuteronomy 11:14 in the Hebrew read literally, "the early rains" and "the late rains." So the appearance of leaves on trees was a sure, and easily read, sign that the warm season was about to replace the cold, rainy season.

5 *Awake!* October 8, 1968, admitted on page 23 that groups "announcing a specific date" in times past "were guilty of false prophesying" as the scheduled end "did not come."

now unchangeable results of imprudent decisions based on false claims. Jesus' warning, "Do not go after them," is sound advice.[6]

In some cases, the failure to recognize the unpredictableness and instantaneousness of the time of the Master's return produces an outlook that allows persons, religious persons not excepted, to conduct themselves in merciless ways toward others, ways that indicate they feel a certain sense of impunity as regards a swift day of divine judgment. They are thus not unlike the slave whose master did not come according to the schedule he had calculated. In that parable it is, notably, only the wicked slave who seems to have some ideas worked out as to a certain time for his master's return. Speaking with his mouth to others he may have said otherwise, but "to himself," in his heart, he viewed his master's return as "delayed." By contrast, nothing is said of the faithful slave's making any pretense of knowing or attempting to figure out whether that arrival was near or far—he simply continued faithfully doing his master's will and dealing justly with his fellow slaves, believing his Lord would in due time return. (Matthew 24:48–50; compare 1 Peter 4:7–10.) He was not 'lording it over others,' but serving their needs as a co-laborer, even as the apostle expressed his own attitude:

> **We are not dictators over your faith, but are fellow workers with you for your happiness; in the faith you are steady enough.**—2 Corinthians 1:24, JB.

Other "non-signs" of which to be aware

There is no reason to limit Jesus' introductory warning against being misled solely to false Christs and false prophets. In Matthew chapter

---

6 *The Watchtower* of December 15, 1984, explained Christian watchfulness to mean paying attention to two things, namely, 1) "the time element" and, 2) "the many-featured sign." But this movement's record of over 100 years of failed dates and failed predictions shows that this cannot have been the kind of watchfulness recommended by Jesus. Yet, instead of deploring and deprecating this kind of prophesying and date-setting, the Watch Tower Society, in the same issue, attempts to elevate it to a Christian virtue by saying: "True, some expectations that appeared to be backed up by Bible chronology did not materialize at the anticipated time. But is it not far preferable to make some mistakes because of overeagerness to see God's purpose accomplished than to be spiritually asleep as to the fulfillment of Bible prophecy?" (Pp. 15, 18) However, Jesus warned of BOTH "spiritual drowsiness" and presumptuous prophesying. *Both were and are wrong.* In their place Jesus urged a watchfulness that governs one's way of life *at all times*, as the time of his *parousía* would not be possible to identify in advance.

twenty-four, verse 6, he went on to other things that he knew might easily lead his followers to jump to false conclusions. He said:

You will hear of wars and rumours of wars; do not be alarmed, for this is something that must happen, but the end [*télos*] will not be yet.—*The Jerusalem Bible.*

The disciples had asked for the sign of the *conclusion* (Greek, *suntéleia*) *of the age.* Jesus says that "wars and rumours of wars" would be no indication of the end. Some, attempting to avoid this plain statement, claim that the "end" (*télos*) of the age is not the same as the "conclusion" (*suntéleia*) of the age. Thus, while agreeing that *télos* here refers to Christ's intervention at the final judgment, the Watch Tower Society holds that *suntéleia* refers to a longer period, a period that currently runs more than seventy years in length, having begun in 1914.

This distinction, though, is wholly artificial. *Suntéleia* and *télos* are often used interchangeably. In the LXX (Septuagint Version), which was contemporaneous with Jesus' time, both words sometimes translate the same Hebrew word for "end," *qēts*.[7] It must be stressed, too, that Jesus in his answer does not use *suntéleia* at all, using, evidently, *télos* as a synonym instead. As Dr. Brunec explains in the article quoted previously (see footnote 1), "the term *télos* with the article in this place can have no other meaning than *hē suntéleia tou aiōnos* ['the conclusion of the age'] or the *parousía*. The term *télos* is in fact a synonym for the word *suntéleia*."[8]

Jesus' disciples were not to be 'alarmed' on hearing of wars. The 'alarm' here evidently does not refer to a natural concern over the dangers of military combat. The word used in Matthew's account is

---

7 Compare, for instance, 2 Samuel 15:7 and 2 Kings 8:3 (*qēts = télos*) with Daniel 12:4, 13 (*qēts = suntéleia*). In the last verse LXX (the Septuagint Version) twice translates *qēts* by *suntéleia:* "But go thou thy way till the end (*suntéleia*) be; for thou shalt rest, and shalt stand in thy lot, at the end (*suntéleia*) of the days."

8 That *suntéleia* does not denote a long period of "last days," as the Watch Tower Society claims, is also proved by the way the word is used at Matthew 28:20. Jesus there promised to assist his disciples "until the conclusion (*suntéleia*) of the system of things." (NW) If the "conclusion" began in 1914, then Christ's help in Kingdom preaching would have been "until" that date and would then have reached its terminus, ending at that time. That this "conclusion" instead refers to the very end and not to a lifetime starting in 1914 and running decades thereafter is so obvious that *The Watchtower* of May 1, 1977, had to admit: "Since the foretold end has not yet come, the command to make disciples continues in force." (P. 276) In this way the "conclusion of the system of things" at Matthew 28:20 closely parallels "the end" (*télos*) at Matthew 24:14!

the same Greek word employed by Paul when, in writing to the Thessalonians he urged them:

> **Do not become easily unsettled or alarmed [excited, RSV; wrought up, AT] by some prophecy, report or letter supposed to have come from us, saying that the day of the Lord has already come. Don't let anyone deceive you in any way.**—2 Thessalonians 2:2, 3, NIV.

Rather than arising from a natural fear that warfare inspires, the alarm against which Jesus cautioned is the excitement and agitating stimulus coming from a false conclusion that such warfare constitutes a "sign" of the end.

Explaining why "wars and rumours of wars" should not be understood as signs of the end, Jesus went on to say:

> **For nation will rise against nation, and kingdom against kingdom; and there shall be famines and earthquakes in various places.**—Matthew 24:7, RSV.

Read in connection with the preceding verse (verse 6), the sense of this explanation can only be: "Since wars, famines, earthquakes and other troubles will regularly characterize man's history in the future (as they have in the past), such things should not be understood as signs of my coming and of the end of the age." As pointed out earlier, this is how leading Bible commentators usually understand Jesus' words:

Professor Carl F. Keil:

> **Jesus' answer starts from the second question, concerning the signs that might have reference to the <u>parusia, to warn the disciples not to be mislead by such events</u>.** (*Commentar über das Evangelium des Matthäus,* Leipzig 1877, page 458.)

Dr. B. C. Butler:

> **Matthew xxiv. 5–14 gives a straightforward anticipation of the whole of future history (in reference to the question about the consummation of the age), warning the disciples that secular catastrophes must not be taken as signs of the imminent end of history.** (*The Originality of St. Matthew,* 1951, page 80.)

It is of great interest to note that this is exactly the way the first president of the Watch Tower Society, Charles Taze Russell, understood Matthew 24:6–8. In his *Studies in the Scriptures* (Vol. 4, 1916 edition, page 566) Russell said:

Thus briefly did our Lord summarize secular history and teach the disciples not to expect very soon his second coming and glorious kingdom. And how aptly: surely the world's history is just this, an account of wars, intrigues, famines and pestilences—little else.

It is to be regretted that the Watch Tower Society did not hold to this explanation given by its first president, but—evidently under the agitating influence of World War I and the Spanish flu—abandoned it in 1920, thus allowing themselves to be misled in the very way Jesus had warned against in the introduction to his discourse.[9]

From Seventh Day Adventist sources, one obtains two quite different views. As seen by quotations from his book *Good-bye, Planet Earth*, Adventist Robert Pierson presents Jesus' statements regarding war, famine, and earthquakes as signs designed to indicate that his coming is at hand, signs so clearly evident today that those doubting this are to be listed among the scoffers described by the apostle Peter. In support of his presentation, he quotes Ellen G. White (whose position among Adventists compares with that of Charles Taze Russell among Watch Tower adherents), speaking of her as "One writer whom thousands believe was inspired." In part, he quotes her as writing:

> We are living in the time of the end. The fast-fulfilling signs of the times declare that the coming of Christ is near at hand. . . . The calamities by land and sea, the unsettled state of society, the alarms of war, are portentous. They forecast aproaching events of the greatest magnitude. . . .
>
> The condition of things in the world shows that troublous times are right upon us. The daily papers of full of indications of a terrible conflict in the near future. Bold robberies are of frequent occurrence. Strikes are common. Thefts and murders are committed on every hand.[10]

In strong contrast to the view advanced in *Good-bye, Planet Earth*, prominent Adventist writer C. Mervyn Maxwell quotes Jesus' words at Matthew chapter twenty-four, verses 6 to 8, and states that Christ was there warning his disciples not to be "confused by any clutter of non-signs." Under the subheading *"Signs that aren't signs,"* he writes:

> Christ's point was that disasters and defeats and wars and famines are not 'signs' of the approaching end, either of Jerusalem or of the world. For our sin-drenched planet, sad to say, such sorrows are business as usual.[11]

9 See *Millions Now Living Will Never Die*, 1920, pp. 17–19.
10 Ellen G. White, *Testimonies*, Vol. 9, p. 11. Quoted in *Good-bye, Planet Earth*, p. 50.
11 C. Mervyn Maxwell, *God Cares*, 1985, Vol. 2, pp. 20, 21.

Since Maxwell wrote these words in 1985, they may represent a more current Adventist position than that of Pierson who wrote in 1976. Otherwise Adventists are faced with two diametrically opposed presentations.

There may be a special reason why Jesus warned his followers against looking upon wars, famines, earthquakes, pestilences, and so forth, as signs of the imminence of his *parousía*. In Jewish apocalyptic writings of that time these identical things were often mentioned as portents of Messiah's advent and the near approach of the end of that age.[12] They said that preceding Messiah's glorious appearance and his leading Israel to freedom, there would be great calamities, which they called "the woes of the Messiah."

Illustrating these Jewish apocalyptic views are the following passages from what is called the "Syriac Apocalypse of Baruch." Believed to be a compilation of writings edited and combined together by orthodox Jews in the latter half of the first century, its contents "furnish records of the Jewish doctrines and beliefs of that period." Consider their predictions about tribulations that would constitute a "sign" of the appearance of Messiah's reign on earth:

> **Thou shalt be preserved till that time till that sign which the Most High will work for the inhabitants of the earth in the end of the days. This therefore shall be the sign. When a stupor shall seize the inhabitants of the earth, and they shall fall into many tribulations, and again when they shall fall into great torments.**
>
> **In the first part there shall be the beginning of commotions. And in the second part (there shall be) slayings of the great ones. And in the third part the fall of many by death. And in the fourth part the sending of the sword. And in the fifth part famine and the withholding of rain. And in the sixth part earthquakes and terrors . . .**
>
> **And He answered and said unto me: 'Whatever will then befall (will befall) the whole earth; therefore all who live will experience (them). For at that time I will protect only those who are found in those self-same days in this land [Palestine]. And it shall come to pass when all is accomplished that was to come in those parts that the Messiah shall then begin to be revealed.[13]**

---

12 Some examples are: 1 Enoch 80:2–8; 99:4–8; Jubilees 23:13–25; Assumption of Moses 8:1 and 10:5. See further, D. S. Russell, *The Method & Message of Jewish Apocalyptic,* London, 1964, pp. 271–276.

13 2 Baruch 25:1–4; 27:2–8; 29:1–4.

The disciples therefore may have had such traditional views and predicted calamities in mind when they inquired about a "sign." Obviously, Jesus did not share the views of these Jewish apocalyptic writers. Instead of being signs of the end or conclusion of the age, he explained these woes to be only a *beginning of the troubles* that were to come:

> But all these things are merely the beginning of birth pangs.—Matthew 24:8, NASB.

The "birth pangs" (Greek, *ōdínes*) have sometimes been taken as another reference to the views of contemporary Jewish rabbis and apocalyptic writers, who sometimes may have spoken of the woes they thought would precede the coming of the Messiah as "the birth pangs of the Messiah," out of which the new Messianic age was to be born. The Greek word *odín*, however, did not refer exclusively to *birth*-pangs. It was often used metaphorically of "any travail, anguish" (Liddell & Scott), without the sense of a birth of one kind or another implied. Thus Acts chapter two, verse 24 speaks of the "agony (*ōdínes*) of death" that Christ experienced.[14]

Jesus' use of the *plural* form ("birth pangs") shows that he knew the period up to his coming and the end of the age would be filled with *many* troubles, of which those just mentioned—wars, famines, pestilences and earthquakes—were merely a *beginning*.[15] By stating this he indicated that the future held many other and even worse evils in store. Thus Dr. Brunec concludes:

> Hence, wars and seditions and pestilences and famines and earthquakes are not presented as signs of the end or of the *parusia*, but as a certain small beginning and minimal part of a long series of particular sorrows.[16]

14 In the Old Testament, too, "birth-pangs" are often used metaphorically of any kinds of anguish and tribulations, for instance at Exodus 15:14; Psalm 48:6; 73:4; Isaiah 26:17; Jeremiah 13:21; 22:23; 49:24; Hosea 13:13 and Micah 4:9, 10.
15 It is quite possible that Jesus' use of the term "birth pangs" did not reflect the Rabbinic usage at all. The earliest known Rabbinic use of the expression is that of Rabbi Elieser (c. A.D. 90). Besides, the Jewish rabbis always spoke of the "birth pang" of Messiah *in the singular*, whereas Jesus used the plural. See the comment on Matthew 24:8 in H. L. Strack and P. Billerbeck, *Kommentar zum Neuen Testament aus Talmud und Midrasch*, Vol. I, Munich 1922–28.
16 Dr. David Hill's comment upon Matthew 24:6–8 excellently sums up the discussion above: "Wars, rumours of wars, and accompanying disasters were regarded as signs of the approaching end in Jewish apocalyptic. In order to curb excited anticipations, Matthew makes two important points: first, these disquieting events must happen according to the

Corroborating this understanding, Jesus went on to describe additional evils that would come and have direct and exclusive bearing upon the disciples themselves.

Tribulations upon the disciples

Having given a general survey of calamities which should not be understood as signs of the conclusion of the age, but which were to mark the whole future history of the world in general, Jesus next turns to troubles that his own followers in particular would have to meet and endure in the future:

> Then they will deliver you to tribulation, and will kill you, and you will be hated by all nations on account of My name. And at that time many will fall away and will deliver up one another and hate one another. And many false prophets will arise, and will mislead many. And because lawlessness is increased, most people's love will grow cold. But the one that endures to the end, he shall be saved.—Matthew 24:9–13, NASB.

The word "tribulation" in this section translates the Greek word *thlīpsis*. This is the same word used for the "great tribulation" in verse 21, where it designates the affliction brought upon the Jewish nation in A.D. 66–70. The Greek term has the sense of "distress," "trouble," even "persecution," and is often used in the NT to denote the sufferings endured by Christians. The apostle John, for instance, writes of himself as "partaker in the tribulation [*thlīpsis*] and kingdom and perserverance which are in Jesus." (Revelation 1:9) The apostle Paul, in 2 Thessalonians chapter one, verses 4 to 10, shows that Christians would have to endure such tribulations or sufferings right up to the revelation of their Lord Jesus. At that time God will "repay with affliction [*thlīpsis*] those who afflict you, and . . . give relief to you who are afflicted and to us as well when the Lord shall be revealed from heaven with His mighty angels in flaming fire." Thus the word *thlīpsis* could be used **1)** of the "great tribulation" that was brought upon the

---

purpose of God (cf. Dan. 2:28) and, since history is under the control of God, believers can and should remain calm; and, secondly, these events will be only the *beginning of the sufferings,* lit. "birth pangs," almost a technical term for the tribulations leading up to the end of the age, which are to be endured by the community of the elect. The disasters experienced are but a prelude, and feverish apocalypticism is out of place." (*The Gospel of Matthew,* Eerdmans, 1981). As to the expression "birth pang," the apostle Paul, too, uses it as a symbol in his reference to "the day of the Lord" at 1 Thessalonians 5:3. But it should be observed that he equates this "birth pang" (in the singular!) with *the sudden destruction itself,* not with any "signs" preceding it.

Jewish nation in the years 66–70 A.D., 2) of the sufferings and persecutions Christ's followers have to endure in this world up to the coming of Christ, and 3) of the destruction brought upon the enemies of God's people at Christ's coming.—2 Thessalonians 1:7–9.[17]

Christ's followers were to be hated, Jesus said, not only by "all the nations," but also by some who claimed to be their own fellow-believers. This especially came true in later centuries after the Church became organized into a hierarchical system governed by a central religious body that laid claim to divinely appointed authority. In later centuries dissenting Christians, such as the Waldenses and Wycliffites, were persecuted as apostates, defamed, excommunicated or banned and even killed by their own alleged Christian brothers. Why? Because they believed that "the Bible is the only source of religious truth" and that, therefore, "ecclesiastical ministries or hierarchies were to be tested against the word of God."[18] Although the Roman Catholic Church has long since changed its policy towards such dissenters, many other religious organizations have appeared that have closely followed the same pattern in dealing with dissenters within their own ranks.

"The Good News must first be proclaimed to all the nations"

In addition to hatred and persecution of this kind, Jesus pointed to false prophets, misleading teachings, and increasing iniquity and love-

---

17 As shown by such texts as John 16:33, Acts 14:22 and 1 Thessalonians 3:23, these sufferings are bound to come upon Christians in this world. The book of Revelation, written in a time of great tribulation for the Christian church, repeatedly focuses on these sufferings (1:9; 2:9, 10; 3:10; 6:9–11; 12:17; 13:7), and points forward to the time when Christians victoriously have "come out of" such "great tribulation" and enjoy the reward for their endurance. (Rev. 7:9–17)

18 *The Watchtower*, Aug. 1, 1981, p. 14; *Awake!* March 8, 1982, p. 8. It is remarkable how often religious organizations assume the same attitude toward dissenters within their own ranks that they constantly condemn in other denominations. Thus the Watch Tower Society, while strongly condemning the way the Roman Catholic Church treated its dissenters during past centuries and regularly praising these dissenters as Christian heroes, treats its own dissenters with the utmost religious cruelty: it classifies them as lawless apostates, defames their characters, excommunicates them and cuts them off from all contacts with former Christian brothers, friends and relatives, the only reason often being that these dissenters like the Waldenses, the Wycliffites and the early reformers, believe that the Bible is the "only source of religious truth" against which all ideas, interpretations and claims of religious authority have to be tested. It is also a fact that the Watch Tower Society, like the Roman Catholic Church, regards its own organization as a separate divine authority along with the Bible. Thus it is held that "unless we are in touch with this channel of communication that God is using, we will not progress along the road to life, *no matter how much Bible reading we do.*" (*The Watchtower*, Dec. 1, 1981, p. 27.)

lessness as other evidences of the spiritual decay he foresaw would occur among the growing numbers of professing followers in the future. Yet, none of these things were to be understood as signs of the imminence of his *parousía* and the end of the age. First, another work of worldwide scope had to be accomplished:

> **And this gospel of the kingdom will be preached in the whole world, as a testimony to all nations; and then the end will come.**—Matthew 24:14, RSV.

True, already in the time of the apostles it could be said that the gospel or good news bore fruit "in all the world" and had been preached "in all creation under heaven." (Colossians 1:6, 23) This, though, was undoubtedly said in a general way, as the gospel at that time (c. A.D. 60) had been brought to many different parts of the Roman world, and doubtless also to some places outside the Roman borders. Throughout the centuries the good news has been brought to many other parts of the world and has reached hundreds of millions of people. According to the *World Christian Encyclopedia,* published in 1982, the number of professing Christians today is close to 1.5 billion worldwide, which is 32.8 percent of the world's population, and the present increase is about 25 million a year. (This increase is, of course, partly owing to births among Christians.) Although these figures are impressive, Christendom is also to a very great extent characterized by the spiritual decay predicted by Jesus: hatred, with resultant injustice and bloodshed, false teachings, iniquity and lovelessness. This is also indicated by the fact that—according to the above-mentioned Encyclopedia—the number of sects and denominations within Christendom are as many as 20,800![19]

---

19 The Watch Tower organization seems to reject virtually all preaching of the gospel done during all the centuries since the death of the apostles and claims to be the only denomination of these 20,800 that preaches the true gospel today! What, then, is the single most important difference between the gospel of the Witnesses and that of other Christians? *The Watchtower* of May 1, 1981, explained on page 17: "Let the honest-hearted person compare the kind of preaching of the gospel of the Kingdom done by the religious systems of Christendom during all the centuries with that done by Jehovah's Witnesses since the end of World War I in 1918. They are not one and the same kind. That of Jehovah's Witnesses is really 'gospel' or 'good news,' as of God's heavenly kingdom that was established by the enthronement of his Son Jesus Christ at the end of the Gentile Times in 1914." However, if this enthronement in 1914—demonstrated in this work to be a delusion—is the most distinctive feature of their gospel, the worldwide preaching of it can hardly have anything to do with Jesus' prediction at all. Moreover, when Jesus spoke of "this" gospel of the kingdom he could only be referring to the gospel he and his apostles were then preaching. Compare Matthew 26:13, where the phrase "this gospel" also occurs. By claiming that Matthew 24:14 was fulfilled on a small scale before A.D. 70, the Watch

The great number of professing Christians in the world today, then, does not necessarily allow us to say conclusively that the good news has now been preached "in the whole world" and that a thorough witness has now been given to "all the nations," so that we should announce that "the end is due to come" at any day now. No one can say to what extent more proclaiming of the good news is destined to be done. All we know is that the extension of time shows that there is still, from God's point of view, work to be done, and that this extended time offers more opportunities for us to share our Christian hope with others.—2 Peter 3:9.

The destruction of Jerusalem

In his survey of calamities and troubles that would mark the future history of the world and the church, Jesus made clear that such things should not be misinterpreted as being visible signs of the end. Having first shown the mistaken views to be on guard against, Jesus now proceeded to answer the questions of the disciples.

They had asked for two things: 1) the *time* and (according to the versions of Mark and Luke) the *sign* of the destruction of the temple in Jerusalem, and 2) the *sign* of Jesus' *parousía* and the end of the age.

Jesus now began answering the first of these two questions, describing events that would lead up to the destruction of Jerusalem and its temple, adding, at the same time, appropriate instructions and warnings to be observed by his followers during that period. It is not necessary for our discussion to go into a detailed examination of this section, the destruction of Jerusalem, which is found in verses 15–22. It was all fulfilled to the letter in the first century, Josephus' *Wars of the Jews* actually being the best commentary on and confirmation of Jesus' prediction. There is, then, no sound reason for assuming a *double* fulfillment of this prophecy, as some have done, one in the first century and another at the end of the age. This theory has no support in the context of the prophecy, and is not necessitated by any other circumstances either. A few comments on some passages will suffice for our present purpose.

Tower Society in effect admits this. Thus Jesus did not have in mind some new, startling gospel to be introduced in this 20th century. Galatians 1:6–8 actually *condemns* "new" gospels that becloud or infringe upon the original, genuine "good news" preached in the first century.

Jerusalem, the capital of Judea, was "the city of the great king." (Matthew 5:35) The common Jewish belief was that Messiah, upon commencing his reign, would do so in Jerusalem, in Judea. They anticipated that Messiah's advent would bring a *literal* and *physical* deliverance of the city. (Compare Luke 2:38.) Since Jerusalem in reality faced destruction, this was another dangerous misconception against which Jesus warned his disciples. In pointing out what would be the evidence of the impending destruction of the temple, Jesus made reference to Daniel the prophet:

> So when you see standing in the holy place 'the abomination that causes desolation,' spoken of through the prophet Daniel—let the reader understand—then let those who are in Judea flee to the mountains.—Matthew 24:15, 16, NIV.[20]

Luke, who often paraphrases in order to explain to his non-Jewish readers the Jewish terms and Old Testament allusions used by Jesus and reported by the other synoptics, shows clearly what this "abomination of desolation" would be by saying:

> But when you see <u>Jerusalem surrounded by armies, then know that its desolation has come near.</u> Then let those who are in Judea flee to the mountains, and let those who are inside the city depart, and let not those who are out in the country enter it.—Luke 21:20, 21, RSV.

In May A.D. 66 Jewish revolts broke out in Caesarea and in Jerusalem. This caused Roman armies under Cestius Gallus to lay siege to Jerusalem in November of that year. When, suddenly, Gallus withdrew, Christians in Jerusalem and Judea saw an opportunity to "flee to the mountains," which they evidently did.[21] This sudden and unexpected withdrawal of the Roman troops from Jerusalem and Judea might be seen as the fulfillment of Jesus' prediction that "those days had been cut short . . . for the sake of the elect," giving these an opportunity to flee and thus save their lives. (Matthew 24:22, *NASB*) By this flight they escaped the "great distress upon the land" that began when Roman forces under General Vespasian returned a few

---

20 The reference is probably to Daniel 9:27, where LXX has the same expression as Matthew 24:15: *to bdélygma tēs eremōseōs* ("the abomination of desolation").

21 Eusebius (*Ecclesiastical History* III,v,3), who may have got his information from the second-century writer Hegesippus, says that the Christians in Jerusalem fled to Pella in Peraea, the modern *Tabakât Fahil*. Although this place is in the valley of the Jordan (actually below sea-level), the way there led across mountain hills. Eusebius' story refers to the Christians *in Jerusalem* only. Other Christians in Judea may have fled to other places in the mountains.

months later to subjugate the rebellious Jews. (Luke 21:23) From the spring to the autumn of 67, Galilee was conquered, and in the spring of 68, Peraea and western Judea had been subdued. In the year 69, Vespasian, having been proclaimed emperor by his troops, entrusted the command to his son Titus. In April 70, Titus besieged Jerusalem, and in September the Romans took the city and destroyed it together with its temple. According to Josephus, who was an eye-witness to the destruction and who published his detailed description of it about five years later, 1,100,000 Jews were killed in this catastrophe, while about 97,000 survived it. (It may be stated, however, that most scholars regard these figures as highly exaggerated.) In harmony with Jesus' statement that this tribulation upon the Jews was to be worse than any other "from the beginning of the world until now," Josephus says that "neither did any other city ever suffer such miseries, nor did any age ever breed a generation more fruitful in wickedness than this was, from the beginning of the world."—Matthew 24:21.[22]

Those who endeavor to make a double application of this prophecy have often given themselves up to the most fanciful speculations, so as to be able to point to a so-called "greater fulfillment" in today's events. Thus some believe that Herod's temple will soon be restored in Jerusalem and that an idol or an image of Antichrist will be placed in it to fulfill the prediction about the "abomination of desolation."[23] The Watch Tower Society identifies the "abomination of desolation" with the United Nations, which, they predict, will soon desolate Christendom, the claimed counterpart of ancient Jerusalem. All such applications are wholly unwarranted and have no support in the text itself. Luke's account shows that this "abomination of desolation" referred to armies that would surround Jerusalem in order to destroy it, and Josephus, probably wholly unaware of Jesus' prophecy, shows how all details of the prediction came true in the years 66–70 A.D. The idea of an additional fulfillment in our days, therefore, is not only

---

22 Josephus, *Wars of the Jews*, V,x,5. Some suggest that the expression "such as has not been . . . nor ever shall be" may have been used for the purpose of emphasis, and should perhaps not be taken too literally. (Matt. 24:21; Dan. 12:1; compare, for example, Ex. 10:14 and Joel 2:2.) It is also possible that the expression "such as has not occurred" (Matt. 24:21) does not refer to the *degree of severity* of the "great tribulation," but to its *unique character*, its meaning and consequences being like nothing else in God's dealings with his people. (Compare Jeremiah 30:7: "Alas! for that day is great, there is none like it; and it is the time of Jacob's distress, but he will be saved from it." [NASB]) On the other hand, it is possible that no city in history has suffered as intensely as Jerusalem did in A.D. 66–70.

23 Oral Roberts, *How to be Personally Prepared for the Second Coming of Christ*, page 38.

foreign to the Biblical context; it turns out to be completely superfluous in the light of the full and detailed fulfillment in the first century.

The visibility of the parousia

Proponents of what may be called a "two-stage coming"—first an invisible coming and presence followed later by a revelation with visible effects—endeavor to find support for their belief in the word found in Matthew's account of the disciples' question, namely the Greek term *parousía*. They focus on the accepted fact that the primary meaning of the term is "presence." It is an equally established fact, however, that in Bible times this term had become the equivalent of "coming" or "arrival," particularly in connection with a kingly or imperial visit, a visitation often accompanied by acts of judgment. A simple comparison of the accounts related to Christ's coming will demonstrate that the term *parousía* is used virtually interchangeably with the Greek words for "revelation" (*apokálypsis*), "manifestation" (*epipháneia*), and "coming" (*éleusis*). (Compare Matthew 24:39 [*parousía*] with Luke 17:30 [*apokálypsis*]; 1 Thessalonians 4:15, 16, and 2 Thessalonians 2:1 [*parousía*] with 2 Timothy 4:8 [*epipháneia*]; Matthew 24:3 [*parousía*] with Luke 21:7 [*éleusis*, in Codex Bezae Cantabrigensis (D)].) All these terms relate to facets of the same event, the royal visitation of a ruler, the king Christ Jesus. For a full discussion of this subject, the reader may consider the detailed material presented in Appendix B. As the evidence there shows, the "two-stage" theory about Christ's coming was first developed by an English banker in the 1820's. Later in that century, many millenarians adopted it, some of whom, including Pastor Russell and his associates, used it as a convenient means to salvage failed predictions based on chronological conjecture, thereby seeking to explain away their failure.

What, then, do the Scriptures reveal as to the visibility or invisibility of Jesus' promised *parousía?*

In times of great crises, interest in the second coming of Christ and the end of the world always increases. The great Jewish crisis of 66–74 would logically be no exception. Evidently due to this, after his prediction of the Jewish catastrophe, Jesus saw fit to repeat his earlier warning against being misled by false Christs and false prophets:

> Then if any one says to you, 'Lo, here is the Christ!' or 'There he is!' do not believe it. For false Christs and false prophets will arise and show great signs and wonders, so as to lead astray, if possible, even the elect.

Lo, I have told you beforehand. So, if they say to you, 'Lo, he is in the wilderness,' do not go out; if they say, 'Lo he is in the inner rooms,' do not believe it. For as the lightning comes from the east and shines as far as the west, so will be the coming of the Son of man.—Matthew 24:23-27, RSV.

The word "then" (Greek, *tóte*) in verse 23 connects the warning that Jesus proceeds to give with his preceding discussion of the "great tribulation" upon Jerusalem. Josephus, when describing the burning of the temple by the Romans, says that "there was then a great number of false prophets suborned by the tyrants to impose upon the people, who denounced this to them, that they should wait for deliverance from God," and that "the miserable people (were) persuaded by these deceivers." (*Wars of the Jews,* VI,v,2,3) Whatever the circumstances may have been, Jesus' disciples were not to be misled by any predictions of Messiah's appearance at such time; they were not to be induced to go to Jerusalem or even to Judea, and if already there, they were to leave, fleeing to the mountains. The warning against such false prophets as well as false Messiahs would apply to all future times as well.

The coming false prophets would "show great signs and wonders." This may, of course, refer to actually performing miracles of some kind. But it is more likely a reference to *false prophesying*. The Greek word translated "show" really means "give" and does not necessarily imply *performing* something. As pointed out by Bible commentator Henry Barclay Swete and others, the words are based on Deuteronomy chapter thirteen, verses 1 to 3, where the giving of signs and wonders refers to giving *predictions,* not to performing miracles.[24] The "false prophets," therefore, include all those through the centuries that have devoted themselves to false prophesying with respect to the second coming of Christ, as by paying undue attention to the "time element," setting dates for the coming and related events, and by claiming ability to interpret with authority what they designate the "signs of the time."

There is another lesson to be learned from the passage before us, a lesson that has to do with the *manner* of Christ's coming. A human being, who falsely claims to be Christ, would not easily be acknowl-

---

24 H. B. Swete, *Commentary on Mark,* the 1977 reprint of the 1913 ed., published by Kregel Publications, Grand Rapids, Michigan, page 310. Professor Alexander Jones also comments: "*Show:* i.e. announce, prophesy (cf Deut 13:1–3), not 'perform'." (*The Gospel of St. Mark,* London-Dublin 1963, 1965, p. 197.)

edged or recognized as such. His followers would have to tell others *where* he is and *who* he is, in effect saying: "Here is the Christ," or "There he is." "He is in the wilderness," or "He is in the inner chambers." But Jesus warned against pretenders who had to be pointed out that way: "Believe it not."

His coming will not be like that. When he comes, his identity or whereabouts will not constitute any problem. On the contrary, his *parousía* will instantly be evident to all. To emphasize this, Jesus likened his coming to the *lightning,* that "comes from the east, and shines as far as the west." A lightning flash that lights up the heavens is seen at once by all from the eastern horizon to the western horizon. It is not necessary for anyone to tell others where or what it is, and nobody needs to "go running off in pursuit" after it. (Luke 17:23, NEB) Similarly, Christ's *parousía* will instantly and directly manifest itself to every individual on earth. This, of course, also excludes all ideas about a secret, unnoticeable coming, and all explanations to the effect that a certain "Bible chronology" and/or certain "signs" show that he has come and has been "invisibly present" since a certain year. Such a conception of the *parousía* is completely opposite to the description of it given by Jesus himself, who presents it as a very noticeable event.[25]

To further emphasize to his disciples that his coming would not be found at or limited to any particular geographical place on earth, Jesus, speaking proverbially, added:

> **Wherever the body is, there the eagles will be gathered together.**— Matthew 24:28, RSV.

---

25 The present authors do not argue that Christ at his coming will be observed from the earth as a *literal* figure sitting or standing on a *literal* cloud in the sky above, as some seem to hold, taking quite literally such a text as Revelation 1:7. Our emphasis is upon the fact that the Bible presents Christ's *parousía,* his glorious appearance, as an event that will at once be *seen and understood by all mankind as a divine, supernatural intervention in human affairs.* Thus it is not necessary to decide whether this event will include the vision of a literal figure on a literal cloud or not. In support of the idea that Christ's *parousía* is invisible to mankind, the Watch Tower Society refers to Jesus' statement in John 14:19: "Yet a little while, and the world will see me no more." (*You Can Live Forever in Paradise on Earth,* 1982, p. 142.) Giving the expression "no more" (Greek, *oukéti*) an absolute sense, "never again," they hold that Christ will be invisible even at his future "appearing." But this argument is untenable in view of what Jesus said at John 16:16: "A little while, and you will see me no more (*oukéti*); again a little while, and you will see me." (Compare also verse 10.) Here the beholding "no more" means beholding no more *for a little while* only. It was not used in the absolute sense of "never again." The "no more" at John 14:19, therefore, could have been used in a similar, limited sense, referring to the period of Christ's absence until his *parousía.*

From the fact that the Romans carried eagles on their standards many expositors conclude that Jesus by this statement refers back to his earlier discussion of the destruction of Jerusalem. The thought, then, would be that the Jewish nation, having become like a lifeless corpse ready for judgment, attracted to itself the "carrion eagles" of Rome. But abruptly bringing in such an idea when discussing the manner of the *parousía* does not only seem wholly uncalled for; the parallel text at Luke chapter seventeen, verses 34 to 37, shows it to be erroneous. According to Luke's account, Jesus' statement about the eagles and the carcass was preceded by a description of the judgment that would take place at the *parousía;* **"In that night there will be two in one bed; one will be taken and the other left. There will be two women grinding together; one will be taken and the other left."** This caused the disciples to ask: **"Where, Lord?"** Jesus answered: **"Where the body is, there the eagles will be gathered together."**

What actually caused the proverbial statement about the eagles and the corpse, then, was the disciples' question as to where the judgment, the separation of the righteous from the unrighteous, was to take place. According to the common view of the contemporary Jews, Messiah at his coming would take his seat in Jerusalem, some even saying this would be on the pinnacle of the temple, and that from there he would perform his office as judge.[26] But if, as Jesus had just explained, that temple was to be destroyed, then the judgment could not take place from there. This may have been in the mind of the disciples when they asked, "Where, Lord?" At any rate, Jesus by his proverbial statement clearly stressed that the judgment would not take place at any particular geographical place, but that "wherever" the sinners would be on earth at his coming, they would be found by his avenging forces, even as eagles would fly to a body wherever it might be. By saying this Jesus again repudiated the view that at his coming he would appear at a particular locality on earth, for instance in the wilderness, or in Jerusalem, or, as many even today believe, on the Mount of Olives. In contrast to such ideas Jesus describes his *parousía* as a manifestation of divine power and glory that will be instantly seen and felt by all everywhere on earth.

Having answered the question about the sign of the destruction of the temple, his connected discussion of the *manner* of his coming forms a natural transition to the next question of his disciples, in

26 Brunec, *ad loc*. Brunec in turn refers to the study by the French scholar J. P. Bonsirven.

which they inquired as to what *sign* there would be of his coming, and of the end of the age.

"The sign of the Son of man"

In terms echoing Old Testament texts that dealt with divine judgements in the past, Jesus presents his future coming as being accompanied by terrifying cosmic upheavals:

> Immediately after the tribulation of those days the sun will be darkened, and the moon will not give its light, and the stars will fall from heaven, and the powers of the heavens will be shaken; then will appear the sign of the Son of man in heaven, and then all the tribes of the earth will mourn, and they will see the Son of man coming on the clouds of heaven with power and great glory.—Matthew 24:39, 30, RSV.

The first problem that confronts us in this text is the word "immediately" (Greek, *euthéōs*). If "the tribulation of those days" refers back to the "great tribulation" of verse 21, then it would seem at first glance as if Jesus (at least according to the version of Matthew; Mark and Luke both omit the adverb *euthéōs*) placed his *parousía* immediately after the destruction of Jerusalem in A.D. 70. If so, we would be obliged to conclude that he was either mistaken or that his *parousía* did take place in A.D. 70. In the latter case we would have to assume an invisible and an essentially unnoticed coming, similar to what the Watch Tower Society claims occurred in 1914.[27]

That the destruction of Jerusalem in A.D. 70 was a "visitation" from God is certainly true. In the parable of the marriage feast, Christ described the disinterest shown by the guests whom the king in the parable had invited and their abuse and even murder of some of the messengers he sent to them. He states that, as a result, "the king was angry, and he sent his troops and destroyed those murderers and burned their city." Thereafter he sent his servants out to invite others "from the street corners" to be his guests at the marriage feast of his son. (Matthew 22:1–10) Since the king here represents God, the Father of Jesus Christ, what took place at Jerusalem could, in some

---

27   Actually, there are a number of commentators who hold that the *parousía* did take place in A.D. 70. The most comprehensive presentation of this idea is that of J. Stuart Russell in *The Parousia*, first published in 1878. See also Max R. King, *The Spirit of Prophecy*, Warren, Ohio, 1971 (2nd printing 1981). In this view the *parousía* is identical with the Jewish tribulation that culminated with the destruction of Jerusalem in A.D. 70. Although this was certainly a "divine visitation" and judgment, Christ himself said his coming would take place "after the tribulation of those days." (Matt. 24:29)

respects be called a royal visitation by God, hence, in that sense, a *parousía*. But even if what took place at Jerusalem in 70 A.D. should be considered as a *parousía*, there are numerous problems with viewing it as THE *parousía*, the promised coming of Jesus Christ, the *parousía* referred to in Matthew chapter twenty-four and parallel texts.

Such a conclusion is difficult to harmonize with a number of points in Jesus' preceding discourse. A major difficulty is that if the *parousía* really took place in A.D. 70, the first resurrection and the changing of the living Christians to be united with Christ must also have occurred at that time. (1 Thessalonians 4:15–17; 1 Corinthians 15:50–52) The sudden disappearance of thousands of Christians from hundreds of congregations spread all over the Roman Empire would certainly have left some traces in extra-Biblical Christian writings preserved from the first two or three Christian centuries. Any evidence of this kind, however, is completely missing. On the contrary, we find that after A.D. 70, even in Christian writings close to the event, such as the letters of Clement and Barnabas and the writings of Justin Martyr, Christ's coming and the resurrection are still being looked forward to as yet future.

The writing of the book of Revelation by John, as also the writing of his three epistles, is commonly believed to have been done toward the close of the first century, toward the close of the reign of Domitian. John's death is believed to have occurred at about the turn of the century in the reign of Domitian's successor, Trajan. It seems difficult to believe that, if Christ's *parousía* had occurred subsequent to the events of 70 A.D., John would not have given at least some reference thereto in his writings. Of course, if it had occurred at that time (70 A.D.) one would be obliged to assume that John ceased his earthly life then, thereafter sharing heavenly life with God's Son. This would mean that John wrote Revelation and his three letters some thirty years earlier (that is, earlier than the time to which the existing evidence points), hence previous to A.D. 70, as some scholars hold. (See John A. T. Robinson, *Redating the New Testament*, London 1976, pp. 221–311.)

Finally, Christ's presentation of his *parousía* as an event as visible as the lightning in contrast to the coming of some of the false Christ's (who sometimes would have to be represented as being in *hidden* places, "in the wilderness" or "in the inner chambers") also seems to weigh against this theory. What other explanation is there, then, for the use of the term "immediately" in the passage under consideration?

Some commentators point out that Matthew quite possibly may have used the word translated "immediately" (*euthéōs*) in a different sense than the usual one. It is widely recognized that Mark in his gospel very often uses the almost identical adverb *euthús*, not in the ordinary sense of "straightway, at once," but in a "weakened" sense.[28] As Dr. David Tabachovitz points out in his careful study of Mark's use of *euthús*, its purpose was often to draw the attention of the reader to something new, and the best translation in such cases, therefore, would be, "Behold,. . . ."[29] For this reason *The New Bible Commentary Revised*, in its comment on Matthew chapter twenty-four, verse 29, suggests that "'immediately' (Greek-*euthéōs*) might have a weakened sense (*euthys*), as it often has in Mark."[30]

Similarly, Dr. Brunec points out that this Greek term has as one of its meanings that of "in sequence," and that while it is generally employed to emphasize the brevity of the interval of *time* between one event and the next, it can also be used to denote *the absence of any intervening event*. Thus, he states, to say that 'after event *x* "immediately" comes event *y*,' can mean either of two things: First, that event *y* takes place after event *x* without any intervening period of *time;* or, second, that event *y* takes place after event *x* without any intervening or intermediary *event*—with no emphasis on the amount of time that may pass.[31] In this latter case, Jesus would be saying that, *in the course of predicted events* (events of the kind that the disciples were inquiring about), after Jerusalem's destruction there would be no other prophesied event of that type until the outbreak of celestial phenomena he described. After that Jewish catastrophe, *the next thing in order*, in sequence, would be the foretold "sign of the Son of man." This would mean that, whatever the things that might happen during the centuries that would intervene between that event and his coming, they were not to be viewed as among the divinely predicted events of Messianic import or construed as constituting a divinely given sign. In

---

28 The two adverbs are practically identical, both being formed from the adjective *euthús* and used in exactly the same way. (See Liddell & Scott)

29 David Tabachovitz, *Die Septuaginta und das Neue Testament*, Lund 1956, pp. 29–35. As Tabachovitz shows, ancient Greek translations of the Old Testament, such as LXX and *Symmachus'* translation, sometimes render the Hebrew word for "behold" by *euthús* instead of *idou* ("see"). *Euthús* and *idou* are sometimes also used interchangeably by the Synoptics. (Compare Mark 7:25 with Matthew 15:22 and Mark 14:43 with Matthew 26:47 and Luke 22:47.)

30 *The New Bible Commentary Revised*, ed. by D. Guthrie and J. A. Motyer, Grand Rapids, Michigan, 1971, p. 845.

31 Brunec, ad loc.

actuality, history has demonstrated the absence of such intermediary events.

While such understanding is entirely in harmony with grammatical and Biblical usage of this Greek term translated "immediately," it is admittedly not the only possible meaning of Jesus' statement. Yet another possible, and relatively simple, solution to the problem merits consideration.

By saying, "Immediately after the tribulation of those days," did Jesus have in mind the tribulation for the Jews in the years A.D. 66–70 only? It should be remembered that this was not the only tribulation he had spoken of in his prophecy. In fact, *the whole speech before the mentioning of the distress upon the Jews had been nothing but an enumeration of tribulations of different kinds,* namely, the wars, famines, pestilences, and so forth, which he called "the beginning of travail" (verse 8), and the hatred, persecution and other troubles—termed "tribulation" (*thlipsis*) in verse 9—that would come upon his followers in the future. Further, the predicted "great tribulation" upon the Jews may not have ended with the destruction of Jerusalem in A.D. 70. This is indicated by the parallel account of Luke. While Matthew and Mark both quote the statement about the coming "great tribulation" from Daniel chapter twelve, verse 1, Luke gives his non-Jewish readers a more detailed explanation of the prediction:

> For there will be great distress in the land and a terrible judgement upon this people. They will fall at the sword's point; they will be carried captive into all countries; and Jerusalem will be trampled down by foreigners until their day has run its course.—Luke 21:23, 24, NEB.

Thus Luke's parallel account seems to show that the tribulation upon the Jews would not come to an end immediately after the destruction of Jerusalem in A.D. 70. Captivity in foreign countries would follow (as it actually did for the Jews who survived the destruction), and the city of Jerusalem would be trampled down or controlled by foreigners for an indefinite period, "until their day has run its course."[32]

32 Those who hold that the *parousía* took place in A.D. 70 are forced to identify this period of the trampling down of Jerusalem until the end of the Gentile times with the five months the Romans besieged Jerusalem, or with the actual destruction of the city and the temple. But it seems strange to say that the Romans "trampled on" Jerusalem during the time they were *outside* of the city. Besides, it seems clear that Luke says that the Jewish captivity in foreign countries would run parallel with the times when the Gentiles trampled upon Je-

It is certainly possible, therefore, that Jesus, by saying that his coming would occur "immediately after the tribulation of those days," did not think of the tribulation ending with the destruction of Jerusalem only, but had in mind the whole period of tribulation that was to follow, not only upon the Jews but also upon his own followers.[33] Christ's coming will quite naturally put an end to or "cut short" this period of tribulation or affliction.[34] (Matthew 24:22) This shortening of the tribulation is said to be done "for the elect's sake." If the tribulation is understood as something that would continue up till the *parousía,* the statement, "for the elect's sake, whom he chose, he shortened the days," is quite understandable, because an important object of Christ's coming is repeatedly said to be for the deliverance of his chosen ones out of their distress.—Mark 13:20; 2 Thessalonians 1:4–10; 1 Thessalonians 4:17, 18; 1 Peter 4:12, 13.

According to this view, then, Christ would come literally "<u>immediately</u> after" the tribulation, as his coming will actually cut it short or put an end to it.

Whatever the case may be, the sign of the imminence of this coming will, in spite of its terrifying aspects, inspire hope in faithful Christians, because they will remember Jesus' words: **"When all this begins to happen, stand upright and hold your heads high, because your liberation is near."** (Luke 21:28, NEB) What will this deliverance mean to the faithful followers of Christ? As shown by many passages in the New Testament it can only mean their *gathering together unto Christ, to be with him forever after that moment.* (1 Thessalonians 4:15–17; 2:1; John 14:3; Philippians 3:20) It was evidently this event that Jesus had in mind when he said that he, at his coming "immediately after the tribulation of those days," "shall send forth his angels with a great sound of a trumpet, and they shall <u>gather together his elect</u> from the four winds, from one end of heaven to the other."[35] Further on in his discourse Jesus pointed out that at that mo-

---

rusalem, thus indicating that these "times of the Gentiles" would be a period of long duration.

33 Dr. Basil F. C. Atkinson, for example, says in *The New Bible Commentary* (2nd ed., London 1954, page 800): "The 'tribulation' did not end with the destruction of Jerusalem. In the present writer's view it includes the subsequent Christian age."

34 It is a mistake to conclude that the "shortening" of the tribulation implies that it would necessarily be of short duration. The Greek word *koloboō* denotes to "dock, curtail, amputate," and so forth and indicates nothing about the length of the period up to the point of cutting it short, only that it would have been longer without the shortening.

35 Although the Watch Tower Society since 1973 holds that the coming "on the clouds of heaven" at Matthew 24:30 is *still future,* it claims that the "gathering together" of the elect

ment "two men (shall) be in the field; one is taken, and one is left; two women shall be grinding at the mill; one is taken, and one is left." (Verse 40, 41) It is also at that coming that Jesus will bless his "faithful and discreet" servants by appointing them "over all his belongings," but will assign the evil servants their part with the hypocrites.[36] (Matthew 24:45–51) Thus, while the coming will mean liberation and exaltation for the faithful servants of Christ, it will also mean judgment and punishment for his unfaithful servants.

---

mentioned in the very next verse (v. 31) has been going on since 1919 by the preaching work performed by the movement! (*God's Kingdom of a Thousand Years Has Approached*, 1973, pp. 327–329) But this reversal of the order of events as set forth by Jesus is made impossible by the parallel text of Mark which, by the word "then" (*tote*), definitely fixes the gathering together of the elect to the time of the coming on the clouds, not to the time preceding it. (Mark 13:27) The Watch Tower Society's view that its preaching work since 1919 is the "harvest" mentioned in the parable of the weeds and the wheat (Matt. 13:24–30, 36–43) falls to the ground when it is realized that the separating of the "weeds" from the "wheat," as well as the separating of the good "fishes" from the bad in the parable of the dragnet (Matt. 13:47–52) is connected with the judgment that will take place at Christ's future coming "on the clouds" with all his angels. In the parable of the dragnet the preaching performed by Christ's nominal followers is illustrated by a net lying in the sea, gathering fishes "of every kind." The point is that the *separation* of the good fishes from the bad does not take place *as long as the net is still gathering fishes in the sea* (even as the separation of the wheat and the weeds does not take place while they are growing but at the harvest time). Furthermore, the gathering of the good fishes into vessels and the casting away of the bad ones is performed by "the angels," not by humans (as is also true with the wheat and the weeds). Christians cannot logically have any part in this separating work, as *they are the ones being separated*.

36 On the basis of the view that Christ's *parousía* began in 1914, the Watch Tower Society holds that Christ (the "Lord" in the parable) at his inspection of the professing Christians at that time found only the anointed members of the Watch Tower movement to be "faithful and discreet," having been giving the members of the "household" their spiritual food "at the proper time." Thus, in 1919, he is thought to have appointed them "over all his belongings." (*God's Kingdom of a Thousand Years Has Approached*, 1973, pp. 349–357) This view is used to justify this movement's claim to divine authority over its members. Since 1973, however, the Society has unintentionally been undermining the theological basis of its own authority. Up to that year it was held that the parable (vv. 45–51) was an expansion of verses 42–44 and related to the same event, namely to Christ's "coming to the temple" in 1918. (*Vindication*, Vol. 3, p. 121, 122) Then, in 1973, the Society *postponed the "coming" mentioned in verses 42–44 to the future "great tribulation."* (*God's Kingdom . . .* , pp. 336, 337) Contextually, however, there is no way to separate the "coming" of verses 42–44 from the following verses (45–51). Hence, if the "coming" of verses 42–44 is future, the "coming" of the master in verses 45–51 is future also, as well as his appointing of the "faithful and discreet slave over all his belongings." Occasionally, therefore, the Watch Tower publications since 1973 have indicated that the elevation of the "slave" is still future, and may even have an *individual* application. (*Our Incoming World Government—God's Kingdom*, 1977, p. 158f.)

The "last days"—what are they?

As pointed out earlier, the popular idea of the "last days" is that they refer to a period of time which precedes Christ's coming for judgment and which serves as an indicator that that event is imminent, about to occur. While popular, is this actually what is taught in Scripture?

Jesus himself never used the expression "the last days" in any of his discussions of what the future would bring. He did refer to "the last day" (singular) but this was in describing what he would do after he actually had come and had begun the final judgment. (Compare John 6:39, 40, 44, 54; 7:37; 11:24; 12:48.) Furthermore, all of his counsel to his disciples explicitly states that there will be nothing about the course of human events that will be so notable, so different and unique, that would enable them to know from such conditions that his coming was about to occur. In reality, the very ordinariness, sameness, and repetitive nature of human events and conditions would present the danger of their becoming spiritually drowsy, complacent— quite the opposite of a period of very unusual conditions and startling events such as produce a state of jittery agitation and wrought-up expectation.—Matthew 24:43, 44; 25:1–6, 13; Luke 12:35–40; 17:26– 30; 21:34–36.

Turning to the writings of his apostles and disciples, what do we find? Peter, Paul, James and Jude all made reference to "the last days." We first find Peter speaking of "the last days" on the day of Pentecost, fifty days after Jesus' death and resurrection. Speaking to the crowd that gathered he told them that what they witnessed—the disciples being filled with holy spirit and speaking in different languages—was in fulfillment of Joel's prophecy, and he then said:

> **God says, 'This will happen in the last days: I will pour out upon everyone a portion of my spirit; and your sons and your daughters shall prophesy; your young men shall see visions, and your old men shall dream dreams. Yes, I will endue even my slaves, both men and women, with a portion of my spirit, and they shall prophesy. And I will show portents in the sky above, and signs on the earth below—blood and fire and drifting smoke. The sun shall be turned to darkness, and the moon to blood, before the great, resplendent day, the day of the Lord, shall come. And then, everyone who invokes the name of the Lord shall be saved.'—Acts 2:17– 21, NEB.**

Peter thus applied the "the last days" as being in effect at that time. In an effort to circumvent this fact, some make the claim that he used the expression only with reference to the last days of the nation of

Israel, leading up to Jerusalem's destruction in A.D. 70.[37] But Peter does not say this and we are hardly warranted to put words in his mouth or assume a meaning that is nowhere stated. The fact is that Peter clearly uses the term in a context which embraces the coming of "the day of the Lord" and the salvation that that day brings. He does not limit "the last days" of which he spoke to the few years up till A.D. 70 but apparently extends them right up to the day of God's judgment through Christ.

In Paul's second letter to Timothy, after counseling him as to difficult circumstances and problems he would have to face in serving his fellow Christians, Paul then said:

> **But understand this, that in the last days there will come times of stress. For men will be lovers of self, lovers of money, proud, arrogant, abusive, disobedient to their parents, ungrateful, unholy, inhuman, implacable, slanderers, profligates, fierce, haters of good, treacherous, reckless, swollen with conceit, lovers of pleasure rather than lovers of God, holding the form of religion but denying the power of it. Avoid such people.**—2 Timothy 3:1–5, RSV.

Was Paul speaking of conditions that were not to prevail until some far-distant period, perhaps down here in our twentieth-century? His own writings indicate otherwise. In his letter to the Romans he writes of the way people were right then conducting themselves and he describes such people in identical terms, as being:

> **. . . filled with all manner of wickedness, evil, covetousness, malice. Full of envy, murder, strife, deceit, malignity, they are gossips, slanderers, haters of God, insolent, haughty, boastful, inventors of evil, disobedient to parents, foolish, faithless, heartless, ruthless. Though they know God's decree that those who do such things deserve to die, they not only do them but approve those who practice them.**—Romans 1:29–32, RSV.

What difference is there in the two descriptions? They are obviously equal in terms of the degree of extremeness and excessiveness. That being so, we can understand why Paul, in writing to Timothy of the conditions of the "last days" (or, as the *New English Bible* renders it, "the final age of this world"), could say—*in the present tense*—that Timothy should "avoid such people." In harmony with this, Paul's subsequent words deal with persons from among "such people" who were even then infecting the Christian brotherhood, and he again does

---

37 This is the standard explanation offered in modern Watch Tower publications.

so *in the present tense*. (2 Timothy 3:6–9) According to Paul's own expressions elsewhere and according to the context of his letter to Timothy, his reference to "the last days" was to an ongoing period already in effect, the period in which Timothy lived, and was in connection with conditions, attitudes and kinds of people Timothy already faced, and would have to face, during his ministry. Efforts to find a way around this evidence result again in placing a meaning on Paul's words that is not there, a meaning that is inserted in an effort to support a preconceived idea and a meaning which does not agree with the context.

James, in his letter, addresses himself to those rich persons who have "laid up treasure for the last days." (James 5:1–3, RSV) This expression allows for varying renderings. Thus, some translations speak of their hoarding wealth "in the last days" (NIV; NW), "in these last days" (Phillips; TEV), "in an age that is near its close" (NEB). The Greek preposition used (*en*) literally means "in." Whichever rendering one may prefer, this statement certainly provides no strong foundation upon which to build a concept of the "last days" as meaning an identifiable period immediately preceding, and signaling, the coming of Christ. The thrust and content of its context is much like that found in the earlier-considered statements of Peter and Paul.

Both Peter and John warn of scoffers who "will come in the last days," questioning the certainty of God's day of judgment. (2 Peter 3:4; Jude 17, 18) Again, however, both of these writers indicate that such scoffing would take place right during the life of those to whom they were writing; they present their mockery as an attitude already to be faced and, as Jude puts it, such unspiritual and selfish persons were at that very time to be guarded against, as "men who divide you."— Jude 19, NIV.

Peter shows that it is the very fact that the overall pattern of human life and of human conditions continues essentially the same which provides the basis for these persons expressing such disbelief; he does not say that they see extraordinary, never-before-witnessed conditions and then refuse to recognize them as a "sign." Rather, he compares their faithless attitude with that which produced the destruction of people in the flood. As Jesus had stated, people in that day were not forewarned by some unusual conditions; they were living in what was for them a time of normalcy, "eating, drinking, marrying and giving in marriage," with nothing to serve as a premonition of the destruction that swiftly, without warning, came upon them. (Matthew 24:38, 39)

Such disbelief, and the scoffing viewpoint it engenders, has existed down through the centuries right to the present day. It is not unique to our time.

There is, then, reason to believe that the apostles and disciples of Christ Jesus applied the expression "the last days" to that period of human history from the appearance, death and resurrection of the Messiah on down to the time of final judgment. Thus, the letter to the Hebrews begins with the statement:

> In many and various ways God spoke of old to our fathers by the prophets; but in these last days [in this the final age, NEB] he has spoken to us by a Son, whom he appointed the heir of all things, through whom he created the world.—Hebrews 1:1, 2, RSV.

The long panorama of human history, from its inception forward, might thus be compared to a three-act drama. In such a drama, the first and second acts lead up to the finale, and when the curtain rises for the third act one knows that the drama has entered its final part and that when the curtain falls the drama will come to its close. From the scriptural evidence, the drama of human history entered its final stage, its "third act," with the coming of the Messiah and his death and resurrection. Those climactic events set the stage for, and marked the commencement of, the final age of this world, its last days.

The true sign and its meaning

Jesus stated that mankind, all mankind, would see a sign in connection with his coming. What is this *sign* that heralds his coming judgment and the eagerly longed-for liberation of faithful Christians? (1 Corinthians 1:7; 1 Thessalonians 1:10) Quite obviously, it is the cosmic commotion described at Matthew chapter twenty-four, verses 29, 30. At the approaching of the Son of man, clothed in divine power and glory, nature is trembling and heaven is darkening. The parallel text of Luke has additional details worth noting:

> And there will be signs [Greek, *sēmeía*, the plural of *sēmeíon*] in sun and moon and stars, and upon the earth dismay among nations, in perplexity at the roaring of the sea and waves, men fainting from fear and the expectation of things which are coming upon the world; for the powers of the heavens will be shaken. And then they will see THE SON OF MAN COMING IN A CLOUD with power and great glory.—Luke 21:25-27, NASB.

When these things begin to happen, Jesus said, "your liberation is near," "at the doors." This cosmic commotion, therefore, is *the sign* the disciples inquired about. It is interesting to note that Luke directly mentions *signs* in sun and moon and stars, while Matthew speaks of the darkening of these heavenly bodies and so on, and adds that "then shall appear the sign (*sēmeíon*) of the Son of man in heaven." It seems clear from this comparison that the "sign of the Son of man" *is* this cosmic upheaval, the "signs in sun and moon and stars," the shaking of the "powers of the heaven," accompanied by the "roaring of the sea and the waves" and so on.[38]

As stated earlier, the language used here reflects the language used in many Old Testament prophecies dealing with divine judgments in the past. It is clear that the language of those ancient prophets was highly symbolic, and that they used physical phenomena to describe catastrophic changes in the social and spiritual world, such as the upheaval of dynasties and destruction of nations hostile to Israel. Isaiah's prophecy of the fall of ancient Babylon, for instance, includes the prediction that "the stars of heaven and the constellations thereof shall not give their light; the sun shall be darkened in its going forth, and the moon shall not cause its light to shine." (Isaiah 13:10) The ancient prophets foretold the destruction of Idumea and Egypt in similar terms. (Isaiah 34:4; Ezekiel 32:7,8) The "roaring of the sea and the waves" is also a common feature in Old Testament texts dealing with divine interventions in man's world. (Isaiah 51:15; Habakkuk 3:8; Haggai 2:6; Psalm 77:17–19)[39] In considering the cosmic upheavals in connection with Christ's coming such parallels are often pointed to— and rightly so—as warnings not to take the description too literally.[40]

---

38 That Matthew 24:29, 30 contains the answer to the disciples' question about the sign of Christ's coming is the conclusion of many Bible commentators. Dr. J. C. Fenton, for example, observes: "*then will appear the sign of the Son of man in heaven* is a Matthean addition, and answers the question in v. 3, *what will be the sign of your coming?*"—*The Gospel of St. Matthew* (Penguin Books).

39 This way of depicting nature as trembling at the "sight" of divine forces or mighty conquerors is also common in extra-Biblical literature from the ancient Orient. The Assyrian kings, for example, boasted that the world "shook" during their attacks. Shalmaneser III (858–824 B.C.) claimed that "at his mighty onslaught in battle the ends of the world are made uneasy, the mountains quiver," and Sargon II (721–705 B.C.) boasted that during his attack "heaven and earth shook, the mountains and the sea writhed." (Samuel E. Loewenstamm, "The Trembling of Nature during the Theophany," in *Comparative Studies in Biblical and Ancient Oriental Literatures*, Neukirchen-Vluyn 1980, p. 183)

40 Christ's coming "on the clouds" (or "in" or "with" the clouds, Luke 21:27 and Revelation 1:7) does not denote *invisibility*, as the Watch Tower Society holds (*The Watchtower* of December 15, 1974, p. 751), but the presence of *divine power and glory*. In the Old

On the other hand, there is also the danger of spiritualizing the *parousía* to mean nothing but great changes in the religious or political world. Other texts, such as 2 Peter chapter three, verses 4 to 13, are not easily explained as mere symbols of such upheavals.[41] Indisputably, our century has seen great social and political commotions, including two world wars. But have these things caused men to "faint from fear and the expectation of things which are coming upon the world?" (Luke 21:26) The authors do not deny that there is much fear in the world today. The Watch Tower Society in particular claims that this fear is something new, and that it uniquely fulfills Jesus' prophecy.[42] As has been aptly demonstrated in this book, however, there have been other periods in the past equally characterized by widespread fear, such as the time of the Black Death in the 14th century. In fact, Pastor Russell, the founder of the Watch Tower Society, held that the foretold "fear" was clearly evident in the latter part of the 19th century![43]

Today, one need only look around him, at his neighbors, at people on the streets, at people at work, in their daily affairs and at leisure, and ask—how many give evidence of some great fearful agitation? The fact is that, despite atom bombs and hydrogen bombs, despite spectacular space activities and trips to the moon, despite political or economic upheavals, the vast majority of people go on as people have in the past, their minds occupied with their daily mundane concerns and their plans for the future.[44] Fear of crime, of war, of disease, or

---

Testament only God himself, aside from the "Son of man" in Daniel 7:13, is pictured as coming on or in the clouds. (Jer. 19:1; Ps. 104:3) (See the discussion by Gustaf Dalman in *The Words of Jesus*, Edinburgh 1902, pp. 241–243.)

41 The apostle Peter clearly contrasts "the present heavens and earth" with those existing before the flood and which had been formed by God on the second and third creative "days." (2 Pet. 3:5, 7; Gen. 1:8, 10) Those dating the parousía to A.D. 70 even conclude that "the present heavens and earth" mentioned by Peter refer to the *nation of Israel*, the temporal and spiritual institutions of which were destroyed and dissolved in A.D. 70. (J. S. Russell, *The Parousia*, p. 320) But Peter clearly indicates that "the present heavens and earth" replaced those existing before the flood. It is reasonable to ask how that ancient world could be viewed as being replaced by the nation of Israel in Palestine only? It seems evident that the judgment and destruction described by Peter will be universal in scope, embracing all mankind.

42 *The Watchtower*, July 15, 1983, pp. 3–7.

43 *The Watchtower Reprints*, pp. 26, 253.

44 Dr. Peter Bourne, president of Global Water, Incorporated, in reviewing a work on pestilences in the past, notes that the constant threat of such uncontrollable and often widespread disasters then created much more fear than the threat of nuclear war does today. He says: "The book reminds us of something we too easily forget, namely the terrifying threat

of any other calamity seldom produces more than a vague sense of unease, not the extreme agitation described in prophecy, and those fears are by and large smothered over by workaday interests. And Jesus foretold that it would be no different from this at the time when, with lightning rapidity, the "trap" snaps shut as the time of divine judgment arrives, bringing genuinely terrifying circumstances.— Matthew 24:36–39; Luke 17:26–30; 21:34–36.

Whatever the fear felt in the past and present, it will be dwarfed by the universal panic that actually will fulfill the prophecy. Jesus did not speak about fear of what *might* happen, but of what men understand *will* happen because of the shaking of the "powers of heaven." (Luke 21:26) This clearly refers to the time when "the sign of the Son of man" is seen, when, according to the parallel text in Matthew chapter twenty-four, verse 30, "all the peoples of the earth will beat their breasts [in lamentation]." (NEB) This situation is not presented as having anything to do with mankind's internal affairs, such as periodically scare people. Rather, it will be caused by *cosmic upheavals* of such proportions that men "will die of fright of what is coming upon the earth." (NAB)[45] Whatever the cosmic phenomena introducing the *parousía* turn out to be, therefore, one thing seems clear from the context. As the unmistakable *sign* of the *parousía* they will certainly relate to acts that all on earth will realize are clearly and undeniably

---

which epidemic disease constantly posed to people throughout all of history until just the last few years. Hanging over everyone, regardless of social level, income or power, was the ever-present fear of sudden and irrational death. In our own time, only the threat of nuclear war remotely approximates what that fear must have been like."—*A Shift in the Wind,*No. 18, May 1984, p. 8 (a paper published by The Hunger Project, P. O. Box 789, San Francisco, California 94101, USA).

45 On the terror caused by the alarming cosmic signs, see further Norval Geldenhuys, *Commentary on the Gospel of Luke* (12th printing, Grand Rapids, Michigan, 1979), pp. 537–540. By using the word *oikouménē*, "the inhabited earth, the world," Luke included the whole earth in the coming judgment. Sometimes, as for example in Luke 2:1, *oikouménē* was used of the Roman empire, "which, in the exaggerated language commonly used in ref[erence] to the emperors, was equal to the whole world." (Bauer's *Greek-English Lexicon of the New Testament*, p. 561) Some earlier scholars, focusing on Luke 2:1 and Acts 11:28, 29, argued that *oikouménē* sometimes was used of Palestine only. This view is not currently favored by modern scholarship. Thus the "great famine" mentioned in Acts 11:28, 29, is now documented also for other parts of the Roman empire outside Palestine. (K. S. Gapp, "The Universal Famine under Claudius," *Harvard Theological Review*, Vol. 28, 1935, pp. 258–265.) Similarly, the census referred to in Luke 2:1 was not unique to Palestine, as similar censuses are known to have been taken in many other provinces in the time of Augustus. (See the discussion in I. Howard Marshall, *The Gospel of Luke*, Grand Rapids, Michigan, 1978, pp. 98–104.)

of *divine* origin, and hence totally distinctive from the age-old, common, human experiences with war, famine, pestilence and earthquakes.

Being of this nature, the cosmic upheavals will be recognized by the followers of Christ as foreboding the supreme and ultimate turning-point in the history of mankind: Christ's coming to terminate forever the present evil age with its wars, famines, pestilences and numerous other troubles, and to bring in a new age, "the age to come," of which he will be the Lord. (Mark 10:30) May we be "considered worthy to attain to that age" to be blessed by its Lord with life, peace, happiness and freedom forever! (Luke 20:35) Until the coming of that age we need to live each day of our lives in a way demonstrating that we keep ever in mind the urgent appeal with which, according to the version of Mark, Jesus concluded his discourse:

> Take heed, keep on the alert; for you do not know when the appointed time is.
>
> It is like a man, away on a journey, who upon leaving his house and putting his slaves in charge, assigning to each one his task, also commanded the doorkeeper to stay on the alert.
>
> Therefore, be on the alert—for you do not know when the master of the house is coming, whether in the evening, at midnight, at cockcrowing, or in the morning—lest he come suddenly and find you asleep.
>
> And what I say to you I say to all "Be on the alert!"—Mark 13:33–37, NASB.

Correspondence With Seismologists

IS THERE even *one* seismologist versed in historical seismicity who agrees with today's end-times expositors, and, notably, the Watch Tower Society, that our century has experienced a uniquely great number of destructive earthquakes?

The authors wrote to a number of reputable seismologists all over the world to find out. The answers received were remarkably unanimous. In fact, we have not found a single seismologist who states that he feels earthquakes have increased dramatically in number during this century.

More than one hundred years of research on historical seismicity seems to have established a general consensus among authorities that the seismicity of the earth is not markedly different today from what it has always been for thousands of years.

From considerations of space we can publish only a selection of the letters received, but those not published convey the same message. In general, we explained the nature of our investigation and put a few questions. The following were the most typical:

1. Do you feel that there has been a tremendous increase of major earthquakes during this century compared with earlier centuries?

2. Do you feel that the earthquake activity in this century is in any way unique?

3. Do you know of any other seismologist who holds that our time has seen an unusually large number of earthquakes?

The first letter here published, from Professor Båth, makes reference to an article by Howard D. Burbank entitled "There shall be earthquakes." That article was published in the Adventist periodical *Review* of December, 1977. It contained a graph designed to show that the number of earthquakes has increased explosively, especially in our twentieth century. We asked Professor Båth to comment on Burbank's statements, which he does in his reply:

SEISMOLOGICAL SECTION
BOX 12019
S-750 12 UPPSALA
SWEDEN

Uppsala, 17th June 1983

Mr. Carl Olof Jonsson
Box 281
433 25 Partille

Hearty thanks for your letter of June 6 and the attached article "There shall be earthquakes" by Howard D. Burbank. - . It is very clear that you are complete-ly right in your objections to this article. The author makes the catastrophic mistake of counting only the number of quakes. Instead he should have tried to go by Richter magnitudes and thus by the released energy. The result would then have been quite different.

As you very correctly point out, it is only in recent times that we have got a better network of seismograph stations and thereby a better observation. Actually, reliable instrumental data extend back only to about 1900. But we can make a statistical examination of the period since then.

For this I enclose a paper - Tectonophysics, 54 (1979) T1-T8 - in which Fig. 2 shows energy release and the number of quakes with magnitudes of 7.0 or more. The first 20 years (until about 1920) had about twice as great an energy release per year as the whole period thereafter. The number of quakes with magnitudes of 7.0 or more does not show any marked increase toward later years either.

For earlier centuries we do not have the same reliable statistics, but there are no indications at all of any increase in the activity in the course of time. - Without the slightest hesitation the article (by Burbank) must .be rejected.

With kind regards,

Markus Båth

Markus Båth

The following quite detailed letter was received from Wilbur A. Rinehart of the World Data Center A in Boulder, Colorado:

WORLD DATA CENTER A
BOULDER CENTERS

SOLAR-TERRESTRIAL PHYSICS
(303) 497-6324

SOLID EARTH GEOPHYSICS
(303) 497-6521

National Geophysical Data Center
National Oceanic and Atmospheric Administration
325 Broadway
Boulder, Colorado 80303 U.S.A.
TELEX: 45897 SOLTERWARN—BDR

MARINE GEOLOGY AND GEOPHYSICS
(303) 497-6487

GLACIOLOGY (SNOW AND ICE)
(303) 492-8171

August 8, 1985

Drs. Wolfgang Herbst &
   Carl O. Jonsson
Box 14037
S-14037
S-400 20 Goteborg, Sweden

Dear Drs. Herbst and Jonsson:

Dr. Gänse left the Data Center about three years ago and I have been asked to respond to the questions you posed in your letter of July 7, 1985.

Instrumental seismology began around the turn of the century. Prior to that, the reporting of both large and small earthquakes fell on a general populace, a small scientific community and the media. Large earthquakes occurring in sparsely populated areas went unnoticed and were seldom cataloged.

Systematic locations of earthquakes began by the International Seismological Survey in England in 1913 by Herbert Hall Turner, following the lead set by John Milne who was regarded as the father of English seismology. Their work was continued by many others, including Miss Ethel Bellamy, and Sir Harold Jefferys who continued publishing annual and five year summaries of earthquakes located by ISS since 1918. They used instrumental data to determine the locations of these earthquakes. At the time, there were less than two hundred seismological observatories in the world and the instruments were all of low gain, in the order of 100 to 200. Even with this major contribution to observational seismology, the instruments were too insensitive to determine even some large earthquakes in remote areas of the world.

Seismology did not really receive an instrumental break-through until the early 1960's when the United States Coast and Geodetic Survey installed a network of 111 exact duplicate sets of instruments throughout the 'free' world, primarily for the purpose of detecting the detonation of underground nuclear bombs. The response of all these instruments were the same; their gain varied depending on the ground noise at the site. At that time, the threshold for

2

detecting all large and significant earthquakes was achieved and probably none go undetected in the world.

The misuse of the statistics which you quote in your letter is common for anyone wishing to prove a point. The occurrence of earthquakes is known not to be uniform in time, but no one knows for sure what is the temporal distribution. Our statistical time period for large earthquakes is just too small to know reoccurrence rates or to suggest that for any one time period, there are more shocks than in another time period. Looking at specific areas, there seems to be clusters of large earthquakes in time and then no others in the area appear in the record. A perfect example of this is the 1811-1812 group of possibly magnitude 8+ earthquakes in the New Madrid area in central United States. Even our famous San Andreas fault has been locked since 1906, yet there were large shocks in 1838, 1857, and 1866.

In answer to your questions, I would not agree with the use of the numbers of earthquakes as reported in the 'Catalog of Significant Earthquakes 2000 BC - 1979' to prove any occurrence or reoccurrence rates of earthquakes. The authors would surely agree that the catalogs completeness varies with time, being poorer in the years before instrumental seismology. I know of no competent seismologists or statisticians who would use the numbers quoted in the way the Watchtower Society used them. I certainly would agree with both Professors Bath and Richter in their assessment that there has been no significant increase in the numbers of earthquakes during this or any other century. And I would conclude with Mark Twain's famous quote:

"There are three kinds of lies - lies, damned lies, and statistics."

Sincerely yours,

Wilbur A. Rinehart
Wilbur A. Rinehart
Seismologist

Since the Watch Tower Society, in its publication *The Watchtower* of May 15, 1983, page 6, expressly appealed to the opinion of Professor Keiiti Aki of the Department of Geological Sciences at the University of Southern California, the following correspondence is doubly significant. After receiving a letter from Professor Aki, we had a kind letter, dated September 22, 1985, sent to the Watch Tower Society, asking them for a copy of Aki's *full* statement to them. Not surprisingly they were unwilling to supply such a copy. We are thus obliged to conclude that they do not wish others to know the precise content of the statement to which they referred in their magazine.

We here present, nonetheless, a copy of Professor Aki's letter to the Watch Tower Society, kindly forwarded to us by Professor Aki himself, and this is followed by other correspondence between Professor Aki and the authors of this current work. (For details as to the manner in which Professor Aki's view was misrepresented in publications of the Watch Tower Society, see Chapter 3, pages 66, 67.)

54-526

30 September 1982

Watchtower Society
25 Columbia Heights
Brooklyn, NY 11201

Dear Sir:

This is in response to your inquiry about earthquakes /EC:ESH
September 24, 1982/. The apparent surge in intensity and frequency
of major earthquakes during the last one hundred years is, in all
probability, due to the improved recording of earthquakes and the
increased vulnerability of human society to earthquake damage. The
main reason is the well established plate tectonics which indicates
a very steady fault motion over the past many millions of years.

A measure of earthquake strength more objective than casualty
is the Richter scale. It is in general difficult to assign the
Richter scale to earthquakes more than 100 years ago. An attempt,
however, has been made in China, where historical records are kept
in better shape than in other regions. Enclosed figure shows the
Richter scale (M) of earthquakes in China during the period of about
2000 years. The past 100 years are certainly active, but there have
been periods as active as that, for example, from 1500 to 1700.

Sincerely yours,

Keiiti Aki

KA:jnb
encl.

The Watch Tower Society's use of a selected portion of the above
letter in its magazine *The Watchtower* resulted in an interchange of
correspondence between the authors of this present work and Professor Aki. We here present this resulting correspondence:

DEPARTMENT OF GEOLOGICAL SCIENCES
TELEPHONE: (213) 743-2717

5 September 1985

Messrs. W. Herbst & C. O. Jonsson
Box 14037
S-400 20 Goteborg
SWEDEN

Dear Messrs. Herbst and Jonsson:

Thank you for your inquiry re my statement in Jehovah's Witnesses. I feel strongly that the seismicity has been stationary for thousands of years. I was trying to convince Jehovah's Witnesses about the stationarity of seismicity using the data obtained in China for the period 1500 through 1700, but they put only weak emphasis in the published statement. Excellent geological evidence for the stationarity has been obtained by Prof. Kerry Sieh of Caltech, for the San Andreas fault.

Sincerely yours,

Keiiti Aki

:jl

Professor Keiiti Aki
Department of Geological Sciences
University of Southern California
University Park
LOS ANGELES
California 90089-0741
U.S.A.

Wolfgang Herbst and
Carl Olof Jonsson
Box 14037
S-400 20 Göteborg
Sweden

April 19, 1986

Dear Sir,

Many thanks for your valuable letter of September 5, in answer to our inquiry about the statement on the frequency of major earthquakes as quoted by the Watchtower Society.

We wanted to find out to what extent the Watchtower Society had misrepresented your professional opinion, so I, Wolfgang Herbst, wrote to the Watchtower headquarters in Brooklyn asking for a photocopy of your full statement to them.

Strangely, instead of sending the desired information to us they sent it to their branch office in Sweden, which in turn sent it to a local Witness elder in Göteborg named Börje Silfverberg. This local representative wrote to me and wanted to meet with me in one of their Kingdom Halls, where I would be shown the information I had asked for. As this was not possible at the time I suggested that he just send a copy of their correspondence with you, pointing out that "when I wrote to Professor Aki he did not propose an inconvenient meeting" but "promptly sent the information I asked him for."

However, Mr Silfverberg, acting in consultation with the Watchtower office, still would not send the information. Twisting matters he wrote that since I had information from you there was no longer any need "to show the correspondence in question" and that he therefore was sending the information back to the branch office.

Naturally we take this strange mode of procedure on their part as indicating that they realize they have misused your statement and that they now are trying to conceal the whole matter. The Watchtower Society claims, even in its latest publications, that the frequency of severe earthquakes has increased twentyfold since 1914!

As we attempt to present the true facts on the matter in our coming book on calamities in human history, we would like to know if you still possess copies of the correspondence you had with the Watchtower Society and if it would be possible for us to get xerox copies of it from you? As you may appreciate the Watchtower Society does not want to give any help. Among other things we would like to determine what you meant when you wrote to them about "the apparent surge in intensity and frequency of major earthquakes during the last one hundred years" - if you wrote anything like that at all. If you did, did you use the word "apparent" in the sense of "seeming" (not real), or in the sense of "evident, palpable", as the Watchtower Society indicates, and even more unambiguously in translations into other languages. The Swedish Watchtower, for instance, uses a word meaning "noticeable".

We already have statements from your colleagues, doctors Båth, Ambraseys, Person, Kanamori and others concurring with what you already have written to us. But the Watchtower Society's misuse of your statements to them makes your opinion significant in a special way. If you can help us once more we will be happy to send you a copy of our book when published in Atlanta, Georgia, later this year.

Yours sincerely,

Wolfgang Herbst

Wolfgang Herbst

DEPARTMENT OF GEOLOGICAL SCIENCES
TELEPHONE: (213) 743-2717

16 June 1986

Wolgang Herbst
Carl Olof Jonsson
Box 14037
S-40020 Goteborn
SWEDEN

Dear Sirs:

Enclosed please find a copy of my letter to Watchtower Society. Although the first paragraph is somewhat incomplete (the main reason why I believe that the earthquake activity is constant is shortened to "The main reason"), it is clear that they quoted the part they wanted, eliminating my main message.

Sincerely yours,

Keiiti Aki

Keiiti Aki

Since the Mediterranean area is one of the major earthquake areas of the world, the following letter from Professor N. N. Ambraseys, of the Imperial College of Science and Technology in London, England, discussing seismicity in that area, is of particular interest:

IMPERIAL COLLEGE OF SCIENCE AND TECHNOLOGY

N.N. Ambraseys
DSc(Eng) FGS FRGS FICE
Professor of Engineering Seismology

Department of Civil Engineering
Imperial College Road
London SW7 2BU
Telephone 01-589 5111 Ext.4718
Telex 261503

9th August 1985

Dear Messrs Herbst and Jonsson,

        Thank you for your letter of 5th August. My general response to your queries is that much of the answers are to be found in some detail in my book with C. Melville, entitled "A history of Persian earthquakes", Cambridge University Press, 1982.

        Most certainly, there has been no increase in the seismic activity of the Mediterranean during this century. Quite the contrary, in the Eastern Mediterranean the activity of this century has been abnormally low when compared with that of the 10th-12th and 18th centuries. I do not think that we have missed out any large event in that region during the last 24 centuries.

        I enclose some publications that you may find of some help in the preparation of your book,

        Yours sincerely

        N. N. Ambraseys

cve/NNA

In its issue of June 8, 1984, page 29, under the heading *"Significant" Earthquakes Up,* the Watch Tower Society's magazine *Awake!* referred to geophysicist Waverly Person at the United States Geological Survey. This is the response to our inquiry by Dr. Person, who is head of the National Earthquake Information Service in Denver, Colorado:

United States Department of the Interior
GEOLOGICAL SURVEY
BOX 25046   M.S.___967___
DENVER FEDERAL CENTER
DENVER, COLORADO 80225
Branch of Global Seismology & Geomagnetism
National Earthquake Information Center

IN REPLY
REFER TO:

October 8, 1985

Dr. Carl Olof Jonsson
Box 14037
S-400 20
Goteborg, Sweden

Dear Dr. Jonsson:

Your letter to Dr. Frank Press, concerning a significant increase in great earthquakes during this century has been referred to me for an answer.

I am not sure of your classification of great earthquakes, but to us great earthquakes are ones having magnitudes of 8.0 or greater.

Our records do not show any significant increase in great earthquakes. Enclosed is a list of all magnitude 8.0 or greater earthquakes we have on file.

If we may be of further service to you, please contact us again.

Sincerely yours,

Waverly J. Person
Chief, National Earthquake
Information Service

Enclosures

Along with his letter, Dr. Person sent a complete list of the "great earthquakes," that is, "all magnitude 8.0 or greater earthquakes," on file. This list covers all "great earthquakes" from 1897 onward, plus seven scattered earthquakes previous to that date.[1] Actually the list shows *a gradually decreasing number of great earthquakes during this century,* with the proportionally greatest number during the period previous to 1914. This is in agreement with the conclusions of other prominent seismologists, as shown in our chapter on earthquakes.[2]

The list supplied by Dr. Person is summarized below in 17-year intervals:

17-year period	*No. of great earthquakes*	*Annual average*
1897–1913	49	2.9
1914–1930	28	1.6
1931–1947	28	1.6
1948–1964	14	0.8
1965–1981	10	0.6

From 1982 to 1985, inclusive, only one "great" earthquake occurred, the one in Mexico on September 19, 1985. Naturally, this gradual decrease in the number of great earthquakes during this century simply represents a normal variation when seen in the longer perspective. The trend may thus quickly shift to an opposite trend at any time in accordance with the cyclical nature of tremors.

Because the Worldwide Church of God publication *The Good News of the World Tomorrow* made the astounding claim that from 1901 to 1944 "only three earthquakes measured magnitude 7 or over," a letter

---

1 The choice of 1897 as the starting point is not accidental. It was in the 1890's that seismographs capable of registering distant earthquakes came into use. Thus a fairly complete record of great earthquakes from all parts of the earth is available only from 1897 onward.

2 Seismologist Seweryn J. Duda, in his thorough study of the period 1897–1964, concludes: "Thus, the annual seismic energy release in the world shows a clear indication of decrease in the interval 1897–1964. . . . The seismic energy release per year has decreased significantly in the 68 years since 1897 both in the circum-Pacific and the non-Pacific regions." (Tectonophysics, Vol. 2, 1965, p. 424) Of these 68 years, those of 1905–1907 saw the greatest number of earthquakes. Geologist Haroun Tazieff explains: "The period 1905–1907 was the most disturbed of modern times, a period marked by eleven shocks of magnitude 8 or more; and during the year 1906 alone the world sustained these successive earthquakes: Honshu, Japan, magnitude 8 . . .; frontier of Colombia and Ecuador, magnitude 8.6; San Francisco, 8.2; Aleutians, 8; Valparaiso in Chile, 8.4; New Guinea, 8.1; Sinkiang, China, magnitude 8. According to Gutenberg and Richter the energy released by earthquakes in 1906 was five times greater than the average for the twentieth century, based upon the years 1904–1952." (*When the Earth Trembles,* London 1964, p. 134)

was written to Dr. Seweryn J. Duda, Professor of Geophysics at the University of Hamburg, requesting his comments. Professor Duda's reply is here presented:

UNIVERSITÄT HAMBURG

INSTITUT FÜR GEOPHYSIK

> Institut für Geophysik
> Bundesstraße 55, D 2000 Hamburg 13

Mr.Wolfgang Herbst
Carl Olof Jonsson
Box 14037
S-400 20 Göteborg
Sweden

Fernsprecher: (040) 41 23 - **4918** } Durchwahl
Behördennetz: 9.38. (.) |

Telex-Nr.: 2 14732 unihhd

Datum und Zeichen Ihres Schreibens	Aktenzeichen (bei Antwort bitte angeben)	Datum
	SJD/ro	7 July 1986

Betreff

Dear Mr. Wolfgang Herbst,
dear Mr. Carl Olof Jonsson,

this is with reference to the letter of Mr. Wolfgang Herbst dated 7 June 1986. Your questions can be answered as follows:

— ad 1) In the time 1901-1944 about 1000 (one thousand) earthquakes with magnitude 7 or over have taken place worldwide.

ad 2) It is not justified to claim that large earthquakes have increased dramatically from the mid-fifties to the present. There are indications that worldwide seismic activity - if expressed in terms of earthquakes with magnitude 7 or over - has decreased steadily in the time from the beginning of the 20-th century until now. It would be however speculative to extrapolate the pattern in any way into the future.

ad 3) There are no indications that the twentieth century is radically different from earlier centuries, as far as the global seismic activity is concerned.

What is different though is the higher density of population (in earthquake-prone areas, and thus the higher potential loss of human life in case of an earthquake, compensated however in general by a better standard of house-construction. Also, the better communication increases the awarness of the calamities incurred in case of a natural desaster.

Thanking you for having asked my opinion on the above problems, I am

Sincerely yours,

Seweryn J. Duda
Professor of Geophysics

All these letters by reputable earthquake authorities thus stand in stark contrast to the extreme, often irresponsible, claims made by various end-times expositors in our day.

"Coming" or "Presence"—What Do the Facts Reveal?

IN THE question put to Jesus at Matthew chapter twenty-four, verse 3, "What will be the sign of your coming," the word "coming" translates the Greek word *parousía*. *Parousía* primarily means "presence," but it is well established today that at the time of Jesus it was also used in a different sense. Despite this, the Watch Tower Society insists on "presence" as the only correct Biblical meaning of the term. In this they clearly have a "vested interest."

Their claim that Christ's *parousía* began in 1914 and that since that year we have seen the sign of this in world events implies that Jesus' disciples asked for a sign indicating that *Christ had come and was invisibly present,* not for a sign that would *precede* his coming and indicate this to be *imminent.* Consequently the Society's *New World Translation of the Holy Scriptures* renders the question at Matthew chapter twenty-four, verse 3, thus:

> **Tell us, When will these things be, and <u>what will be the sign of your presence</u> and the conclusion of the system of things?**

The idea underlying this translation is that Christ's second coming consists of two stages, the first being an *invisible presence* for a period until the second stage, that of his final revelation of this presence to the world at the battle of Armageddon. This idea did not originate with the Watch Tower Society. It can be traced back to the 1820's, when it was first suggested by the well-known London banker and Bible expositor *Henry Drummond,* who was later to become one of the founders of Edward Irving's *Catholic Apostolic Church.* The "invisible presence" or "two-stage coming" theory, better known today as the "secret rapture" theory, was quickly picked up by other expositors of the prophecies. It was adopted not only by the Irvingites but also by the followers of John Nelson Darby, the *Plymouth Brethren,* through whom it was widely spread in England, the U.S.A. and other countries. It became very popular especially among the *millenarians,* Christians who believe in a literal, future millennium on earth.[1]

For many of the defenders of the "two-stage coming" idea the Greek word *parousía* became a crucial point in the discussion. It was commonly held that this word referred to the first stage of Christ's coming, his invisible presence "in the air." The Greek words *ephiphánia,* "appearing," and *apokálypsis,* "revelation," on the other hand, were usually said to apply to the second stage of the coming, Christ's intervention in world events at the battle of Armageddon. Changing the translation of *parousía* from "coming" to "presence" radically alters the sense, not only of the question of the disciples, but also of Jesus' answer. This is illustrated by the arguments put forth in 1866 by Reverend Robert Govett, the most prominent British champion of the secret rapture idea in the last century:

> If we say, 'What is the sign of Thy *coming*?' (Matt, xxiv. 3) then, . . . we are enquiring for a sign of the Savior's future movement from the highest heaven. If we say, 'What is the sign of thy *presence*?' we are enquiring for a proof of Jesus' *existence in secret in the air,* after his motion towards earth is for a while arrested.
>
> The disciples inquire, 'What shall be the sign of thy Presence?' (verse 3). This, then, assures us that they imagined that Jesus would be present in *secret.* We need no sign of that which is openly exhibited.[2]

These arguments made in 1866 were picked up by many other expositors, among them Charles Taze Russell. In 1876, under the influence of the Adventist Nelson H. Barbour and his associates, Russell had adopted "presence" as the only acceptable meaning of *parousía* to explain how Christ could have come in 1874 (as had been predicted by Barbour) without being noticed by anyone. The adoption of this view, then, was due to a failed prediction and it was used as a means of explaining away their 1874 failure. This explanation was retained

---

1 For a detailed investigation into the origin and development of the "invisible presence" idea and how it came to be adopted by Russell and his followers, see C. O. Jonsson, "The Theory of Christ's *Parousía* As An 'Invisible Presence'," *The Bible Examiner,* Vol. 2, No. 9, 1982, and Vol. 3, No. 1, 1983, Box 81, Lethbridge, Alberta, Canada T1J-3Y3.

2 The British millenarian journal *The Rainbow,* June 1866, p. 265 and July 1866, p. 302. *The Rainbow,* more than any other millenarian journal in England, granted space to the expositors of the secret rapture idea, and Govett had many articles published in it. Govett's main work on the subject was his 357-page work, *The Saints' Rapture to the Presence of the Lord Jesus,* published in 1852. The whole discussion throughout the book rests on Govett's changing the word "coming" into "presence"!

by Russell's followers on up into the early 1930's, when it was suddenly "discovered" that Christ's "invisible presence" had begun in 1914 instead of 1874!

However, such stress on "presence" as the only correct Biblical meaning of *parousía* appears to find very little support among Bible translators. In fact, all but a very few Bible translators prefer instead the renderings "coming," "advent," "arrival," or similar terms, instead of "presence." A Witness researcher and Bible collector, William J. Chamberlin of Clawson, Michigan, U.S.A., carefully checked how *parousía* is rendered at Matthew chapter twenty-four, verses 3, 27, 37 and 39, in hundreds of different Bible translations all the way from William Tyndale's New Testament in 1534 to translations released as recently as 1980, and he prepared extensive lists of the renderings of 137 translations from this period. An examination of these lists gave some very interesting results.

"Parousía" in Bible translations

Before the middle of the nineteenth century apparently few Bible translators were inclined to render *parousía* by "presence." Of the English translations of the New Testament from Tyndale in the sixteenth century to Robert Young in 1862, Chamberlin found only one translator, Wakefield, who in his New Testament (1795) used "presence" as a translation of *parousía* at Matthew chapter twenty-four, verse 39. But still Wakefield preferred to render it "coming" at verses 3, 27 and 37 in the same chapter. Further, Daniel Scott in his translation of Matthew published in 1741 (*New Version of St. Matthew's Gospel*) gives "presence" in the notes, while retaining "coming" in the running text.

The first translator in the nineteenth century to translate *parousía* as "presence" in Matthew chapter twenty-four was probably Dr. Robert Young in his *Literal Translation of the Holy Bible* (1862), the reason being, as the title indicates, that he attempted to present the *strictly literal* meanings of the Greek words instead of the meanings in modern idiom. Two years later, Benjamin Wilson, an early leader of a small religious body known today as the Church of God General Conference, published his *The Emphatic Diaglott* (1864), which likewise renders *parousía* as "presence" throughout all the 24 occurrences in the New Testament.[3]

---

3 See the book *Historical Waymarks of the Church of God*, published by the headquarters of the movement in Oregon, Illinois 61061, in 1976. The group holds views similar to the

Then, in 1868–1872, Joseph B. Rotherham published his *The Emphasized New Testament*. But it was not until in the third revised edition, published in 1897, that Rotherham changed his translation of *parousía* from "arrival" to "presence." Why? The reason he gives in the *Appendix* to the third edition indicates that he, at least partially, had come to embrace the "two-stage coming" idea. He explains that Christ's *parousía* may not only be an *event,* but also "a period—more or less extended, during which certain things shall happen." Undoubtedly, Rotherham had been influenced in his thinking on this subject through his close friendship with some of the contributors to *The Rainbow* magazine, of which Rotherham himself became editor during its last three years of existence.[4]

Other translators of the last century who used "presence" for *parousía* at Matthew chapter twenty-four were W. B. Crickmer (*The Greek Testament Englished,* 1881), J. W. Hanson (*The New Covenant,* 1884) and Ferrar Fenton, who began publishing the first parts of his translation, *The Bible in Modern English,* in the 1880's.

In our century translations that render *parousía* as "presence" in Matthew chapter twenty-four are A. E. Knoch's *A Concordant Version* (1926), Ivan Panin's *Bible Numerics* (2nd ed., 1935), the Watch Tower Society's *New World Translation of the Christian Greek Scriptures* (1950), James L. Tomanek's *New Testament* (1958), the *Restoration of Original Holy Name Bible* (1968), Donald Klingensmith's *Today's English New Testament* (1972) and Dr. Dymond's *New Testament* (1972; in manuscript form only).[5] Other translations occasionally give "presence" as the literal meaning of *parousía* in footnotes, but prefer "coming," "arrival" (or the like) in the main text.

With these comparatively few exceptions, then, both older and modern translators have preferred to render *parousía* by "coming," "advent," "arrival," or some similar term instead of "presence" in texts dealing with the second coming of Christ. They do this despite the fact that all of them agree that "presence" is the *primary* meaning of the word. Why? Is it logical to believe that so many experts on the

---

Christadelphians and Jehovah's Witnesses on such doctrines as the trinity, the soul and hell-fire.

4 See earlier footnote 2. Rotherham was editor of *The Rainbow* from 1885 through 1887. See also Rotherham's *Reminiscences,* compiled by his son J. George Rotherham (London, shortly after 1906), pp. 76–79.

5 That at least some of these translators were influenced by their adherence to the "invisible presence" doctrine is illustrated by Dymond's translation of Matthew 24:3: "But in the meantime tell us what other events will indicate that you have returned to earth to be invisibly present."

original language of the New Testament have somehow failed to grasp the true sense of this Greek term?

What of the *earliest* versions of the New Testament, the Latin, Syriac, Coptic and Gothic versions, which were produced *while the original koiné Greek of the New Testament was still a living language?* What do they reveal as to how those ancient translators understood the word *parousía?*

"Parousía" in the earliest versions of the New Testament

As is well known, the Latin *Vulgate* Version was produced by the great fourth century scholar Hieronymus, better known today as St. Jerome. He carried out his translation work toward the end of the fourth century, starting with the Gospels in A.D. 383. Interestingly, in 20 of the 24 occurrences of *parousía* in the New Testament, Jerome chose the Latin word for "coming," *adventus,* from which the English word "advent" is derived. The four exceptions are 1 Corinthians 16:17; 2 Corinthians 10:10; Philippians 2:12 and 2 Peter 1:16. In these instances the Vulgate uses the Latin word for "presence," *praesentia.* It is noteworthy that only the last of these four texts deals with the *parousía* of Christ. In all the other sixteen instances where *parousía* refers to the coming of Christ, Jerome preferred the Latin word *adventus.* Why? Evidently he felt that in texts dealing with the *parousía* of Jesus Christ the word meant "coming" rather than "presence." Was he wrong in this understanding?

Actually, the Latin *Vulgate* was not the earliest Latin version of the Bible. It was preceded by numerous other Latin translations, some of which were produced as early as in the second century. Jerome's Vulgate was, in fact, not a translation but a revision of these earlier Latin versions (although compared against the original Hebrew, Aramaic and Greek texts), a revision produced in order to create an authoritative Latin version out of the diversity of old Latin versions. These older versions are with a common name termed the *Old Latin Bible* or (in Latin) *Vetus Latina.* Like the *Vulgate* they, too, usually render *parousía* by *adventus.* The five exceptions (2 Corinthians 10:10; Philippians 2:12; 2 Thessalonians 2:9; 2 Peter 3:4, 12) include only two passages dealing with the *parousía* of Christ. Thus, like the *Vulgate,* the Old Latin versions prefer to render *parousía* by the word *adventus,* doing this in 15 out of the 17 texts dealing with the *parousía* of Christ.[6] (See the accompanying table on page 255.)

The Latin word *adventus* literally means "a coming to," although it, too, sometimes could be used in the sense of "presence." In the above-mentioned Latin versions, though, *adventus* is clearly used in the sense of "coming," in contrast to *praesentia,* the Latin word for "presence."

The Syriac *Peshitta* version was produced in the fifth century, but like the Latin *Vulgate* it was preceded by older versions, as shown, for instance, by the Curetonian and Sinaitic Syriac manuscripts.[7] If, as is commonly held, the native language of Jesus and his apostles was *Aramaic,* these Syriac versions may actually reflect words used by Jesus and the apostles themselves, including the Syriac word for *parousía* in Matthew chapter twenty-four, *me' thithá!*[8] Like the Latin word *adventus, me' thithá* literally means "coming," being derived from a verb meaning "come."

The *Gothic Version* was produced by Wulfila in the middle of the fourth century, being therefore slightly earlier than the Latin Vulgate translation. This version translates *parousía* by the Gothic noun *cums,* a word related to the English "come." It means, quite naturally, "coming."[9]

The remarkable conclusion, then, is that the earliest versions of the New Testament—produced when *koiné* Greek was still a living language and by translators some of whom knew that language thoroughly from their childhood—preferred to render the Greek noun *parousía* by words meaning "coming" rather than "presence" in passages relating to the second coming of Christ. They did this in spite of the fact that *parousía* primarily means "presence" and was so translated at other places. The question is: Why did they render the word

---

6 See D. Petri Sabatier, *Bibliorum Sacrorum Latinae Versiones Antiquae,* originally published in 1743. The facsimile printed in Münich in 1974 has been consulted for this discussion.

7 See the extensive discussions by Bruce M. Metzger in *The Early Versions of the New Testament,* Oxford 1977, pp. 3–82, and by Matthew Black in *Die alten Übersetzungen des Neuen Testaments,* K. Aland, editor, Berlin, New York, 1972, pp. 120–159.

8 Pieter Leendert Schoonheim, *Een Semasiologisch onderzoek van Parousia met betrekking tot het gebruik in Mattheus 24* ("A Semasiological Research into Parousia with special reference to its use in S. Matthew 24"), Aalten, Holland, 1953, pp. 20–22, 259. The Curetonian manuscript is generally believed to be a recension of the earlier Sinaitic Syriac text, which in turn was originally produced in Antioch in northern Syria. The Syriac of these manuscripts, therefore, being a dialect of Aramaic, is probably very close to the Palestinian Aramaic dialect used by Jesus and his apostles.

9 The early Coptic, Ethiopic and Armenian versions have not been investigated.

PAROUSIA IN THE OLDEST LATIN TRANSLATIONS OF THE NEW TESTAMENT

Texts using parousia:	*Vulgate* (4th century)	*Old Latin* (2nd century)	*Church fathers (1st–5th centuries)*	
			Adventus	*Praesentia*
Matthew 24:3	adventus	adventus	many	none
24:27	adventus	adventus	many	none
24:37	adventus	adventus	many	none
24:39	adventus	adventus	many	Victorinus, d. 303
1 Cor. 15:23	adventus	adventus	many	Augustinus, d. 430
16:17	*praesentia*	adventus	none?	Ambrosiaster, 5th century, *et al*
2 Cor. 7:6	adventus	adventus	Ambrosiaster	none
7:7	adventus	adventus	Ambrosiaster	none
10:10	*praesentia*	*praesentia*	none?	Ambrosiaster
Phil. 1:26	adventus	adventus	Ambrosiaster	none
2:12	*praesentia*	*praesentia*	none?	Ambrosiaster
1 Thess. 2:19	adventus	adventus	Tertullianus d. after 220 Ambrosiaster	none
3:13	adventus	adventus	Tertullianus Ambrosius, d. 397 Ambrosiaster	none
4:15	adventus	adventus	many	none
5:23	adventus	adventus	Irenaeus, d. after 190 Tertullianus, in many places, *et al*	Tertullianus, in one place
2 Thess. 2:1	adventus	adventus	Tertullianus	none
2:8	adventus	adventus	Tertullianus Ambrosiaster *et al*	Irenaeus Hilarius, d. 367 *et al*
2:9	adventus	*praesentia*	many	Augustinus
James 5:7	adventus	adventus	none	none
5:8	adventus	adventus	none	none
2 Peter 1:16	*praesentia*	(missing)	none	none
3:4	adventus	*praesentia*	none	none
3:12	adventus	*praesentia*	(Pelagius)	(Auctor)
1 John 2:28	adventus	adventus	none	none

(The variants of the Church fathers are taken from Sabatier's footnotes.)

as "coming" when it referred to the *parousía* of Jesus Christ, but as "presence" when it referred to the *parousía* of, for instance, the apostle Paul (2 Corinthians 10:10; Philippians 2:12)? For centuries this remained somewhat of a mystery, until—at the dawn of our own twentieth century—new discoveries enabled modern experts on New Testament Greek to find the answer to this riddle.

The technical use of parousía

During the last century excavations on the sites of ancient settlements of the Graeco-Roman world brought to light *hundreds of thousands* of inscriptions on stone and metal and texts on papyrus, parchment and potsherds.

These new finds revolutionized the study of the original Greek language of the New Testament. It was discovered that the Greek of the New Testament was neither a special "Biblical Greek" as some believed, nor the literary, archaizing Greek used by contemporary authors, but to a great extent was colored by the Greek vernacular used by ordinary people at home and elsewhere, the common language of daily life, the spoken form of the *koiné* Greek.

The consequences of this discovery as regards the understanding of the original Greek language of the Bible was first explored in detail by Adolf Deissmann, later Professor at the University of Heidelberg (still later at the University of Berlin), who began publishing his findings in 1895. Other scholars, who realized the importance of the discovery, soon joined in scrutinizing the newly discovered texts. New light was thrown upon the way many Greek words were used and understood at the time the New Testament was written.

One of the words, whose meaning was illuminated by the new texts, was the word *parousía*. The new insights were summarized by Professor Deissmann in 1908 in his now classic work *Licht vom Osten* (*Light from the East*). His discussion of the word *parousía*, covering several pages, opens with the following explanation:

> Yet another of the central ideas of the oldest Christian worship receives light from the new texts, viz. παρουσια [*parousía*], 'advent, coming,' a word expressive of the most ardent hopes of a St. Paul. We now may say that the best interpretation of the Primitive Christian hope of the Parousia is the old Advent text, 'Behold, thy King cometh unto thee.' [Matthew 21:5] From the Ptolemaic period down into the 2nd cent. A. D. we are

able to trace the word in the East as a technical expression for the arrival or the visit of the king or the emperor.[10]

Professor Deissmann then gives many examples of this use of the term. At the occasion of such an official, royal visit, as for example when the Roman emperor made a *parousía* in the provinces in the east, "the roads were repaired, crowds flocked to do homage, there were processions of his white-garbed subjects, trumpet blasts, acclamations, speeches, petitions, gifts and festivities."[11] Often a new era was reckoned from the *parousía* of the king or emperor, and coins were struck to commemorate it. At the visit or *parousía* of Emperor Nero, for instance, in whose reign Paul wrote his letters to Corinth, the cities of Corinth and Patras struck "advent-coins." These coins bore the inscription *Adventus Aug(usti) Cor(inthi)*, demonstrating that the Latin *adventus* was used as an equivalent of the Greek term *parousía* at those occasions.[12]

Since then, additional research by numerous scholars, such as Professors George Milligan, James Hope Moulton and others, has further confirmed conclusions of Deissmann, who first demonstrated this technical use of *parousía*.[13] This use of the term clearly explained why the early versions of the New Testament rendered it by words meaning "coming" in texts dealing with the *parousía* of Jesus Christ. Greek lexicons and dictionaries today all point out this sense of the word in addition to its primary meaning ("presence"), and there is a general consensus among modern scholars that *parousía* in the New Testament, when used of the second coming of Christ, is used in its technical sense of a royal visitation.[14]

Will his coming be "a visit of a king?" Certainly it will. Repeatedly,

---

10 Quoted from the English translation by L. R. M. Strachan from the 4th edition, *Light from the Ancient East*, reprinted by Baker Book House, Grand Rapids, Michigan, 1978, p. 368.

11 B. M. Nolan, "Some Observations on the *parousía*," *The Irish Theological Quarterly*, Vol. XXXVI, Maynooth 1969, p. 288.

12 Deissmann, p. 371. Notably, the Greek word *epipháneia*, "appearing," usually applied to the second stage of Christ's coming by the adherents of the secret rapture notion, was also used at times on Greek "advent-coins" as an equivalent of the Latin *adventus!* (Deissmann, p. 373.)

13 The most extensive linguistic study of the term *parousía* is that of Pieter Leendert Schooheim, *Een semasiologisch onderzoek van Parousia*, Aalten, Holland, 1953. This work covers about 300 pages, including a 33-page summary in English.

14 See for instance Kittel/Friedrich, *Theological Dictionary of the New Testament*, Vol. V, pp. 858–871, and the lengthy article in the French *Dictionnaire de la Bible, Supplément*, ed. by L. Pirot, A. Robert and H. Cazelles, Paris-VI, 1960, pp. 1332–1420. Another interesting study is that by J. T. Nélis in *Bibel-Lexikon*, Tubingen 1968, pp. 1304–1312.

the Bible presents Christ's *parousía* as a coming "with power and great glory," when he will be sitting "upon the throne of his glory" and be accompanied by "all his angels." (Matthew 24:30; 25:31) A mighty "voice" of an archangel, "a great trumpet sound," and other noticeable signs further contribute to the description of Christ's *parousía* as an *official, royal visit,* noticed by all and causing "all the tribes of the earth" to "beat themselves in lamentation" at his sight. In no way is his coming presented as an invisible, secret presence unnoticed by the great majority of mankind.—Matthew 24:27, 29–31; 1 Thessalonians 4:15, 16; Revelation 1:7.

Scholarly support claimed

In support of its insistence upon "presence" as the only acceptable meaning of *parousía* in the Bible the Watch Tower Society sometimes quotes a few Bible translations and an occasional Greek scholar. It is significant, though, that most of these references are obsolete, dating from a time when the technical use of the term was still unknown.

Thus the most recent discussion of the word *parousía,* published in 1984 in the revised *New World Translation of the Holy Scriptures with References,* pages 1576 and 1577 (Appendix 5b), starts by citing four Bible translations that render *parousia* as "presence" at Matthew chapter twenty-four, verse 3, three of which (Wilson's *The Emphatic Diaglott,* Rotherham's *The Emphasized Bible* and Fenton's *The Holy Bible in Modern English*) were produced before the discovery of Deissmann and his colleagues. The fourth is the Society's own *New World Translation of the Christian Greek Scriptures* from 1950! The article that follows is wholly dominated by a quotation from the work *The Parousia* written by Dr. Israel P. Warren, who argues in defense of "presence" as the correct Biblical meaning of *parousía.* Unfortunately, Dr. Warren's work dates from 1879![15]

The article, however, also refers to three modern Greek lexicons. It is pointed out that Liddell and Scott's *A Greek-English Lexicon* and Kittel/Friedrich's *TDNT* (*Theological Dictionary of the New Testament*) both give "presence" as the meaning of *parousía.* But why are the readers not told that both these same lexicons go on to explain that *parousía* was also used in the technical sense of "the visit of a king"? Why are they not told that these same lexicons emphasize that this is how the word is used in the New Testament when it refers to the

---

15   Israel P. Warren, D.D., *The Parousia,* Portland, Maine, 1879, pp. 12–15.

parousía of Jesus Christ? The last of the two lexicons, the *TDNT*, actually spends only a few sentences on the primary meaning "presence." *The rest of the article, covering 14 pages in all, is a discussion of the technical use of the term, demonstrating that this is how the word is used in New Testament texts dealing with the parousía of Jesus Christ!* The reader of the Watch Tower's publication would never know this and would be unlikely to have the means to find it out. Argumentation that finds it necessary to employ such obviously slanted use of evidence certainly has little to recommend it.

Finally, Bauer's lexicon is quoted as saying that *parousía* "became the official term for a visit of a person of high rank, esp(ecially) of kings and emperors visiting a province." Curiously, this statement is cited as if it gave additional support to the claim that the Bible uses *parousía* only in the sense of "presence," despite the fact that Bauer's lexicon here gives *the technical use of the term*, the official visit of a king or emperor (or a person of high rank).

There is one modern Greek-English dictionary, however, that seems to lend some support to the Watch Tower Society's understanding of Christ's *parousía* as a period of "invisible presence," to be followed by a final "revelation" of this presence at the battle of Armageddon. That is W. E. Vine's *Expository Dictionary of New Testament Words*, which defines the term *parousía* in the following way:

> **PAROUSIA . . . denotes both an arrival and a consequent presence with. . . . When used of the return of Christ, it signifies not merely his momentary coming for His saints, but His presence with them from that moment until His revelation and manifestation to the world.**

This description of the *parousía* sounds very much like that of the Watch Tower Society. It is no surprise, therefore, to find that Vine's definition of the word is quoted at length on page 1335 of the Society's Bible dictionary *Aid to Bible Understanding*. It may be a surprise to some, however, to learn that Vine was one of the most assiduous advocates of the "secret rapture" doctrine in our century. This apparently caused him to define the word *parousía* in a way that supported his theological views. However, this only served to bring him into conflict with the results of modern scholarship.

As noted earlier, the "secret rapture" idea found its most zealous champions among the followers of John Nelson Darby, called the *Brethren*. In 1847 a schism between Darby and George Müller, the leader of a group of Brethren in Bristol, England, split the movement in two: the *Exclusive Brethren*, headed by Darby, and the *Open Breth-*

ren, who sided with Müller. Although Müller himself rejected the "secret rapture" concept, the Open Brethren movement stuck to the idea and continued to preach it. W. E. Vine, who was born in 1873, was associated with the Open Brethren and seems to have been that from his youth. He was a great scholar, and his *Dictionary* is invaluable as a handbook to the study of the New Testament. His definition of the word *parousía,* however, was clearly influenced by his adherence to the "secret rapture" doctrine, a doctrine that may have been dear to him since his early days. He defended it in several works written in collaboration with a fellow-believer, Mr. C. F. Hogg, such as *The Epistles of Paul and the Apostle to the Thessalonians* (1914), *Touching the Coming of the Lord* (1919), and *The Church and the Tribulation* (1938). The last-mentioned book was published as a reply to Rev. Alexander Reese's broadside against the "secret rapture" idea, *The Approaching Advent of Christ,* published in the previous year (1937). The well-known exegete and Bible commentator, Professor F. F. Bruce, although of the same religious background as Dr. Vine, gives the following critical comments on Vine and Hogg's use of the word *parousía* in their eschatological system:

> **Perhaps the most distinctive feature of *Touching the Coming* was their treatment of the word *parousía.* They insisted on the primary sense of 'presence' and understood the word in its eschatological use to mean the presence of Christ with His raptured Church in the interval preceding His manifestation in glory. . . .**
>
> **It may be questioned whether this interpretation of *parousía* does adequate justice to the sense which the word has in Hellenistic Greek. The writers did, indeed, appeal in support of their view to Cremer's lexicon; but Cremer wrote a good while before the study of vernacular papyri revolutionized our knowlege of the common Hellenistic speech.**[16]

The Watch Tower Society's reference to Dr. Vine's definition of *parousía,* then, does not carry great weight. At a closer look it proves to be essentially as obsolete as their other references.

What does the Biblical context show?

When a word has more than one meaning, the context must always be considered in determining how it should be understood. Does the context of Matthew chapter twenty-four, verse 3, indicate that Matthew

---

16 F. F. Bruce in Percy O. Ruoff, *W. E. Vine, His Life and Ministry,* London 1951, pp. 75, 76.

used *parousía* in its technical sense or in its primary sense? The Watch Tower Society claims that the latter sense, "presence," is indicated by the context. Said *The Watchtower* of July 1, 1949, on page 197:

> The fact that the arrival or visit of a king or emperor was one of the technical meanings of *parousía* does not deny or disprove that in the Holy Scriptures it has the meaning of *presence* respecting Christ Jesus. To show the meaning of the word the Scriptural context is more powerful than any outside papyrus usage of the word in a technical sense.

Agreed, Scriptural context is more powerful in such circumstance. The question is, Does the context of Matthew chapter twenty-four, verse 3, really show that the disciples asked for a sign that would indicate Christ to be *present,* and not for a sign that would indicate he was *coming?* Is there any reason to believe that they actually thought of Christ's coming as an "invisible presence," one that could be recognized only by means of a visible sign?

When this question was put to the Watch Tower Society, they had to admit that the disciples "had no idea that he [Christ] would rule as a glorious spirit from the heavens and therefore did not know that his second presence would be invisible."[17] If the disciples had no idea that Christ in the future would come to be invisibly present, how could they have asked for a sign of such an invisible presence? This alone shows that Matthew cannot have used *parousía* in the sense of "presence." Evidently they asked Jesus to give them a sign that would announce that Christ's promised coming or arrival was imminent. They wanted a sign, not to tell them of something that would already be in effect, but a sign that would give *advance* notice that the desired event was about to occur, was indeed at hand. Their language, the words they used to express their question, would be in harmony with that desire.

That this is the correct understanding is clearly verified by the way Mark has recorded their question. In Mark's version, the question for a "sign" refers to the *destruction of the temple* only. It certainly is impossible to think that they needed some "sign" to convince them that the temple had been destroyed or that its destruction was taking place. They wanted some indication *in advance* of that event![18]

---

17 *The Watchtower,* September 15, 1964, p. 576. The same conclusion was drawn in *The Watchtower* of January 15, 1974, on page 50: "When they asked Jesus, 'What will be the sign of your presence?' they did not know that his future presence would be invisible."

18 This refutes the argument sometimes employed by the Watch Tower Society that 'there would be no need for a sign if the parousia were to be visible and tangible.' See *Awake!* December 8, 1967, p. 27.

The way Jesus answered their question fully confirms this. After his survey of future events that also included the destruction of Jerusalem, Jesus, in verses 29 and 30, described the sign that would accompany his future coming "on the clouds" and added:

> Now learn from the fig tree as an illustration this point: Just as soon as its young branch grows tender and it puts forth leaves, you know that summer is near. Likewise also you, when you see all these things, know that he is near at the doors.—Matthew 24:32, 33, *NW.*

It should be noted that Jesus did not say that when they saw the young branch of the fig tree growing tender and putting forth leaves, they would know that "summer is present." These signs would *precede* the summer and prove it to be *near.* Similarly, the sign of the coming of the Son of man would prove that "he is near at the doors," not invisibly present. The comparison is between the summer as *being near,* and Christ as *being near.* Clearly, Jesus told his disciples to look for a sign that would *precede* his arrival or "royal visit," not for a sign that would *follow* his coming and show him to be invisibly present. From the *context* of Matthew chapter twenty-four, verse 3, then, it is very clear that the disciples asked for the sign of Christ's imminent *coming,* not for a sign of his *presence.* The context, therefore, strongly supports the conclusion that Matthew used the word *parousía* in its technical sense, to signify the arrival or visit of a king or high dignitary.[19]

It is remarkable, also, that of the four Gospel writers, Matthew alone uses the word *parousía,* and this only in chapter twenty-four. The four verses containing the term (3, 27, 37 and 39) have parallels in Luke, but instead of *parousía* Luke usually has "day" or "days." When Jesus compares his coming to the lightning, which immediately lights up in a flash the entire visible heaven from the east to the west and adds, according to Matthew chapter twenty-four, verse 27, "So shall be the coming (*parousía*) of the Son of man," Luke instead, at

---

19 In the book *God's Kingdom of a Thousand Years Has Approached* (1973) the Watch Tower Society makes an attempt on page 169 to adapt the technical use of *parousía* to its "invisible presence" doctrine by stating that, "A 'visit' includes more than an 'arrival'. It includes a 'presence.'" This is certainly true. But they try to obscure the obvious difference between the two uses of *parousía.* At a royal visit the *arrival* of the king or emperor was the most spectacular phase of the visit, something that called for the attention of all. If the disciples, as the evidence shows, asked for the sign of the *official, royal, visible visit of Christ,* they must have had in mind something that would *precede* such a visit. It would be pointless to ask for a sign that would show that the king had already arrived.

chapter seventeen, verse 24, has, "so shall the Son of man be in his day." Thus Christ's *parousía* and Christ's *day* (*hēméra*) are used interchangeably for the time of Christ's appearance or revelation. This is brought out even more clearly in Christ's comparison of his coming with the coming of the Flood in the days of Noah, when men "knew not until the flood came; so shall be the coming [*parousía*] of the Son of man." (Matthew 24:37, 39) Luke's version adds also the destruction of Sodom in the days of Lot and says: "after the same manner shall it be in the day the Son of man is revealed."—Luke 17:26–30.

It is obvious that Jesus here is not comparing the *parousía* with the periods *preceding* the Flood and the destruction of Sodom. This is how the Watch Tower Society explains it, referring to the expression "the days of the Son of man" at Luke chapter seventeen, verse 26. To the contrary, Jesus clearly compares his future coming with the surprising coming of the Flood, and with the sudden destruction of Sodom. Like those two events, his *parousía* will be a revolutionizing event, a divine intervention that will immediately change the situation for all mankind in a most perceptible way. The comparison between Matthew chapter twenty-four, verse 39, and Luke chapter seventeen, verse 30, shows that the *parousía* denotes "the day that the Son of man is revealed." The linking together of "the days of Noah" with "the days of the Son of man" at Luke chapter seventeen, verse 26, therefore, means only that, as men in the days of Noah were swiftly taken unawares in the middle of their daily occupations, so it will be also in the days when the Son of man is to be revealed. His sudden intervention will come with nothing to alert people beforehand, shocking them into the reality of the situation.

At first glance it might be concluded that the clause, "What will be the sign of your coming (*parousía*)," at Matthew chapter twenty-four, verse 3, has no clear parallel in the Gospel of Luke. The question of the disciples as reproduced at Luke chapter twenty-one, verse 7, seems to be related to the destruction of the temple only: "What shall be the sign when these things [the destruction of the temple, verses 5 and 6] are about to come to pass?" However, one of the most important manuscript witnesses to the early text of the Gospels, the *Codex D* (*Bezae Cantabrigensis*), frames the question differently, bringing it into close agreement with the reading of Matthew 24:3, with one important exception:[20]

---

20 Although the manuscript dates only from the 5th or 6th century A.D., its textual variants often find support by the second-century Fathers and the Old Latin and Syriac versions.

Matthew 24:3: "What shall be the sign of your coming [*parousía*]?"
Luke 21:7: "What shall be the sign of your coming [*eleuseōs*]?"

As shown, the only difference is that Luke according to this manuscript does not use *parousía* but *éleusis,* the common Greek word for "coming." Dr. Schoonheim, after a close examination of these parallels, even concludes that, "Luke 21:7, according to D, presents a more original tradition," being a translation of the Syriac or even Aramaic *me'thitha'* ("coming").[21]

The Biblical context, then, gives no support to the claim that *parousía* has to be translated as "presence" in Matthew chapter twenty-four. The fact that the disciples did not imagine Christ's coming as an "invisible presence," the way Jesus answered their question, as well as the parallel texts in the Gospel of Luke, all show this translation to be untenable. In Luke, Christ's *parousía* is spoken of as Christ's "day," or even as "the day that the Son of man is revealed." And, as shown by Codex D, the word *parousía* could also be exchanged for the common Greek noun for "coming," *éleusis.* Similar parallels may be found in other texts dealing with Christ's *parousía,* in which texts terms relating to Jesus' manifestation or revelation are employed. Thus, the apostle John, at 1 John 2:28, exhorts the Christians to "abide in him; that, if he shall be manifested [Greek *phaneróō*], we may have boldness, and not be ashamed before him at his coming [*parousía*]." Here John clearly parallels Christ's *parousía* with the day of his appearing or manifestation. Similarly, the apostle Paul prays that the Christians in Thessalonica may have their hearts established "unblameable in holiness before our God and Father, at the coming [*parousía*] of our Lord Jesus with all his holy saints." (1 Thessalonians 3:13) This coming of the Lord with all his holy saints or angels is also spoken of at Jude verse 14 and in Matthew chapter sixteen, verses 27, 28, but instead of *parousía* Jude and Matthew both use forms of *érchomai,* the most common verb for "come," and cognate with the

---

Some scholars even regard it as a more faithful representative of the original text than Vaticanus and Sinaiticus. As demonstrated by A. J. Wensinck it is colored by Aramaic constructions and idioms more often than Vaticanus and Sinaiticus and, according to Dr. Matthew Black, it represents, therefore, "the Aramaic background of the Synoptic tradition more faithfully than do non-Western manuscripts."—Matthew Black, *An Aramaic Approach to the Gospels and Acts,* 2nd ed., 1954, pp. 26–34, 212, 213.

21 Schoonheim, pp. 16–28, 259, 260. This would refute the statement in the 1984 revised *New World Translation,* page 1577, that "The words *parousía* and *éleusis* are not used interchangeably."

noun *éleusis*. All three texts refer to one and the same occasion, the Lord's coming with all his holy ones for executing judgment, and to translate *parousía* by "presence" at 1 Thessalonians chapter three, verse 13, as the Watch Tower Society does, ignores this interrelation with other, parallel, passages.

In those parables in which Jesus emphasized the need for his servants to be alert and on the watch, we may note that he presents his judgment as like that which follows a master's returning to his household. The master's *coming* or *arrival,* not some "invisible presence," is what he describes. It is not as if the master slipped into the area and invisibly proceeded to pass judgment on what his servants were doing, only later revealing himself to them. To the contrary, the master's return, though perhaps unexpected, is quickly evident to all his servants, the faithful and the unfaithful, manifest from the beginning, and his judgment is not made from some invisible hiding place but in a most open manner.—Compare Matthew 24:45–51; 25:14–30; Mark 13:32–37; Luke 12:35–48; 19:12–27.

The evidence, then, from the earliest translations, as well as from modern translations and lexicons of the Greek language, and particularly from the context and related passages, all testifies that the use of *parousía* at Matthew chapter twenty-four, verse 3, cannot refer to an "invisible presence" of a "two-stage coming," but does refer to Christ's future arrival and appearing for judgment as King, "with power and great glory" and accompanied by his holy angels.

APPENDIX C

The Four Horsemen of the Apocalypse

WAR, FAMINE and pestilence also meet us in the book of Revelation in the guise of three riders sitting respectively on a red, a black, and a pale (literally, yellowish-green) horse, headed by a fourth rider, an archer, sitting on a white horse.—Revelation 6:1–8.

The major question here is whether the vision involving these four riders represents an end-times description applying to some period just precedent to the final day of judgment and therefore constituting a sign of the proximity of that day.

A reading of the account itself reveals nothing that ascribes the ride of these horsemen to any specific period. It is true that the vision of these riders forms part of a series of "seals" that were opened, seven in all, and that after the opening of the sixth seal, dealing with a great earthquake, men seek to hide, recognizing that 'the great day of God's wrath has come.' (Revelation 6:12–17) But this alone gives no sound basis for saying that the previous "seals" all fit within some particular time frame immediately preceding that day of judgment. There is nothing said to indicate that these seals form part of a "sign" designed to alert persons to the nearness of divine judgment. War, famine, pestilence have, as already shown, been a regular part of the human scene throughout all ages. They are not more so in our time than in previous generations.

In an effort to assign the ride of these horsemen to a specific period, the Watch Tower Society focuses attention on the rider on the white horse. The claim is made that he represents Christ Jesus and that the fact that he is spoken of as being "given a crown" fixes the time of the prophecy to the period from and after 1914 when, according to Watch Tower doctrine, Christ Jesus was enthroned in heaven and began to exercise kingly rule toward all the earth. What validity does this teaching have?

Who is the rider on the white horse?

The riders do not represent literal persons, of course. They are symbols, as are their horses and the colors of the horses.[1] Three of them are easily identified. There is a general consensus among commentators that the second rider, bearing a large sword, is a symbol of *war*, most often *civil war*, fittingly illustrated by the red color of his horse, a reminder of bloodshed.[2] The third rider is a symbol of *famine*, and this affliction is also well-depicted by the color of his horse, black being the color of crops in the field blackened with blight. The fourth rider symbolizes death by *pestilence*, and the pale or yellowish-green color of his horse denotes the color of a sick, plague-stricken person. These identifications are all confirmed also by the missions given to each of them. But who is the archer riding on the white horse?

Here the problems start, and various suggestions have been given by different commentators. Some believe this rider is a symbol of Christianity, or the triumphal progress of the Christian gospel. Others think he stands for military conquest, in contradistinction from the second rider who, according to this interpretation, symbolizes civil or internecine war. Dr. Graham presents his argument for believing that

---

1 As noted by most commentators, these symbols parallel those found at Zechariah 6:1–8, although some of the details differ. The colors evidently have different meanings in the two visions. In Zechariah's vision the four groups of differently shaded horses are interpreted by the angel as being "the four winds of heaven, which go forth from standing before the Lord of all the earth." (Verse 5, ASV) These winds in turn apparently represented the wrath of God sent out against the enemies of God's people in the days of Zechariah.—Compare Isaiah 66:15; Jeremiah 4:13; 23:19; 30:23; 49:36.

2 To the rider of the red horse it "was given to take peace [literally, "the peace"] from the earth, and that they should slay one another." (ASV) Has there ever been universal peace on earth? As argued in chapter five, there has hardly been any total peace year on earth throughout history. Yet, at the time John wrote down his visions there was, actually, a kind of "peace." This was the well-known *Pax Romana*, the "Roman peace," a period of peace and stability within the Roman borders lasting from 29 B.C. to about A.D. 162. True, there were constant wars at the borders of the vast empire, with the Teutons (Germans) in the north, and especially with the Parthians in the east, the Parthian kingdom being the only remaining great power aside from Rome itself. But these wars at the borders were not viewed as a threat to the peace prevailing within the Roman borders. So, when John's addresses read that the rider on the red horse was assigned to "take the peace from the earth," this *Pax Romana* or Roman peace might naturally come to mind. Further, as pointed out by J. M. Ford's commentary on Revelation (*The Anchor Bible*, Vol. 38, New York 1975, p. 106), "The phrase *allelous sphaxousin*, 'to kill one another,' indicates civil strife." Civil wars within the Roman borders would, of course, "take the peace from the earth," with the "earth" being understood as a reference to the Roman Empire. Whatever the precise application, it goes without saying that, in the world as a whole, civil strife and turmoil, often accompanied by bloodshed, have been destructive of peace throughout all the centuries of the Christian era.

the rider symbolizes deception, having a surface appearance that is deceptive, and bent on greedy conquest.[3] Still others, including the Watch Tower Society, identify him with Jesus Christ himself. Since the Watch Tower Society sees the whole vision as a parallel of the visitations described by Jesus at Matthew chapter twenty-four verses 6–8, and since they proclaim that those verses apply from 1914 forward, their claim is that the four riders began their devastating gallop on earth in that year. A particularly strong evidence of this is said to be found in *the crown* given to the first rider:

> The rider of this speedy means of travel signified a newly installed king, for a <u>royal crown</u> was given him. . . . Inescapably, then, the rider of the white horse who rides on victoriously must be <u>Jesus Christ at his coronation in heaven at the close of the Gentile Times in 1914</u>.[4]

This interpretation cannot be correct, however, because *it is founded upon a serious linguistic mistake*. The Greek language had two different words for "crown." One is *stéphanos*, the other is *diádēma*. It is *diádēma* that signifies a "royal crown." It is used, for instance, of the many crowns worn by Jesus at Revelation chapter nineteen, verse 12:

> And his eyes are a flame of fire, and upon his head are many diadems [*diadēmata*].

These many diadems evidently symbolize Christ's royal authority over all other kings, emphasized also by the name written on his garment and on his thigh according to verse 16, "KING OF KINGS, AND LORD OF LORDS."

This meaning of the word *diádēma* is brought out by all Greek dictionaries. Thus, for instance, *Vine's Expository Dictionary* says on page 260:

> DIADĒMA . . . is never used as *stephanos* is: it is always the symbol of the kingly or imperial dignity, and is translated 'diadem' instead of 'crown' in the R.V., of the claims of the Dragon, Rev. 12:3; 13:1; 19:12.

But the "crown" given to the rider of the white horse in Revelation chapter six, verse 2, was not a *diádēma*. It was a *stéphanos*. What, then, does this word mean, as it was not used in the same way as *diádēma?* Vine further explains on the same page:

---

3 *Approaching Hoofbeats*, pp. 78–81.
4 *The Watchtower*, May 15, 1983, pp. 18, 19.

STEPHANOS . . . denotes (a) the victor's crown, the symbol of triumph in the games or some such contest; hence, by metonymy, a reward or prize; (b) a token of public honour for distinguished service, military prowess, etc., or of nuptial joy, or festal gladness, especially at the parousia of kings.

A *stéphanos*, then, usually denoted the crown of victory, and this is true in the New Testament, where it is used in connection with the figure of athletic contests. (Compare 1 Corinthians 9:25; 2 Timothy 2:5.) It is this kind of crown that Christians receive as their divine reward from God through his king Christ Jesus, even as individuals were honored by the bestowal of a *stéphanos* at the royal visitation or *parousía* of a king or emperor.—2 Timothy 4:8; James 1:12.

Interestingly, the *stéphanos* was not only given as a prize *after* a victory. As in the case of the archer on the white horse, it was also given to warriors *before* the battle as a promise of victory. Thus the Spartans crowned themselves with a *stéphanos* when they went out to battle as a sign of promised victory. So also did the Roman generals. The crown or wreath was supposed to influence the outcome of the battle. Both among Greeks and Romans the *stéphanos* was the symbol of victory, and Nike, the goddess of victory, was depicted as coming with a crown of victory in her hand.[5]

When the rider of the white horse is given a *stéphanos*, then, he is not, as the Watch Tower Society claims, given a "royal crown." The scene does not describe any coronation ceremony in heaven, and there is certainly no reason for attaching the wreathing of the riding archer to the year 1914. The vision depicts an armed warrior riding out to battle, and as a promise of victory in this battle he is given a crown, not a royal crown but *a victor's crown*. The words that follow—"and he came forth conquering, and to conquer"—immediately explain the purpose of the crown given to him. As the second rider was given *a great sword* as a symbol of his mission—to take peace from the earth—so this first rider was given *a victor's crown* as a symbol of *his* mission: to conquer. The archer, therefore, may symbolize or stand for *victorious conquest*. And this would be in harmony with the color of his horse. How so?

---

5 Kittel/Friedrich, *Theological Dictionary of the New Testament*, Vol. VII, pp. 620, 621. The Watch Tower Society knows, of course, that *stéphanos* means a crown of victory and, in fact, admits this when dealing with texts other than Revelation 6:2. Commenting upon James 1:12, the *Watchtower* of July 1, 1979, page 30, states that *stéphanos* "is taken from a root meaning 'to encircle,' and so it is used to refer to a crown, wreath, prize or reward that a victor in a race receives."

It is certainly true that white often stands as a symbol of purity and righteousness, as for instance at Revelation chapter nineteen, verse 8. But this is not automatically the case. In Zechariah chapter six, verses 1–8, where we find chariots drawn by four groups of horses, three of them having identical colors with their counterparts in Revelation, there is no particular virtue assigned to the chariot drawn by the white horses. Quite to the contrary, it is of the chariot drawn by the black horses that it is said that these "have given my Spirit rest in the land of the north."—Zechariah 6:6, 8.

White was also an ancient symbol of triumph and victory. **"When a Roman general celebrated a triumph,"** says Bible commentator William Barclay, **"that is, when he paraded through the streets of Rome with his armies and his captives and his spoils after some great victory, his chariot was drawn by white horses, for they were the symbols of victory."**[6] At Revelation chapter six, verse 2, therefore, the white color of the horse may well symbolize military victory and triumph, in accordance with the mission given to its rider.

It might be argued that, even if the riding archer is a symbol of victorious conquest, he could still be a symbol of Jesus Christ, especially in view of the fact that Christ is also represented as riding on a white horse in Revelation chapter nineteen, verses 11 onward. It should be noted, however, that the two visions are wholly different, and the two riders also differ. In chapter nineteen the rider wields a sword rather than a bow; he wears many diadems or royal crowns (*diadēmata*), not a *stéphanos* or wreath of victory. As has sometimes been pointed out, "the two riders having nothing in common beyond the white horse."[7]

Even more significantly, the other three riders in Revelation chapter six are all symbols of *calamities* or *visitations* (war, famine, pestilence), not of actual individuals. It would be both logical and consistent, then, to understand the first rider in a similar way, as suggested, possibly picturing the concept of military conquest. This is, in fact, also the conclusion of the majority of well-known commentators. Dr. Otto Michel, for example, explains the first two riders as follows:

---

6 William Barclay, *The Revelation of John*, Vol. 2, 2nd ed., Philadelphia 1960, p. 4. H. B. Swete, also, in his *Commentary on Revelation* (1977 reprint of 1911 3rd ed., Grand Rapids, Michigan, p. 86) confirms that "white was the colour of victory," giving several examples of this from ancient Roman sources.

7 Swete, p. 86.

The white horse represents the conqueror who comes from without with an alien host and oppresses the kingdom. It is followed by the fiery red horse which takes away peace and unleashes civil strife.[8]

Space does not permit a more detailed examination of this vision. The information presented above, however, clearly shows that the Watch Tower Society's attempt to tie this vision to its 1914 date has no support in the text itself. Basing its interpretation on a mistranslation of the word *stéphanos* it tries to turn the wreathing of the archer into a *coronation ceremony,* an idea that is completely foreign to the context. If applied to Jesus, the most reasonable application of his receiving a *stéphanos* or crown of victory and conquest would be to the time of his resurrection, the time when he had achieved his greatest victories, having conquered the world, sin, death and the Devil by his faithful course—not to some time nineteen centuries later. (Compare John 16:33; Revelation 3:21; 5:5.) The symbolic language of the vision of the horsemen is drawn from different texts of the Old Testament, such as Zechariah 6:1–8; Ezekiel 5:12–17; 14:21 and Jeremiah 49:36, 37, texts dealing with divine judgments brought on the enemies of Israel in ancient times. For our present purpose it is not necessary to go into an explanation of when and how the judgments described symbolically in Revelation chapter six would come upon the oppressing powers that figure in the visions of John. It suffices for us to realize that the four riders cannot be shown to have more to do with 1914, or, for that matter, with this twentieth century, than any previous time period in history.

---

8 Otto Michel in TDNT, Vol. III, p. 338. In a footnote he further adds: "We misunderstand the destructive activity of the horsemen if we identify the first with the avenging or warring Messiah of 19:11–16, or with the Gospel in its incursion into the world (Mk. 13:10)."

Acknowledgements

In the course of the production of this work, much help has been received from scholarly friends and colleagues, in the form of constructive criticism, suggested improvements, and additional findings and information. One of them also helped in working out some of the illustrations. We would like to take this opportunity to gratefully acknowledge their assistance.

When producing the chapter on earthquakes, a number of leading seismologists were consulted. We especially thank Professor N. N. Ambraseys in London, and Professor Markus Båth at Uppsala, Sweden, two of the world's most renowned seismologists. Both of them generously shared their knowledge and research and provided important source material. Professor Båth also carefully went over the entire chapter on earthquakes and added important observations and improvements.

While writing the chapter on famines, we profited much from our contact with the **Hunger Project** (Global office: One Madison Avenue, New York, New York, 10010, U.S.A). Suported by millions of people around the world, this movement has as its goal the effectual elimination of hunger on the planet by the turn of the century. Officials of the movement generously shared their information and material.

Finally, and most importantly, we wish to thank the One whose guidance has been constantly sought and relied upon: the God of truth. We both feel strongly that He has blessed our search for truth and facts.

The authors

For information regarding additional or future publications of Commentary Press, send your name and full address to:

Commentary Press
P.O. Box 43532
Atlanta, Georgia 30336